Capitalism with a Human Face

Capitalism with a Human Face

Samuel Brittan

Edward Elgar

Published by
Edward Elgar Publishing Limited
Gower House
Croft Road
Aldershot
Hants GU11 3HR
England

Edward Elgar Publishing Company
Old Post Road
Brookfield
Vermont 05036
USA

British Library Cataloguing in Publication Data
Brittan, Samuel
   Capitalism with a Human Face
   I. Title
   330.122

Library of Congress Cataloguing in Publication Data
Brittan, Samuel.
   Capitalism with a human face/Sir Samuel Brittan.
     p.   cm.
   Includes bibliographical references and index.
   1. Capitalism. 2. Comparative economics. 3. Post-communism.
   I. Title.
   HB501.B7865 1995
   330.12'2—dc20   94–28484
                                                 CIP

ISBN   1 85278 446 6
        1 85278 449 0 (paperback)

Printed and bound in Great Britain by
Hartnolls Limited, Bodmin, Cornwall

Contents

Figures

Tables

Acknowledgements

It is unfortunately impracticable to thank everyone who helped me in every one of the essays, some of which go back a long way. But I must thank Walter Allan for helping to launch the project, when he was at the IEA and for editing some of the chapters, and Alan Hamlin for invaluable advice and guidance on the organization of this book. Geoffrey Wood read a draft of Chapter 9, and Steven Webb and David Willetts a draft of Chapter 13. Peter Jay, Richard Lambert, Nigel and Therese Lawson and my brother Leon commented very helpfully on a draft of the Introduction.

The *Financial Times* Graphics Department kindly provided the charts, some of them specially drawn by Christopher Walker.

The original publications in which some of these essays appeared are mentioned on the first page of the appropriate chapter. These mentions are also intended as acknowledgements.

The quotation from W.H. Auden at the beginning of Chapter 4 is reprinted from *English Auden*, edited by Edward Mendelson, with permission from Faber and Faber and Random House Inc.

Last, but by no means least, Mrs Anne Shotts and Mandy Bentley and her helpers were indispensable in transcribing my thoughts on to various word processors.

SAMUEL BRITTAN

Introduction: footfalls in the memory

THE CONTENTS OF THIS BOOK

Those who have always disliked capitalism have found it expedient since the fall of the Soviet Union to talk about forms of capitalism alternative to the western individualist variety. They will find, however, that the individualist ethic is not merely defended but celebrated in this collection of essays, as a humane approach which allows plenty of scope for altruism and fraternity. Indeed individualist liberalism comes first. The market comes second as an instrument of human co-operation; and capitalism third, as the only known working embodiment of the market system.

I shall be told that one of the main features of the post-communist world is the spread of attitudes such as religious fundamentalism and extreme nationalism. Even adherents of these creeds have, however, to acknowledge the mundane problems of inflation, unemployment and the distribution of income and wealth, which are also discussed in these pages.

This book originates with a suggestion that some of my extended articles of recent years should be collected in a single volume. I gladly accepted. The painter J.M.W. Turner is said to have asked what was the use of his pictures except when seen together; and I feel the same way about my own lesser works in another medium.

I soon realized that I could not just throw at people a miscellaneous collection of essays written for different occasions; and I have taken trouble to make it reader-friendly and to ensure some continuity between the chapters. There has been some updating and rewriting, without I hope losing the flavour of the original time and occasion. Complete updating is of course a chimera, like the proverbial painting of the Forth Bridge: by the time I had updated the final chapter it would be time to start again on the first.

The book begins, as my publisher requested, with a short account, following this Introduction, of how I came upon my ideas and to what extent they have changed. The order of presentation of the main chapters is by subject matter rather than order of composition. The movement is from the general to the particular; but the reader will find his way around the volume according to his own inclinations.

The first chapter is one of the most recent and is an account of how I see the relation between economics and ethics, prepared as the presidential address for

Section F of the British Association at the BA's annual meeting in Keele in 1993. It is one example of lectures which turn out to be far too long to deliver and which I recommend my friends to read rather than attend. It happens also to be the starting point of the Section F conference book, also to be published by Edward Elgar, in which a variety of different authors develop this theme. In the present volume it is a stepping stone to some more personal thoughts in which I tackle some of the puzzles about the role of self-interest in market systems. This leads to some questions going beyond political economy to utilitarian ethics and the contractarian alternative. Finally in Part One I commit the unpardonable offence of defending Margaret Thatcher's celebrated saying 'There is no such thing as society', although not in terms of which she would necessarily approve.

Part Two attempts a bridge to more specific issues by a look at two rival modern thinkers, Keynes and Hayek. Despite his recent vogue in limited circles, Hayek is still much the lesser known and too frequently dismissed as just a synonym for the outlook of Margaret Thatcher and Ronald Reagan. The essay on Hayek therefore aims to give a reasonably rounded critique of his later work. The one on Keynes, on the other hand, deals mainly with his attitude to democratic government.

My assessment of Keynesian economics is to be found in the more impersonal Part Three. That Part is concerned with what many people wrongly think of as the entire subject matter of economics: inflation, depression, monetarism, exchange rates and so on. Although I have never been able to take too seriously slogans about the balance of payments, the unique importance of manufacturing and 'competitiveness', the newly written Chapter 8 is my first published attempt to put my heresies (which are really restated orthodoxies) coherently in one place. The key is that deficits are experienced by companies and individuals – and indeed governments – but not by such strange entities as 'the UK' or 'Europe'. This theme provides a useful link with the discussion of basics in Part One. There is in Part Three some onward momentum. For I wrote or rewrote these macroeconomic chapters in more or less the order they appear. Their subject matter is so intertwined that I have treated them as a whole; and readers might well find what appear as glaring omissions in one chapter analysed in the following one.

Part Four moves further towards the specific with a still interim assessment of the Thatcher government's economic legacy. It naturally leads on to one of the main problems not so far successfully tackled by any regime or system, that of unemployment. Chapter 11 is another attempt to put together thoughts on the link between pay and jobs.

Part Five, which gives the book its name, starts with a concise statement 'Redistribution: yes. Equality: no'. It should be useful for those who have not the patience to plough through the earlier, more analytical material, as well as to those who want to see it further developed. It naturally leads on to the question 'What do we do if some market-clearing wages are unacceptably low?' Is it to provide all citizens with the equivalent of unearned income, independent of pay? Chapter 13 takes another look at this topic, and seeks a way of promoting some of the objectives gradually without the horrendous cost of the pure Basic Income proposal.

The final essay uses my Mais Lecture, given in 1989, to pull together, as far as possible, the subject matter of the whole volume. There is therefore some slight unavoidable repetition of earlier themes.

FOOTFALLS IN THE MEMORY

Early Enthusiasms

My publisher has suggested that I preface these essays with 'an intellectual autobiography'. I have interpreted this to mean an account of how I came to adopt the positions outlined. Thus what follows is emphatically not a full personal autobiography.

My father was a general practitioner in north-west London. Both he and my mother were of Lithuanian Jewish extraction, although naturalized before I was born. As a child I was precocious without being a prodigy. For instance, I worried that the hottest places were not always those nearest to the equator and that the coldest were not always at the poles. Then I switched from an obsessive observance of Jewish rituals to proclaiming my disbelief in religion. What I have retained from this period is a selective liking for ceremony and observance. I attended the last Christmas Eve Latin mass at the Brompton Oratory when a Mozart work was sung.

My early political instincts were more childlike. I started to say I was a Liberal because my mother was one. One family legend has it that I said to a 16-year-old girl: 'The Liberals gave you your old age pension.' But I did as a post-war teenager declare that I wanted to be an economist. That was because I supposed it to be the part of politics from which one could make a living.

Nevertheless, I did believe even in these tender years that mass unemployment was not merely an evil, but a huge illogicality: unsatisfied wants existed side by side with unused labour. I was impressed by a book, which I picked up by accident, by the popular science writer Gordon Rattray Taylor who maintained that the cause of pre-war unemployment – both in reality and according to Keynes – was oversaving. I did not leap with joy to learn this. My iconoclasm stems in part from a frustrated desire to identify with authority and I could not easily believe that all the propaganda about National Savings was rubbish.

Another extracurricular influence was the now forgotten G.D.H. Cole's *Intelligent Man's Guide to the Post-war World*. He maintained that regular business cycles existed entirely in the eyes of the beholder and that there was simply an irregular wave-like movement. Cole also made scathing remarks about *a priori* economists who made more and more refined models of perfectly working free markets and who should be left to spin out their fancies in peace.

Moving on from Liberalism, I brought myself up on a watered-down non-communist semi-Marxism which was then in vogue. One influence was Lancelot Hogben's *Mathematics for the Million*. I am afraid that I absorbed the sugar on the pill – such as the author's opposition to knowledge for its own sake – much more than I did the mathematical core. But I did take more seriously than many real Marxists the insistence of the *Communist Manifesto* that capitalism was objectively progressive for its time; and eagerly embraced the Cobdenite vision of world peace through free trade.

My politics became 'left wing Labour' or 'Bevanite'. This was because I wanted 'a socialist foreign policy'. This included a wishful belief picked up from my reading that western hardline policies had pushed the Soviet Union into repressive policies. Embarrassingly, one of my domestic duties was to take to a distribution centre parcels for a relative who had been deported from Lithuania to Siberia for no crime other than that of being a bourgeois element.

More creditably, I disliked the support given to repressive and corrupt regimes in Asia and Africa for the sake of anti-communism or oil. I had a whole litany, probably taken from some left wing MP, of 'sultans, pashas and effendis' that the west had no business supporting while prating about freedom and democracy. Here I have not changed and was very uneasy about fighting the Gulf War of 1990 to restore the al-Sabah dynasty to Kuwait. As Cobden said: 'In all my travels … three reflections constantly occurred to me: how much unnecessary solicitude and alarm England devotes to the affairs of foreign countries; with how little knowledge we enter upon the task of regulating the concerns of other people; and how much better we might employ our energies in improving matters at home.'

With such attitudes I could not bring myself, either then or later, to admire Clement Attlee. I did once take part in a dinner with Attlee when he came to address the Cambridge Labour Club near the end of his period as Leader of the Labour Opposition. He was asked about Indo-China, which the French were on the point of losing. His reply was, 'Don't know enough to say.' He was also asked (not by me) about the economy. 'Why should I bother?' he replied, 'I have got Gaitskell and Wilson.'

At the age of 15 or 16 I ceased to see politics as the way to promote human happiness. This was not obvious to other people, as the reaction was taking place inside my own head. For a while I wanted to become a psychologist, as psychologists were the people most likely to understand the causes of human happiness and to initiate the reforms which would improve people's prospects.

Of course, I have long since absorbed the common wisdom that the way to achieve happiness is not to pursue it directly; but there are many resulting paradoxes.

Among my parents' circle there were several medical consultants, who were hardly aware of psychology except as a poor relation of clinical psychiatry. My brother Leon and I can still chant their offputting refrain: 'Psychology without medicine means nothing.'

Cambridge Retrospect

I went up to Cambridge on a history exhibition, having nearly spoilt my interview by saying that I liked the quadrangles. ('The quads are in Oxford. Here we have courts.') I took the path of least resistance and read economics, influenced by reports that psychology in Cambridge had a laboratory and physiological basis.

A near-contemporary, Walter Eltis, has written in his own intellectual odyssey that those who went on to study economics in their second and third years were then 'firmly convinced that they were among the privileged 80 in number a year who were learning economics in the world's leading university, which offered both the highest theory and the key to policies that worked.' I could not work myself up into the same elevated opinion. The Cambridge Economics Tripos was a spiral, the same subjects being covered in all three years, supposedly in more advanced fashion. I soon concluded that the Oxford PPE course (politics, philosophy, economics) was more civilized, and just as good for somebody later wanting to become a specialist economist.

I was given a thorough grounding in economic analysis by Peter Bauer, but I still reflected that the famous tutorial system in which individual tuition was given to one or two undergraduates at a stretch was surely a waste of the time of world-famous scholars. In my second year I was taught by Milton Friedman, then on a sabbatical at Cambridge, but not yet the celebrated leader of a particular school. Friedman proved a charming person; but at first I did not like being tutored by a far-out Republican and missing the true Cambridge Keynesian wisdom.

It was not until the first term of my third year that I went to 62 Grange Road, beyond the Backs, to study with that fount of left-wing Keynesian wisdom, Joan Robinson. As in the case of another lady of forthright, but very different, opinions, it was fatal to forget that she was a woman. She was then developing the ideas later embodied in her book, *The Accumulation of Capital*. Her point was that the marginal productivity theory could not be used to explain the distribution of the national income between capital and labour, because it was impossible to measure capital independently of labour. She then proceeded, however, to rebuild the theory with the aid of a complicated saw-tooth diagram which became a bookmark in the published volume. I puzzled whether the theory was meant to be a rough approximation to how a capitalist economy works, or whether its purpose was to show that such an economy could not work because of the highly unrealistic assumptions required. The same question has arisen decades later with modern general equilibrium theory (see Chapter 14). Later I discovered that Friedman had been frozen out of the long-established 'secret seminar' where the new ideas on capital were discussed and where he could surely have helped by cutting through some of the mathematical problems.

Joan Robinson did have some individual words of wisdom for many of her pupils. Those I received were, 'You have plenty of good ideas; but they come to you in a muddle and you need help in sorting them out.' Unfortunately, I have rarely received that sort of help and have had to do the sorting myself. Later in my third year I was supervised by Harry Johnson, who was a genuine prodigy – on the surface flashy and Americanized – and not yet the feared economic personality he later became. He was the supervisor from whom I probably derived most benefit.

Illiberal Liberals

Friedman would sometimes say: 'You can advocate this so long as you believe that the state should decide for the individual.' I regretted the lack of embarrassment of too many other people at this charge. An example was Denis Robertson (once commended in the Peterborough column of *The Daily Telegraph* for not having followed Keynes 'hook, line and sinker'). Robertson was prepared to countenance surprising policies for a classical liberal. At a session of the Political Economy Club he vigorously defended the right of County Agricultural Committees to dispossess supposedly inefficient farmers; 'and more power to their elbow', he added.

Outside the macro-sphere, Cambridge economics still stemmed from Alfred Marshall, a quintessentially Victorian Cambridge figure whose *Principles of Economics* was first published in 1890. Even Keynes revered Marshall, although he also mocked him: and Friedman remarked that if the *Principles* had come out in the 1950s they would have been hailed as the best advanced textbook on price theory – quite extraordinary for a subject claiming to be a science.

My extracurricular activities in Cambridge were too much concerned with the Labour Club and with the Union (an undergraduate debating society). 'Too much' because I was not really cut out for either politics or public speaking. I did, however, make one successful address at the Union, giving the lead speech in favour of the motion 'This house would rather be red than dead'.

My time at Cambridge also saw the last fling of the aesthetic snobs before the 1960s arrived. Most students interested in the arts – and also the 'funny' speakers at the Union – had a term 'drear' which they flung at anyone with serious political or intellectual interests. I should perhaps have called this introduction 'Recollections of a Drear'.

The *Financial Times*

As an undergraduate, I had dabbled a little in writing for the press to the extent of discovering that editors of hard-pressed weeklies could not always afford to pay contributors. Nevertheless, it was not an interest in journalism as such which caused me to respond to a *Financial Times* notice at the Cambridge Appointments Board. I had been rejected by Shell, who could not imagine me standing in shorts selling oil cans in Lagos. The Bank of England had then no graduate recruitment scheme and told me I would spend my first few years copying documents 'with meticulous accuracy': I might prefer to start elsewhere. I had gone to see Manning Dacey, the economic adviser to Lloyds Bank, about possibilities in banking. But when he heard I was a possible First he thought it was not a good idea. On the economic side of Lloyds Bank, he remarked, 'there is only me'. His advice was firm: 'financial journalism'.

I therefore went to see Gordon Newton, the editor of The *Financial Times*, whose interviewing technique has been described exhaustively elsewhere, together with his role in bringing to London Oxbridge graduates who would otherwise have had to start in provincial journalism. I went in saying to myself, 'Let me see if I can't get this job'; and to cut the story short, I did.

Like many recruits, my first few years were spent in the general features department. While my near-contemporary Eltis was writing refereed papers on subjects such as 'Investment, Technical Progress and Economic Growth', I wrote features on the furniture industry or the efforts of a small firm at Hawick to enlist its labour force against a takeover. I was also sent on trips to Israel and Morocco, and to a French automated car plant in response to one of the periodic alarms about machines displacing human beings.

Newton was admirably patient most of the time. But I remember one particular outburst. I wrote a feature on the economics of the egg, which concentrated on market factors. Newton wanted the 'real economics of an egg': so much cost for feeding stuff, so much for heating, so much for labour – all illustrated on a sliced-up egg – which I had almost to invent because of the protestations of trade spokesmen that it all 'varied so much'. In the course of this project I had occasion to ask on the telephone, 'Is that the Society of Objectors to Compulsory Egg Marketing?', which drew hoots of laughter from my colleagues, loudest of all from Nigel Lawson, who afterwards became a prominent ministerial advocate of deregulation.

There was one shortcoming to my training, which I recognized even then. Unlike some other recruits I was not forced to spend a period in the companies section. I would never have been brilliant there; but at least I would have been forced to read a balance sheet despite having been taught at Cambridge that capital could not be measured. To this day, when I hear that the economy is being held back by weak balance sheets, I never know whether this mysterious disease corresponds to something real for which we have no alternative but to suffer, or to accounting conventions which we could surmount.

David Kynaston has, in his centenary history of the *FT*, named some of the contemporary graduate recruits many of whom became well known. The influences from these years were greater than anything at Cambridge. Nevertheless on balance we were pushing in the wrong neo-corporatist direction; and if the UK missed a chance of a dash for economic freedom at the right time, there was no prodding in the correct direction from the congregation of *FT* graduate journalists.

Not many years later I used to amuse myself by imagining the kind of leader that the *FT* would write if the Communists came to power in Britain. The article would acknowledge misgivings, but would point out that good Marxists were, like the *FT*, in favour of a high priority for investment. Eventually the new government would find fresh methods of allocating investment funds. Meanwhile, however, the leader would conclude, it already had an instrument to hand in the Stock Exchange which it should consider retaining until a long-term substitute was found. Unfortunately, I delayed putting this skit down on paper before the Berlin Wall fell in 1989, after which it was too late.

Morality and Foreign Policy

The event which did most to stir me up was not an economic one but the Suez invasion. This has been analysed to death in many places; and I will just focus on one aspect: the assertion made in letters to *The Daily Telegraph* that foreign policy could not be judged morally. This linked up with another hobby-horse of mine. Oxford moral philosophy was widely criticized for analysing moral language instead of providing moral guidance. My complaint was the opposite: that under the guise of analysing moral language, it was smuggling in some highly conventional morality. The result of my cogitation was 'Morality and Foreign Policy', finished in 1957, but not published until 1973 when it became part of *Capitalism and the Permissive Society*. This essay explains the difference between my own rejection of war on most occasions and pure pacifism. This thinking is also reflected, but not repeated, in the much more recent 'Choice and Utility', which is reprinted here as Chapter 3 of the present volume.

The next traumatic experience was indeed in the economic field. In September 1957 the Conservative Chancellor Peter Thorneycroft raised Bank Rate out of the blue from $5\frac{1}{2}$ to 7 per cent, an almost unheard-of Rate not reached since the 1920s. I was away at the time and first heard about it on the telephone from

Nigel Lawson who, allowing for differences of temperament, was as horrified as I was.

Much of the economic world was shocked because Thorneycroft, on the advice of Professor Lionel Robbins, insisted on making speeches about the supply of money, which was supposed to be the basic cause of inflation. Having come across pre-Keynesian economics at Cambridge, this doctrine was not the thunderbolt for me that it was for so many commentators when it came up in 1957, and more seriously in the late 1960s and 1970s. In the Thorneycroft period it was verbiage, as the actual policy was a conventional squeeze.

It was the apparent abandonment of full employment policies that shocked me most. (The whole episode is recounted in *Steering the Economy*.) In the end Thorneycroft resigned at the beginning of 1958, although over public spending and not monetary policy; and the quasi-monetarist rhetoric was dropped. Since I afterwards came to be associated with positions similar to that of Thorneycroft in 1957, a word of explanation is needed. My slowness in seeing the light can be explained, but not excused, by the appallingly unconvincing way in which sound-money policies were then defended. They were put forward in terms of defending the sterling exchange rate (and with it the sterling area), not as a convenient intermediate objective but as a matter of honour. Above all, the distinction between a steady inflation and an accelerating inflation, and the likelihood of 'full employment' policies producing the latter, was not made by the sound-money men who were too shocked by the very idea of inflation to go further into the matter.

In 1960 Newton made me economic correspondent, as he had been intending to do all along. He was primarily interested in my writing features and leaders. As far as I know, I was the first economics correspondent as such on any paper. Previously the economy had come under City editors. Lord Drogheda, then managing director, had queried the idea, asking, 'Are not all our stories economic?' He had a point. With my limited typing abilities, and secretaries going home at the end of office hours, there was no chance of my attempting more than a sample of economic news stories, however narrowly defined. Newton's attitude was simple: 'Write them when you have something to add.'

My main intellectual influences did not, however, then come from economics. I was much more swayed by Karl Popper's *The Poverty of Historicism,* which put into analytical form the teachings of *The Open Society* which I had read at Cambridge. I was also absorbed by Thomas Mann's novel, *The Magic Mountain,* first published in 1924. There are two characters who battle in an alpine sanatorium for the soul of a young engineer, Hans Castorp, and who brought out for me the age-old fundamental division between liberty and authority, hidden from public view by the superficial Conservative–Socialist argument. One is Settembrini, a somewhat operatic Italian liberal who proclaims, 'Democracy has no meaning whatever if not that of an individualistic corrective to state absolutism of every kind.' He favours both national self-determination and the abolition of war through international law. A passionate ascetic 'who lives in a garret', he loves 'form, beauty, freedom, gaiety, the enjoyment of life'. His more formidable antagonist is a would-be Jesuit, Naphta, who believes in 'discipline, sacrifice, the renunciation of the ego, the curbing of the personality'. He is also a revolutionary socialist, who looks forward to a new authoritarian order to be achieved by the proletariat. His favourite quotation is from Pope Gregory the Great: 'Cursed be the man who holds back his sword from the shedding of blood.'

I would still summarize my creed as a battle against the shades of Naphta, although allowing myself the odd laugh at Settembrini. But I do not enjoy being constantly on the ideological front line. One reason why I have never made the leap from economic to general journalism is that not everyone need know what I think about everything; and those who read economic journalism receive it in suitable wrappings.

The Move to the *Observer*

In 1961 I moved to the *Observer* as economic editor. This had been suggested by Andrew Shonfield, who was himself moving from that post to Chatham House. Alas, I cannot say that my time at the *Observer* was the happiest for me professionally. The paper needed someone who could take charge of all its financial coverage, which was not my *forte*. In the end the *Observer* did more for me than I did for it, as it established my name as an economic commentator. The paper should have chosen Robert Collin, who was the other *FT* candidate interviewed, who himself wrote a City column in the *New Statesman*.

Despite the frustrations at the *Observer,* it was then that I wrote my first longer published article, which appeared in the *Banker* under the title 'Too Many Regulators'. The theme was that demand management had destablized rather than stabilized the economy. It was illustrated by a chart (reprinted in all editions of my *Treasury* book) of industrial production, showing that the government had squeezed the economy when it was going down or stagnating and had stimulated it when it was already on the way upwards.

It would have helped my reputation if I had found someone to collaborate on an econometric appendix. But such an appendix could not have solved the basic problem. The undeclared purpose of stop–go measures was not to stabilize the domestic economy but to maintain the $2.80 sterling parity. The Treasury relaxed when it could do so consistently with that purpose. So long as the USA remained a low-inflation country, as it did up to the Vietnam war, the dollar exchange rate was a good proxy for either a money supply target, or a domestic inflation one. If this had been frankly acknowledged there might have been fewer speculative capital flows and policy might not have had to be so destabilizing.

The Treasury under the Tories

The most important event in my *Observer* period was being commissioned to write a book on the Treasury. The idea of going to ask ex-Chancellors and other former ministers to talk of their experiences was given to me by none other than Sir William Armstrong, the Treasury's friendly but intense Permanent Secretary. Armstrong, who came from a Salvation Army background, was different from the popular conception of a Treasury figure. He would talk to me freely at home in the evenings, but none the less warn me the following morning not to delve too deeply in my book into Treasury advice. He once observed that my real *forte* was as an in-depth reporter.

A mistake I made was to show my manuscript to Armstrong. The result was that Reginald Maudling, the usually genial Chancellor who succeeded Selwyn Lloyd, read the Riot Act to me (at a lunch for the two of us for which the *Observer* paid) for mentioning the content of official advice. My suspicions that the official Treasury had put Maudling up to it were confirmed when, once in Opposition, he reviewed a subsequent edition in the *Spectator* very favourably, saying, 'So far as he is dealing with matters of which I have personal experience, I find his account very fair.'

This refrain about 'advice given by civil servants to ministers' being on a par with the confessional has recurred throughout my journalistic life. All the talk of open government is so much hot air while the Whitehall line remains that officials will not give frank advice if it is liable to be reported, even with a lag. It is just as easy to argue that better advice will be given if those who provide it can be held to account.

The purpose of the title, *The Treasury under the Tories, 1951–64*, was to make a virtue of the historical aspect so that it would not seem to have been overtaken by events if Labour was in power by the time the book was published – as it was. Harold Wilson said that the book should have been called *The Tories under the Treasury*.

The policy recommendations of the 1964 edition are, from my present standpoint, too inflationary and countenance too much government intervention. What, however, still gives me retrospective satisfaction is that I distanced myself from the prevailing clamour for a more dynamic economic or production ministry to take over economic steering, with the Treasury as a subordinate instrument. 'If the Treasury remains responsible for the balance of payments, for taxation, for the Bank Rate ... it is likely to remain the effective economic ministry, whatever nominal changes are made.' Yet even as I write this introduction, a recent director general of the CBI, John Banham, advocates the abolition of the Treasury as the key to overcoming Britain's economic problems – like killing the messenger who brings bad news.

George Brown's DEA

I had been wondering how to get out of the *Observer* when Donald MacDougall, then economic director of the National Economic Development Council (NEDC), asked me how long I wanted to remain a journalist. It was common knowledge that MacDougall was likely to move to a new Department of Economic Affairs if Labour won the election and that he was looking for recruits.

My time at the Department of Economic Affairs (DEA) – basically the calendar year 1965 with a month tagged on to both ends – was important mainly for the contacts I made and the subsequent belief of people that I was writing about Whitehall from experience. Treasury officials would say to me, 'Why don't you go back to the *FT* and we can talk to you again?', so distrustful were they of the DEA.

The DEA did not hold any of the levers of power and its influence depended entirely on George Brown's voice in Cabinet. Brown would occasionally talk to me about 'the government which you don't support'. His instinct was right. I had voted Labour in 1964 because I hoped without much confidence that Wilson would honour his own pledge and strike a blow against nuclear proliferation by abandoning the British deterrent. But on the economic side, I had backed Maudling's dash for growth as the most radical show in town and was horrified that the incoming Labour government shattered confidence by shouting from the rooftops about the overall payments deficit it had inherited – very minor by later standards.

On my arrival MacDougall asked if I would mind going to the Information Department. My instinct not to argue was confirmed when I found the working economists sitting in a large room at desks all equipped with hand calculators which looked like pencil sharpeners. It is only in posts near to the level of Chief Economic Adviser that an economist who is not a statistician at heart can make an impact.

Some of my friends say that someone less introverted would have concentrated on getting close to George Brown. There were points in Brown's favour and he was often nearer the mark than the more erudite Wilson; but he did not have the genius that would have made his faults forgivable. Much has been made of his tendency to be the worse for wear after liquor. But he was at his most bullying when sober, especially with Labour Party officials whose jobs were at risk.

I left the DEA when the *Financial Times* offered me the post of economic editor and I returned like a homing pigeon. At first I was inhibited by the self-denying ordinance of the British press in not mentioning devaluation. Nevertheless, I did write for PEP a pamphlet entitled *Inquest on Planning in Britain,* which was devoted to showing how nothing else would work unless the UK devalued or floated sterling. Even PEP had to be prodded into publishing. It was some months after the November 1967 devaluation that Newton at last agreed that I should write a weekly *Economic Viewpoint.*

The Bogus Dilemma

My most productive years were around 1968–72. I doubt if I thought of anything original. Nowadays most ideas in political theory as well as economics inevitably come from the academic world. But I was interested in taking them seriously for the light they shed outside the academic game. My first venture in that period was a book called *Left or Right: The Bogus Dilemma*, published in 1968. The theme in stark simplicity was this: Hitler and Stalin were seen as at opposite ends of a left–right spectrum, while in fact they had more in common with each other than either had with more middle-of-the-road politicians. I did not suggest that terms such as 'left' or 'right' could be dropped. My main objection was to their use as a one-dimensional calibrating scale.

My own book had a subtext. This was a protest against 'socialists in the literary and theatrical world, who rightly leap into protests when civil liberties or freedom of expression are threatened', but did not realize that the end of competitive private enterprise would bring every form of artistic expression under state control. The contemporary Labour government had imposed savage travel restrictions to save foreign currency. 'Yet one of the severest restrictions it is possible for governments to impose on personal liberty in times of peace was greeted with hardly a word of protest from Labour's intellectual camp followers.'

On the other hand, *Left or Right* was strongly critical of Conservatives for combining relatively permissive attitudes in economic policy with an authoritarian approach to questions of personal conduct. While I was writing, the Tory Conference carried by an overwhelming majority an extreme resolution disapproving not merely of legalization but any re-examination of the law covering soft drugs. Quintin Hogg expressed the charitable Christian wish that 'addicts of hashish and marijuana would be pursued with the utmost severity the law allows. I hope that they find themselves in the Old Bailey, and however distinguished their position in the Top Ten, that they will be treated as criminals deserve to be treated.'

It took me a long time to get used to the fact that my first book (that on the Treasury) sold far more than any of the others I wrote, even when I had moved from what I thought was a specialist subject to one of general interest. I always imagined that the philosopher A.J. Ayer must have felt rather similarly when all his life he was far more famous for the first book he wrote in his mid-twenties, *Language, Truth and Logic,* than for any of his later works.

My Own U-turn

It was soon afterwards that I made my only big conscious U-turn. At the suggestion of Charles Goodhart, then of the Bank of England, I read Milton Friedman's 1967 Presidential Address to the American Economic Association.

I had always been sufficiently hard-headed to accept the Phillips curve, which showed that the lower the level of unemployment, the faster wages would rise and the worse inflation would be. It took Friedman, however, to demonstrate that the Phillips curve could never be stable. Eventually workers would take into account the higher inflation, and in a sufficiently tight labour market would insist on still larger wage increases to catch up. This doctrine was sometimes called the 'vertical Phillips curve', sometimes the 'accelerationist hypothesis' and sometimes the 'natural rate of unemployment'. The latter was changed by some economists to the NAIRU – the non-accelerating inflation rate of unemployment – to banish the idea that there was anything natural about it.

The basic propositions are now very familiar among macroeconomists and are summarized in Chapter 7 of this volume; but at the time they were explosive stuff. They dealt a death blow to unreconstructed Keynesian demand management. For if there was only one rate, or range, of unemployment consistent with either price stability or even a stable rate of inflation, attempting to run the economy at a higher pressure through demand management was asking for disaster. For it would lead not only to faster inflation, with which one could live, but to accelerating inflation, with which one could not.

My U-turn had little to do with the much-better-known Friedman doctrines about controlling the money supply. If there was some special angle to my own position it was in seeing that the NAIRU and the vertical Phillips curve were the key points of the counter-revolution and that arguments about the monetary transmission process were second-order.

By about 1969 I had grasped the explosive potential of the Friedman address and was indeed sorry that it had not been fully evident in the second edition of my Treasury book, now entitled *Steering the Economy*. Indeed, I went to the length of writing a critical review of that edition in the *Banker* under the pseudonym of 'A. Shepherd'. As a consolation I was able to state my new beliefs in the final edition of *Steering the Economy*, published by Penguin at the beginning of 1971.

The Not-So-Great-and-Good

There was one belief which carried over for a while from my radical Keynesian phase to my counter-revolutionary one: that was in flexible exchange rates. In the summer of 1967 the Conservatives held an open conference on economic policy with speakers of all persuasions. I had been assured of free speech and I delivered an ideological tirade against the City for being willing to surrender every other kind of freedom, and indeed every other policy, for the sake of a particular currency ratio.

The men in grey suits became alarmed that the conference would turn into a demonstration on behalf of devaluation. During the lunchbreak, Edward Heath, who had not heard my speech, said to me: 'If you must talk bollocks, talk bollocks in private.' By the afternoon, the counter-attack was under way. Paul Bareau – a very senior City journalist – eloquently warned that the Tories would 'rue the day' if they ever became the party of devaluation, which of course they did. But first Harold Wilson himself was forced to devalue in November the same year.

In 1970 a short book of mine appeared entitled *The Price of Economic Freedom: A Guide to Flexible Rates.* The mistake was to issue it as a hardback, when it simply put forward what was by then a well-known academic point of view. A work designed to popularize, in however serious a way, an existing intellectual position is best issued as a think-tank paper or broadside.

My activities were not confined to public advocacy. In 1969–70, Keith Joseph, then Shadow Trade and Industry Secretary, asked me to join a small group, not limited to Conservatives, to consider UK balance of payments policy. Somehow I was able to persuade the committee to report in favour of a floating exchange rate – which may have contributed something to Heath's subsequent decision to make Joseph Secretary of State for Social Services instead of Trade and Industry.

It was also at the end of the 1960s that I got on to a few academic establishment committees such as those of the Royal Economic Society, the National Institute and PEP. I did not enjoy arguing about research frameworks for other people's work; and I had far too bloated a respect for the senior economist members. Moreover, in practice, these committees spent time on matters such as determining the secretary's salary while she was out of the room. Although the committees were concerned with economics, I realized that any proposals to pay staff according to the state of the market would not have been welcome.

My membership several years later of the Armstrong Committee, set up by the Institute for Fiscal Studies to report on UK budgetary reform, was more interesting, although I was very much in the back seat. I took a, greater part in the Peacock Committee which sat in 1985–6, ostensibly to consider the future of the licence fee. The basic idea of the Committee's Report was to establish in broadcasting the equivalent of a publishing market where viewers and listeners could pay directly. The detail can be found in an article I wrote for the *Political Quarterly.* But I was left with the following reflections. First, the establishment of this market would depend far more on the growth of technology than anything we recommended. Secondly, committees of this kind waste most of their time listening to interested parties and pressure groups, whose views are known before they enter the room. Thirdly, the projections of the researchers were largely irrelevant to the findings, which depended much more on how people lined up on paternalism versus consumer choice. Fourthly, too many broadcasters reminded me of the Oxford don, who when asked by a soldier in 1915 what he was doing to defend their common civilization replied: 'My dear sir, you do not realize that I *am* the civilization that you are defending.' Fifthly, I remain pleased with my role in entrenching an indexed licence fee, which did more to protect the BBC from political interference than all the actions of the public service broadcasting lobby. Sixthly, the Home Office blamed me personally for what it regarded as the Committee's overwide interpretation of its terms of reference and blackballed me from future investigations. This was excessively flattering.

The Role of Economics

I had long mulled over a book which would adjudicate the claims made by writers such as Hayek and Friedman identifying a free society with a free economy. The idea was to extract the kernel of truth and to say in what respects they were right or wrong. Previously I had put off the endeavour as too daunting. But I was impelled into the breach by the hysterical media reaction to the first overt Conservative flirtation with market-based policies.

This related not to the Thatcher government but to the Heath government of 1970–4 in its first 'Selsdon' phase. The Selsdon Park hotel was where Conservative leaders met privately before the 1970 election campaign and afterwards briefed political reporters in an abrasively pro-market fashion. The phase lasted until the celebrated U-turn towards pay and price controls and industrial intervention, following the government's alarm at rising unemployment and the loss of the first miners' strike in early 1972.

I tried to introduce an empirical content into my projected work on the market economy by an attitude survey among economists. I had seen multiple-choice questions for students in which, to take one example, the correct answer to a question about below-cost housing for the poor was that it was less efficient than direct social security payments 'because it will result in too much housing and too little of the other things consumers want.' If this statement – so opposed to everything that Labour MPs preached – really did represent an economic consensus, then this would not only be powerful ammunition but would also show that there was a distinctive economic view of public policy 'different from that of politicians, journalists or other educated laymen'. In the end the survey was published separately as another slim volume.

Since I was subsequently asked by the Institute of Economic Affairs (IEA) to write a preface to a much larger survey of economists' opinions published in 1990 it is illuminating to take the two surveys together. Both did show a kind of economic orthodoxy embodied in a belief in competitive markets, use of the price mechanism and cash redistribution of income. The outlook was also pretty Keynesian in the English post-war sense of believing that demand management affected output and employment and that fiscal policy made a big difference here.

In both surveys the majority of respondents took every opportunity to show that they were opposed to anything like a minimal state approach, to endorse the slogan of more equality and to reject cuts in government spending. There was something goody-goody in the economists' attitudes. In 1973 the approved correct answer, given by a large majority, was that a freely operating market system could perform efficiently even in communist countries. Some doubts might have occurred to economists even in the early 1970s if they had been more familiar with works on the economics of property rights or public choice.

One of Margaret Thatcher's most popular remarks may have been when she intervened in a *Yes, Minister* television programme to say that all government economists should, without exception, be sacked. Tempting though it would be to agree, generalized attacks on the economics profession amount almost to a category mistake. For if all economists were put painlessly to sleep, human curiosity about matters such as the wealth of nations, booms and slumps, or why some people are rich and others poor would remain, and the profession would re-emerge.

What has gone wrong with economics is the over-emphasis on technique as opposed to underlying ideas. Perhaps the time has come for a less strenuous insistence on economics as a science. Most of the hard-core economic doctrines about the gains from international trade, analysis of opportunity costs, and the linking of prices to costs to allocate resources are neither falsifiable propositions nor just political value judgements. They are ways of looking at the world. Economists do not need to pose as *ersatz* physicists. Philosophers and literary critics know more about their subjects than lay outsiders without their being in a position to supply authoritative answers; and economists may be nearer to them than they are to hard scientists.

Capitalism and the Permissive Society

My full-length study of the relation between a free market and a free society was eventually published in 1973 under the title *Capitalism and the Permissive Society*. It is still available under the title *A Restatement of Economic Liberalism* and its conclusions are summarized in Chapter 14 of the present volume. But its main value lies in the detailed explorations *en route*.

The conclusion of my study of Hayek and Friedman (as well as others) was that neither had supplied adequate criteria for differentiating between good and bad types of government intervention, although I drew from both of them and from the then new school of public choice, better labelled 'the economics of politics'. I went to press before the appearance of Rawls's *Theory of Justice*, but was able to pick up his guiding ideas from his earlier articles and managed to formulate for myself a distinction between his contractarian method – which still provides the best hope of disinterested discussion of contentious public issues – and his much more dubious specific principles.

The part of my book in which my heart lay, however, was the less formal prologue, which identified with the permissive values of the 1960s, but attacked the radicals of the time for the failure to see that market capitalism embodied their emphasis on 'doing your own thing'. While *Left or Right* is my favourite among my books, *Capitalism and the Permissive Society* is the one by which I would want to be judged.

Perplexities and Convexities

There have been no dramatic changes in my standpoint since then, but mainly evolution, investigation, elaboration and endeavours to disseminate and recycle.

I spent a year in 1973–4 as a temporary Fellow at Nuffield College, Oxford, and in 1978 a semester at Chicago University (although based on the Law School, not the Economics Faculty). My main gain during this period was in contacts, ideas for further reading and so on, rather than in any specific work which I undertook then.

My tendency to get lost when trying to follow a mass of symbolic computations has long haunted me. When I took my degree at Cambridge I decided at the last moment to add public finance to political theory and applied economics as a third optional subject, knowing that the two best would count. There was a similar syndrome at Nuffield.

On Friday nights there was an economics seminar, which could be on a wide variety of topics, provided that the treatment was sufficiently mathematical. On the same evenings there were more immediately appealing seminars, for instance David Butler's on Modern British Politics, where I once had to hold the fort because of the late arrival of Harold Wilson. Even seminars on British Commonwealth History seemed more appealing than the technical economic ones. Yet there was an unspoken assumption by the economic Fellows that unless I attended their advanced sessions I was just a dilettante.

I was at first surprised to be asked about economic matters by dons in other subjects within earshot of great economic authorities. It was only afterwards that I realized they were afraid of being fobbed off or having their heads bitten off by these very authorities. The low point was reached when I met at dinner a crew-cut young American who told me that his seminar had been 'on convexities'. (A convex curve bulges outwards. One was expected to know the economic context from the mathematical shorthand.)

Later still I gave a talk at Warwick (where I had become a visiting professor of Politics) on such matters as the relative credibility of money supply and exchange rate targets and the role of an independent central bank. I was followed by a celebrated specialist visitor who was preparing to fill the board with symbols. He was talking about credibility: which I thought I had already been doing under a different title.

During these years I was frequently embarrassed by the appalling rudeness of my supposed allies among the monetarists. Somewhat earlier I attended a dinner organized by the patiently enquiring Geoffrey Crowther, a former editor of *The Economist*, to bring himself up to date on the debate between floating and fixed exchange rates. On the fixed-rate side was Harold Lever, Labour's engaging financial expert and later Cabinet adviser to Wilson and Callaghan. On the floating side were Harry Johnson and myself. It would have been better to have heard either of us alone. For I had to defer to Johnson, who was not only my senior in every sense, but from whom I had derived many of my own ideas on the subject. Yet instead of presenting the case in a straightforward way, he started attacking Harold Lever, almost personally, unwisely challenging Lever's competence and showing annoyance at having to debate with him. Afterwards Lever said to me: 'I am sorry if I annoyed Harry.' Any apology should have been the other way round.

On one occasion Richard Kahn was publicly attacked for writing articles for *The Times* not based on journal articles 'refereed' by other economists. On another occasion I had to listen at coffee to a still-unconvinced Oxbridge economist being abused by an American monetarist along the lines of 'Why should I explain it to you?' Not that the unconverted British mainstream were without spots. Their favourite attitude was to be puzzled, to 'not understand' and to treat the monetarists with not merely intellectual, but even a touch of social, condescension.

Contradictions of Democracy

On a different planet from the squabbling technicians are the prophets of doom. There were predictions of the end of the world as the end of the first Christian millenium approached. Alarms since then have been too numerous to list. Every tremor in the financial markets has been greeted with cries of 'another 1929' or another Great Depression. I have often been asked by broadcasting producers whether I agreed. When I have replied, 'No; but there are still problems worth discussing', the reply has usually been, 'Can you tell me of anyone who *does* think we are in for a Great Depression?'

During the mid-1970s, following the Heath defeat in the second miners' strike, there was much talk about the 'ungovernability of Britain'. This provided the right climate for a paper of mine written in 1974, entitled 'The Economic Consequences of Democracy'. It began: 'The conjecture to be discussed is that liberal representative democracy suffers from internal tensions, which are likely to increase in time, and on present indications the system is likely to pass away within the lifetime of people now adult.' Eventually I reproduced it as a chapter in a book of essays, *The Economic Consequences of Democracy,* published in 1977. After the Treasury book it is probably my best-known work (although not among economists).

In truth I was agnostic about my own conjecture. In another essay in the book I cited Popper's views on the mistaken identification of scientific method in social studies with historical prophecy. My real aim was to exploit the prevailing mood to propagate some observations in Schumpeter's *Capitalism, Socialism and Democracy,* first published during the Second World War. Schumpeter saw democracy as a market in which politicians competed for votes, as business-men competed for customers. Political and economic theorists have treated him as a precursor of their own formal models of political competition. What they overlooked were his more fundamental statements of the conditions under which democratic competition would work. These included a limit to the effective range of political decisions, a well-trained bureaucracy as a constraint (I instanced the pre-1914 Bank of England) and above all tolerance and democratic self-control.

I was hitting at the sacred cow of unfettered representative democracy – what Hailsham was later to call 'elective dictatorship'. Majority – or still more, plurality – voting is in reality simply a convenient decision rule. Nothing, however, was heard from Hailsham on elective dictatorship after the Tories returned in 1979.

The 'Jay–Brittan' Period

In the middle years of the 1970s, Peter Jay, who was then economic editor of *The Times*, and I were regarded by many in the British economic establishment as two terrible monetarist twins because of our scepticism of the Heath dash for growth. The charge was that, because of the coincidence of two people with such views having prominent positions in two heavyweight newspapers, half-baked journalism was undermining proper economics. Some of our articles were even given to students as set-pieces for demolition. But if British academics only knew of the post-Keynesian counter-revolution from press articles, they had themselves to blame for their own professional lag.

Jay and I had slightly different starting points. Nevertheless, unlike many purely technical monetarists, Jay never flinched from the implications of the new (or rediscovered) ideas on the ultimate futility of traditional full employment policies – witness his role in James Callaghan's famous speech to the 1976 Labour Conference in which the former Prime Minister delivered his much-cited speech about governments not being able to spend their way to prosperity.

The possibility of a government more committed to a market approach and less inclined to buying off the unions came into prospect when Margaret Thatcher first won the leadership of the Conservative Party in 1975 and then seemed to have a chance of winning the coming election, which she duly did in 1979. I did not, however, want to be considered for an advisory post.

One very modest part I did later play was as a member of the 'Gooies' (group of unofficial economic advisers), whom Nigel Lawson had assembled to advise him once every couple of months or so in the last two or three years of his Chancellorship in 1987–9. The mistake of the Gooies was not to insist on written minutes, as a lot could be learned about who was right and who was wrong on which issues and when. I was irate to find at my first meeting, when I warned of overheating, that I was fobbed off by other Gooies, because the monetary numbers were not then worrying them. Later on, my views on overheating were lost to sight because of the support I gave Lawson both in his campaign for Exchange Rate Mechanism (ERM) membership and in shadowing the Deutschmark.

It is clear from my *Financial Times* articles that I believed in 'playing it long' on the valid grounds that, if sterling were linked to the Deutschmark, the UK could not have in the long run a faster rate of inflation in traded products than Germany. But I should have paid more attention than I did to the official Treasury's line, which was to downplay inflationary threats even in the short term. The lesson throughout my career has been that I should pay more attention to subtle differences with my allies of the moment and not worry about a common front against the rest.

The Thatcher government's economic record is discussed in the main body of this book, but to me personally the period was an embarrassment. I dreaded the name 'Thatcher' coming up before the soup. I found most of the attacks on her ignorant and condescending. But as Margaret Thatcher sold a version of market economics as part of a package containing national reassertion abroad (symbolized by the Falklands victory) and something she called Victorian values at home, I could not line up as 'one of us'.

There was, however, a minefield for me in the core economic area. When the Keynesian establishment had earlier said that tackling inflation by monetary policies without an incomes policy would lead to one million unemployed, it was indignantly denounced by some of the more unwise monetarists. Yet in the early 1980s unemployment had shot up to near 3 million or $10\frac{1}{2}$ per cent. There was no shortage of *post hoc* rationalizations; but I almost avoided social occasions at which economic questions might arise.

I was, however, much less embarrassed than the technical monetarists by the coincidence of a very sharp, perhaps excessive, squeeze on inflation with a bad upward overshoot of monetary targets. This gave me an opportunity to write for the IEA 'How to End the Monetarist Controversy', which I afterwards incorporated in a book of essays, *The Role and Limits of Government*. The paper was associated with the slogan of a nominal GDP objective. But too many participants in the debate treated this as if it were an alternative to existing monetary targets rather than the higher-order goal which it was.

By then I was pretty sure that my natural mode of expression was something shorter than a book but longer than a newspaper column or speech; and I could not understand the aversion of publishers (with honourable exceptions such as Temple Smith and Edward Elgar) to collected writings. I find it much easier to absorb material reprinted in decently bound books than in the dreadful piles of copied conference papers, so much in vogue, which are difficult to store and impossible to find afterwards.

Presentational tactics apart, there was a sea-change in the financial press during the 1980s. A recent writer, Wayne Parsons, compares it with the advent of the trans-Atlantic cable in 1866, which together with the growth of a wider investing public, encouraged a new brand of journalism for readers more interested in personal financial gain than in great debates on tariffs or currency theory. The change was also abetted by the professionalization of economists, who became keener on academic respectability than on policy discussion.

The wheel has since turned full circle several times. Parsons believes that economic pundits have been among the casualties of the information revolution. Market economists should not complain about changes in the market they themselves face. But I cannot believe that the instant comment on the latest indicator by a City dealer in front of a computer terminal is the last word in human wisdom.

Egg on My ERM Face

The exchange rate which loomed so large in my early writings came to haunt me in the last few years. Just before the European Exchange Rate Mechanism was launched in 1979, I wrote an article for the *Journal of Common Market Studies,* criticizing the ERM for providing the worst of both the fixed and the floating exchange rate worlds.

But as the 1980s wore on I could not help feeling, in view of the extreme difficulty the British authorities had in establishing satisfactory monetary guidelines, that there was much to be said for an exchange rate link with a known sound-money country, namely Germany. This was not any profound revelation, but mainly a second-order reflection on how to achieve a nominal framework for macroeconomic policy. The same thought occurred to the Chancellor, Nigel Lawson, and to many others.

But because I took Lawson's side on what became a high-profile issue and coupled it with a principled objection to Thatcher's attempt to settle the matter by Prime Ministerial *ukase,* Lawson and I were regarded as a conspiratorial duo, reminiscent of the equally imaginary Jay–Brittan duo of the 1970s. Some people assumed that Lawson had inspired my articles while others thought I was a sinister backstairs influence on him. I was even asked to give interviews on what his views were, when he was unavailable.

Where, however, I took my eye off the ball was in failing to appreciate how the German handling of unification completely changed the balance of the argument after 1989. Like most others, I celebrated the fall of the Berlin Wall but saw the inflationary threat in Germany. But I both misjudged how much and how soon German interest rates might come down from their post-unification peak and how much harm high German rates would inflict on other countries with a large debt overhang. For many reasons, the German Mark was no longer the ideal anchor for the currencies of other countries that it had been earlier.

As it was, these events took the shine off the knighthood I received from a much friendlier post-Thatcher British government in 1992 and even from the *Légion d'Honneur* that I received from France a few months earlier. I was left with a feeling of a lot of egg on my face and all kinds of unexpressed reservations on the part of colleagues and readers. Chapter 9, newly written for the present book, represents my attempts to pick up the pieces. The demonstration that a floating exchange rate does not provide full freedom for a government 'to manage our own interest rates for our own benefit' is novel, at least outside the more esoteric literature.

As for the political aspect of the European Community – or 'Union' as it now misleadingly calls itself, I would just recall the lines from Alexander Pope:

> For forms of government, let fools contend,
> What e'er is best administered is best.

This quotation puts too much weight on the question-begging word 'administration'; but it does make the point that governments are workaday organizations to provide those services which are better secured by collective action than by either the profit motive or by voluntary co-operation. If we have a functional attitude to government we shall neither worry about the shedding of national sovereignty nor actually desire to do so just for the fun of creating new institutions.

Talking to economic liberals on the Continent, I have found quite a lot of sympathy for British opposition to centralization and Brussels-imposed regulation – combined with amazement that this arises in the name of an outmoded nationalism from which they are trying to escape. If I had to give a snap judgement now, I would favour a European executive with minimal state functions, confined to security, external and trade policy and, yes, the issue of a common currency.

The complications created by the end of European communism for Western European monetary policy are, however, trivial compared with its wider implications. The enormous difficulties that the former communist countries have had in establishing successful market economies surely shows that reflection on the foundations of market liberalism is still required.

REFERENCES

Samuel Brittan: Selected Publications

NB: Journal articles, booklets and so on are not – with one exception – listed if they have been incorporated in books.

Books
The Treasury Under the Tories 1951–64, Harmondsworth, Middx: Penguin, 1964; Rev. edn published as *Steering the Economy*, London: Secker & Warburg, 1969; final edn: *Steering the Economy,* Penguin, 1971.
Left or Right: The Bogus Dilemma, London: Secker & Warburg, 1968.
The Price of Economic Freedom: A Guide to Flexible Rates, London: Macmillan, 1970.
Is There an Economic Consensus?, London: Macmillan, 1973.
Capitalism and the Permissive Society, London: Macmillan, 1973; 2nd edn published as *A Restatement of Economic Liberalism,* 1988.
The Delusion of Incomes Policy (with Peter Lilley), London: Temple Smith, 1977.
The Economic Consequences of Democracy, London: Temple Smith, 1977; 2nd enlarged edn, Aldershot, Hants.: Wildwood House, 1988.
The Role and Limits of Government, London: Temple Smith, 1983.

Articles, booklets, etc.
Inquest on Planning in Britain, London: PEP, 1967.
'A People's Stake in North Sea Oil' (with Barry Riley), *Lloyds Bank Review*, April 1978; 2nd edn, Unservile State Papers, no. 26, 1980.
'A Compromise that is Worse than Either Extreme', *Journal of Common Market Studies*, March 1979.
How to End the Monetarist Controversy, 2nd edn, London: Institute of Economic Affairs, 1982.
'The Politics and Economics of Privatisation', *Political Quarterly*, April 1984.
'Privatisation – a Comment', *Economic Journal*, March 1986.
'The Fight for Freedom in Broadcasting', *Political Quarterly*, March 1987.

Other Works Cited

Banham, J., *The Anatomy of Change*, London: Weidenfeld & Nicholson, 1994.
Brittan, S. and A. Hamlin (eds), *Market Capitalism and Moral Values*, Aldershot, Hants.: Edward Elgar, forthcoming.
Cobden, Richard, Letter to John Bright, 16 September 1847, cited in John Morley, *Life of Richard Cobden*, London, 1896.
Cole, G.D.H., *The Intelligent Man's Guide to the Post-war World*, 1947.

Eltis, Walter, *Classical Economics, Public Expenditure and Growth*, Aldershot, Hants.: Edward Elgar, 1993.

Hogben, Lancelot, *Mathematics for the Million*, London: Allen & Unwin, 1936.

Kynaston, David, *The Financial Times: A Centenary History*, London: Viking, 1988.

MacDougall, Donald, *Don and Mandarin*, London: John Murray, 1987.

Marshall, Alfred, *Principles of Economics*, London: Macmillan, 1890.

Parsons, Wayne, *The Power of the Financial Press*, Aldershot, Hants.: Edward Elgar, 1989.

Popper, Karl, *The Poverty of Historicism*, 2nd edn, London: Routledge & Kegan Paul, 1960.

Rawls, John, *A Theory of Justice*, Cambridge, Mass.: Harvard University Press, 1972.

Ricketts, M. and E. Shoesmith, *British Economic Opinion: A Survey of 1,000 Economists*, London: Institute of Economic Affairs, 1990.

Robinson, Joan, *The Accumulation of Capital*, London: Macmillan, 1956.

Schumpeter, J.A., *Capitalism, Socialism and Democracy*, 1942; final edn, London: Allen & Unwin, 1952.

Taylor, Gordon Rattray, *Economics for the Exasperated*, 1947.

PART ONE

Political Economy

1   Economics and ethics[*]

INTRODUCTION

A well-known and fair-minded television commentator stated that he found it odd to begin a television series on the background to the conflict and misery in Bosnia 'with a lecture by currency manipulator George Soros, of all people, on ethics'.

The commentator in question, Christopher Dunkley, immediately qualified his observation by reminding us that Soros had in fact 'spent some of the millions he had made in speculating against the pound [in 1992] on liberal and humane charities in the area in question'. He added that the content of Soros's lecture 'on the need for a new world order based on the Open Society ... where minorities and minority opinion are respected' was 'wholly laudable'.

But the impression remained that, however praiseworthy the financier's other actions, these were an offset to immoral professional behaviour. As against this was the view, particularly widespread in the English-language anti-EC media, that speculators deserved a medal for helping to bring down unrealistic currency parities and systems.

I start with an unresolved headline issue to make the simple point that the relation between moral evaluation and economic analysis has come back into fashion. It went underground in the heyday of the belief in economics as a purely technical guide to action; but it has now resurfaced.

A sign of the change in the academic sphere is that the lead article in the June 1993 issue of the *Journal of Economic Literature* was entitled 'Economics and Contemporary Moral Philosophy'. The authors consider the relationship important for four reasons (I have changed the order):

1.   Some moral commitments are necessary to evaluate either whole economic systems or more limited policy proposals.
2.   The study of positive economics – of what is – turns out to be extremely difficult to separate from normative economics – of what should be – for reasons that go deep into the structure of human language and action.

---

[*] Presidential Address to Section F (Economics) of the British Association, August 1993.

3. The highly technical subject known as 'welfare economics' – which is only remotely connected with the welfare state – rests on complex and disputable moral presuppositions.
4. The moral beliefs of economic agents influence their behaviour in the market place.

It is on the last of these aspects that I wish to concentrate, even though it has received the least academic study.

One reason why the whole subject was for so long underemphasized was a little bit of what I can only call economists' do-it-yourself philosophy. This is the prejudice that it is impossible to have a reasoned discussion of alternative ends, because such a discussion would depend on value judgements which are supposed to be a pure matter of personal taste: so that disapproval of disparities of income and wealth is regarded as like a taste for strawberry ice cream, about which no argument is possible.

People can and do argue about moral beliefs without violating Hume's law that you cannot derive an 'ought' from an 'is' statement. If the consequences of holding beliefs play any part in your moral outlook, then you should be prepared to modify your beliefs in relation to what you discover these consequences to be.

Perhaps the best way of demonstrating how this can be done is still Amartya Sen's distinction in *Collective Choice and Social Welfare* between a basic and a non-basic value judgement. A basic judgement is one that applies in all conceivable circumstances. If circumstances can be envisaged where a judgement would not apply, it is non-basic. Take the statement 'men and women should be allowed to dress as they like'. This may appear to be an ultra-liberal, but undiscussable, basic judgement. Suppose, however, that the person who utters it flinches when asked if he or she would still hold to it, even if it turned out that mini-skirts cause cancer in the eye of the beholder. In that case, the judgement turns out to be non-basic. The fundamental point is that there is no way of demonstrating in advance that a judgement is basic, as no one would have occasion to consider all conceivable circumstances in forming a judgement. Where we have not had to face a concrete choice we may simply not know what our real values are.

THE POST-COMMUNIST WORLD

The importance of the moral aspects of economics should have been brought home by the events in the former communist countries, and especially the former Soviet Union. More thoughtful economists have always known that markets need a background not only of formal laws, but also of accepted rules of behaviour, if the invisible hand is to work.

Unfortunately, the content of these rules has been taken for granted rather than studied by most mainstream economists. The influence of beliefs on behaviour was for too long confined to discussions over coffee, and their study left to sociologists and others, often unsympathetic to the market process. Yet it is just this aspect, which economists have neglected in their formal work – such as the domain of permissible actions which can be taken against competitors, or the rules and conventions governing private and state property – which have proved crucial in Russia and its neighbours rather than the theorems which have been the predominant study of high-level professional economists. The most important understanding needed in the newly emerging market economies is not of the refinements of marginal cost pricing or of general equilibria, but of the difference between criminal behaviour and legitimate profit-seeking.

The need is for an empirically grounded study of how market institutions are built up from the Hobbesian 'war of all against all' which otherwise emerges from the destruction of a central dictatorship. So-called soft subjects, such as cultural history, may have more to tell us about the different outcomes of the breakdown of central planning in the Czech Republic, Russia, the outlying former Soviet republics and China, than mainstream economics.

IMMORAL MORALITY

An extremely important point to clarify is that the influence of moral beliefs is not necessarily for the good. This statement is not self-contradictory, so long as we use the word 'moral' to describe beliefs to which we are not necessarily committed ourselves. The alternative usage, which is sometimes difficult to avoid, is to employ terms such as 'moralistic' to describe other people's moral beliefs which we consider to be misguided.

For many years I have carried around a quotation from Bertrand Russell:

> If men were actuated by self-interest, which they are not – except in the case of a few saints – the whole human race would co-operate. There would be no more wars, no more armies, no more bombs ....
>
> I do not deny that there are better things than selfishness, and that some people achieve these things. I maintain, however, on the one hand that there are few occasions upon which large bodies of men, such as politics is concerned with, can rise above selfishness, while on the other hand, there are a great many circumstances in which populations will fall below selfishness, if selfishness is interpreted as enlightened self-interest. And among those occasions on which people fall below self-interest are most of the occasions on which they are convinced that they are acting from idealistic motives. Much that passes as idealism is disguised hatred or disguised love of power.

More atrocious deeds may well have been committed through the self-righteous commitment to ill-conceived moral codes than through deliberate selfishness and greed. The Grand Inquisitor in sixteenth-century Spain sincerely believed that the highest moral goal was the protection and advancement of the faith. When Philip II asks, in *Don Carlos*: '*La natura, l'amor tacer potranno in me?* [May I not heed the voice of nature and love?]' the Inquisitor replies: '*Tutto tacer dovra per esalter la fe* [Everything must be silenced at the command of the faith].'

If moral codes can have perverse effects when the stakes are so high, can they not also be pernicious in the normal business of economic life?

BUSINESS ETHICS

The subject known as business ethics is a sub-branch of economics and ethics. But it is a branch that is immensely more prosperous than the rest of the business. The subject has blossomed since the mid-1980s in the wake of a number of corporate scandals. Some 500 business ethics courses are said to be available in the US, and the subject is taught in 90 per cent of business schools. Europe's first publication in the area was, no one should be surprised, in Italian. The spirit of the subject is captured by an *Economist* headline, 'How to be ethical and still come top'. John Kay, himself a professor of business economics, has remarked:

> If Aristotle, John Stuart Mill and G. E. Moore could not sort our ethical problems once and for all, it is unlikely that today's business gurus can solve them with a few trite phrases. But, untroubled by these concerns, they go on earning more for a single lecture than Aristotle, Mill and Moore were paid in their entire lifetime.

If we want to be more charitable, we can say that business ethics is a celebration of the modern corporation – which is why corporate executives devote shareholders' funds to it. I shall come back later to discuss the supposed social responsibilities of business.

In the last resort, however, business ethics is not a real subject, as distinct from ethics generally. Some philosophers make a distinction between morality itself, which concerns how we should behave, and ethics, which they see as a more abstract analysis of the language of moral discourse. But in ordinary language ethics is used to cover both aspects, as it is here.

In this sense there is only ethics and its application to different spheres. Business, medicine, politics and law all throw up their special problems; but whatever our basic morality, it should apply to all of these fields as well as personal behaviour.

A frequent business conundrum concerns bribery. A business executive may be strongly opposed to the practice, but if he refrains from bribing some overseas government official, his competitors will obtain a lucrative order. This dilemma is but a particular instance of the difficulty of applying the Golden Rule, 'do unto others as you would have them do unto you', when others do not observe it. In this case the practice you would like to see observed is: do not give or take bribes.

But what do you do if others will not follow? Become a martyr; or do as others actually do, even though you are endorsing a pernicious practice?

Those who are genuinely interested in moral reasoning rather than striking attitudes will not stop there. The maxim against bribery is a lower-level rule of everyday morality, not a basic principle. We merely think that human welfare would be greater in a world without bribery.

To say either 'never give or take bribes though the heavens fall' or, at the other extreme, 'grow up and do what others do' is an evasion. Circumstances need to be examined, including the validity of the maxim itself. In the would-be Soviet command economy the only way of matching supplies to requirements was by a series of side payments and unofficial deals between officials in state enterprises. In these circumstances, it may have been a duty to encourage such payments to help Soviet citizens lead a slightly less impoverished life. Of course, at a later stage when the command economy broke down, the legacy of these habits did a great deal of damage. But it would hardly have been a realistic obligation to have had to guess how many decades would elapse before the collapse of the Soviet system.

How about more standard cases where we believe that the community in question would benefit from less bribery or no bribery at all? Even then we should pause before inflicting known and measurable damage on our own family's standard of living for the sake of a hypothetical gesture towards reform in a society which we may imperfectly understand.

But then reflect a little more: for the cost of observing the Golden Rule is often much less than it appears, especially in open, developed capitalist countries where the long-run returns from different kinds of enterprise tend towards equality. An example comes to mind of an Oxbridge college whose investments had plunged in a stock market slump. The head of the college glowered at his Fellows, who had insisted on a boycott of South African shares in the Apartheid period, saying that this was the kind of gesture the college could no longer afford.

In fact the cost was negligible in a highly liquid market such as the stock exchange. Market prices tend to move in such a way as to equalize prospective returns on different securities, allowing for risk. So by holding the next best alternative to South African securities the college was making a negligible sacrifice.

THE ECONOMICS OF POLITICS

My own interest in economics and ethics comes from a different area, the subject known in the US as public choice but best understood as the economics of politics. This study arose as a reaction to the pious notion that government somehow stands above the sordid self-interest of the common market place and is subject to higher motives and purpose. This view was labelled by Harry Johnson the Fabian-Benthamite view of government. By contrast, practitioners of public choice treat politicians as operating in their own market place, seeking votes rather than cash, in a market place that has its own distinctive kinds of failure.

This general approach has been a salutary one, whatever one may think of the specific contents of public choice theory. But it needs to be complemented by an analysis of the positive effects of moral beliefs. Just as political actors have their normal share of self-interest, so economic actors are influenced by their view or assumption on what is right and proper. David Hume, who has already been cited on 'ought' and 'is', penned the following observation:

> Force is always on the side of the governed, the governors have nothing to support them but opinion. It is therefore on opinion that government is founded: and this maxim extends to the most despotic and the most military of governments, as well as the most free and the most popular. The soldan of Egypt, or the emperor of Rome might drive his harmless subject, like brute beasts, against their sentiments and inclinations; but he must at least have led his mamalukes, or praetorian bands, like men, by their opinion.

Hume himself does not provide too much help in developing these observations further, partly because in that particular essay he is concerned mainly with political behaviour, and even there does not attempt any systematic theory. So we have to carry on ourselves.

THE DEBATE ON SELF-INTEREST

While there have been many discussions of economics and ethics over the last 200 years, they have all too rarely come to grips with the effect of specific moral beliefs on behaviour. Instead we have had a ferocious but highly generalized debate on the self-interest assumption that was supposed to underly classical political economy, and the message of selfishness which market economists were supposed to preach, 'Every man for himself and the devil take the hindmost'.

Throughout most of the debate there has been a confusion between self-interest and materialism. One can imagine a world in which material desires were satisfied with the product of a very few hours' work and most people spent most of their time reciting poetry and playing the harp to each other, perhaps charging for their performances. This would be a non-materialist world, but it could still be heavily influenced by self-interest. Modern economists have tried to remove this misunderstanding by saying that people try to maximize not material prosperity, but an abstract quality called utility – which is defined in a circular way to cover whatever it is that people seek or prefer.

With this amendment, many economists down to our own day have been happy to say, in George Stigler's words, that a person's utility 'depends upon the welfare of the actor, his family, plus a narrow circle of associates'. Many other thinkers, including some economists have, however, been enraged by this assumption.

Political defenders of capitalism and competitive markets have clutched at the inclusion of family and close associates as at a straw to absolve them from the sin of preaching selfishness. But the straw cannot bear the weight. From the genetic point of view, the pursuit of one's family's welfare is just a more extended form of selfishness. A greater concern for children, brothers or sisters than for the human race in general makes sense if survival is substituted for satisfaction as the main goal, and if the gene is substituted for the individual human being as the maximizing agent.

There is clearly much common ground between the 'selfish gene' and the self-interested economic man, and critics who dislike one usually dislike the other.

RATIONAL PROBLEM-SOLVING

An attempt has been made by some writers (such as G. Radnitzky) to overthrow any kind of self-interest assumption and to redefine economics as the rational problem-solving approach. From this point of view people's utility depends on self-chosen objectives of any kind. These may include leading saintly lives, maximizing charitable donations or promoting their church. Moreover, their utility may depend not just on their own welfare but on that of any group, even all mankind and generations yet unborn.

The rational problem-solving approach gets rid of the spectre of pure self-seeking, but at the same time provides the foundation of 'economic imperialism' – that is the attempt to colonize other subject areas. Radnitzky terms this approach 'universal economics', and argues that the 'bare building blocks of the Economic Approach (EA) are optimising and equilibrium, scarcity, opportunities, cost, preference and choice. Universal Economics is basically an invitation to straight thinking', recognizing that there are always such things as costs and benefits.

Defined in this way, economics becomes identical with what is often called decision theory. In fact this territory is no longer the monopoly of economists.

Mathematicians, theoretical statisticians, biologists, cyberneticists and philosophers have all made contributions. There is of course nothing more trivial than the faculty building in which studies are carried out. The point is that rational decision-taking is consistent with any behaviour that is not random, motiveless and therefore demonstrably irrational. Rationality by itself is insufficient to explain the key features of economic life, for which we need both more restrictive assumptions about motivation and more information on institutions such as markets, government, property rights and so on.

SUCCESSIVE CIRCLES

Why not move to a more realistic view of motivation, which avoids tautology, which is wider than the self-interest of the economist but narrower than the universal love of the preacher? Why not accept that most people have strong feelings of obligation towards relations and close friends, and some feelings towards colleagues, members of the same class or cultural group, race, nationality or creed? Different people would place these latter groups in different orders, so that the ordering of the successive circles of concern may vary; but the majority would have stronger feelings towards all than towards the human race in general. Why not then accept these circles as a basis for studying behaviour and assessing the performance of public authorities, as argued in more detail in Chapter 3?

The strength of obligation towards the outer circles will vary according to the person, the time and the issue at hand. When responding to tax changes we can expect something like John Stuart Mill's economic man who, 'prefers a greater proportion of wealth to a smaller'. When it comes to blood donations, people are motivated by a desire to help their fellows at modest cost. There are also high-pressure periods such as war or an old-fashioned miners' strike, when group or national loyalties override everything else. The adverse side is of course the intensification of hostile feelings towards outsiders: and it is fortunate that most people cannot live too long under such pressure-cooker conditions.

A test case of the strength of self-interest versus other loyalties is the so-called voting paradox – the question of why people vote when there is a vanishingly small chance that their action will influence the result. The self-interest model should have no difficulty in accommodating motives like self-expression, or the desire to be a good citizen, so long as the cost of voting is trivial – say a pleasant evening stroll to the polling booth. The self-interest model is in trouble, however, if people will go considerable distances on foot in discomfort in bad weather or in the face of attractive alternatives such as watching the 'match of the season' on television. I would expect the cost that people are prepared to bear to vote to vary a great deal: and maybe the only theories that we can generate about this will be low-level and culture-based.

One amusing result, which has been frequently replicated by Robert Frank and others, is that students of economics give more narrowly self-interested answers to attitude questionnaires than other students, and tend to go for the selfish behaviour in prisoner's dilemma games. If their textbooks tell them that it is how people act for the most part, they will be afraid of looking like suckers if they act differently. They may also believe that the results of such motivation will in the end not be too bad for the others, appearances to the contrary notwithstanding.

THE INVISIBLE HAND

Moralists have long been upset by Adam Smith's invisible hand doctrine, epitomized by the well-known quotation: 'It is not from the benevolence of the butcher, the brewer, or the baker that we expect our dinner, but from their regard of their own advantage.' Smith goes on to claim that in serving themselves they serve their fellows better than had they consciously striven to do so.

What bothers many people is the suggestion that free market economists in the tradition of Smith are urging people to be selfish. They are bemused rather than appeased by numerous other citations in which Smith emphasized the importance of sympathy with fellow men and women, and, despite the work of Smith scholars, I do not think he achieved a rounded doctrine.

Extolling selfishness would, however, be a very peculiar thing for a political economist to do. Not even the most libertarian economist would urge the shooting of competitors. Nearly all economists have accepted that there are many areas where the invisible hand does not work and, even where it does, it will only work successfully against a background of laws, habits, customs and institutions – as we have already noted in the context of the former communist countries.

As I go into this extensively in the next chapter, let me just say here that the invisible hand makes most sense as a *prima facie* rule of conduct within a wider system of morality. My suggestion is that in matters such as buying and selling, or in deciding what and how to produce, we would do others more good if we behave *as if* we were following our own self-interest rather than pursuing more altruistic goals. Some market-type process is necessary to yield the information that even a community of altruists would require to decide what to produce and by what methods it should be produced. Contrary to popular superstition, technology alone does not provide the answers.

The *as if* injunction must be applied with care. Even where it applies, the pursuit of self-interest must be limited by side constraints, such as the observance of contracts, honesty, non-violence and so on. Moreover, there are such things as public goods which will not be provided in sufficient quantity in the market place, because of the temptation to free-ride on the efforts of others. Obvious examples are defence and police. Indeed, there are many spheres where self-interest will only yield good results if there are appropriate adjustments made to the price structure by public policy, for example the enforcement of the principle that the polluter pays.

THE PRISONER'S DILEMMA

An intellectual device – invented nearly two centuries after Adam Smith – illustrating a situation where the invisible hand argument does not apply is known as the prisoner's dilemma. The danger is that anything I say on this topic will seem naive and over-simple to practitioners of game theory, while still puzzling those who are new to the topic. Let me use the simplest representation.

The dilemma runs as follows. Two prisoners, held in separate cells, have been accomplices in a serious crime, for which the sentence is 20 years. The prosecutor does not have the evidence to convict either person; but he can convict both on a lesser charge involving a sentence of one year. If prisoner X confesses and incriminates Y while Y remains silent, X will go free and Y will get 20 years. If Y confesses and X does not it will be the other way around. If both confess, each will get five years. If both stay silent, each is convicted on the lesser charge and gets one year. These various possibilities are summarized in Figure 1.1.

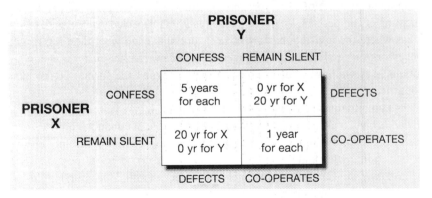

Source: Adapted from R. Frank, *Passions within Reason*, 1988.

Figure 1.1   The prisoner's dilemma

If X consults only his self-interest he will confess. He examines what Y might do. Read down the columns. If Y confesses, X will get five years if he also confesses, but 20 years if he does not. If Y remains silent, X will go free if he confesses, but will get one year if he too remains silent. So, whatever Y does, X is better off confessing. Prisoner Y applies parallel reasoning. So they both confess and go to jail for five years. But if they had trusted each other and neither had confessed, they would each have received a sentence of only one year.

This story has been generalized to apply to numerous other situations – even though the prisoner's dilemma is only one of many types of game. To get away from the criminal example it is best to replace 'confess' and 'remain silent' by the less specific 'co-operate' and 'defect'.

One obvious application is that of two neighbours whose litter blows into each other's gardens unless they take precautions. The first preference of each neighbour is that the other should take precautions, allowing himself a free run. The second is that they both take precautions. The third is that neither take precautions. The fourth and worst is that one should take precautions, allowing the neighbour a free run. If each reasons in isolation on the basis of self-interest, each will end with the third-best outcome and litter-strewn gardens.

A different area of application is industrial training. Employer A may prefer that employer B should train workers, so that he can bid them away fully trained. Employer B may reason similarly. But if each reasons in this manner, they will end up in a situation which no one would prefer, with neither firm training workers.

A full theory of behaviour would have to divide human interactions into those where the invisible hand produces the best result and those where a more co-operative norm works better. It might often be possible to make a two-stage division. The retail market for bread and meat will work best if certain norms of good behaviour, such as 'do not sell contaminated meat' and 'do not lie about the freshness of your bread', are observed. But once these background rules are in operation, the consumer may indeed do better if the butcher and the baker follow the profit motive than if they try consciously to do something of a higher nature. They might then, for instance, try to force some food fad on us, or keep their shops open so long that their own exhaustion far outweighs any benefit to the consumer.

This ties up with the classic argument of von Mises against state planning. It is not just that workers and managers would lack the incentives to provide the right products by the right methods. Even if they were saints they would lack the information to do so.

SELF-INTERESTED CO-OPERATION

So long as the game is played only once, the prisoner's dilemma remains. Each prisoner would be better off trusting the other not to confess. But unless there is fellow feeling between the two prisoners (or a gang boss threatening punishment in the background) neither will find any reason to do so.

Now assume that there is not one game, but that the game is repeated many times: then the situation is transformed. A celebrated study of repeated games of this sort was carried out in the early 1980s by an American political scientist, Robert Axelrod. He organized tournaments in which distinguished game theorists, as well as computer enthusiasts and others, played against each other on the basis of submitted computer programs. The results were surprisingly clear-cut. It paid to follow a co-operative strategy whenever your partner/opponent was co-operative, but to retaliate quickly if your partner/opponent defected. Indeed, by far the most robust strategy, which did best in a variety of environments, was the simple 'tit-for-tat' strategy that offers co-operation on the first round of the game and then reciprocates the other player's last action. Co-operate if he co-operated, defect if he defected. This strategy was submitted to Axelrod's tournaments by only one player, the distinguished game theorist and psychologist Anatol Rapaport.

Axelrod's results caused a sensation in a limited circle and, indeed, featured in a celebrated *Horizon* television programme in 1986 entitled *Nice Guys Finish First*. These results have illuminated an astonishingly diverse range of subjects. One example is the 'live and let live' system which developed in the trench warfare of the First World War, in which – to the fury of the high commands – front-line soldiers refrained from shooting to kill, provided that their restraint was reciprocated.

Some of the initial enthusiasm went quite over the top. Those who had never liked economic models based on utility-maximizing individuals or competitive markets thought that they could have a great time burning the textbooks. But a careful reading of Axelrod's own book showed this triumphalism to be unjustified.

The players in these games are in no sense altruistic, but simply maximize long-term self-interest. As Axelrod writes: 'The foundation of co-operation is not really trust but the durability of the relationship.' Moreover, 'tit-for-tat' is far from a perfect rule. Once a feud is generated – I defect on one round and you defect on the next – it can go on indefinitely. The rule was just more effective than any other that had emerged.

Writers in this area have identified several kinds of altruism. Here are a few varieties in ascending order of concern for others:

- *kinship altruism* covers close relations and is often explained by the demands of genetic preservation. J.B.S. Haldane once said that he should be willing to die to save eight first cousins, who between them would have the same genetic material.

- *reciprocal altruism* is based on anticipated or actual reciprocity, as in the tit-for-tat strategies in repeated prisoner's dilemma games. Examples are frequent in the animal world, as in mutual grooming.
- *hard-core altruism* is the set of actions which are genuinely independent of personal reward or reciprocation.

The most celebrated example of hard-core altruism is the Golden Rule. The well-known problem is that turning the other cheek provides an incentive for others to exploit you.

But there are also many problems with merely reciprocal altruism. It is insufficient to explain many frequently performed actions, such as returning a wallet full of money to its rightful owner, tipping in a restaurant that the diner will never visit again, or removing litter from a beach where the holiday-maker is unobserved.

The apparent success of reciprocity in repeated prisoner's dilemma games depends on there being an indefinite sequence of games. If the players know that they are in the final round of the sequence, it would pay each of them to defect in the penultimate round, knowing that each will defect in the ultimate round so that co-operation will not be reciprocated, players will also defect. Thus, it is argued, the whole sequence of games will unravel back to the non-co-operative solution. A real-life temptation would be for the retiring baker to lie about the freshness of his bread, and for this to influence the trust that customers would place in bakers even before retirement .

An American economist, Robert Frank, has provided what he calls a 'commitment model' to account for apparently selfless behaviour. The problem is that people, including the purely self-interested rationalist, would benefit from living in a world where people behave well even without the promise of reward or the threat of punishment.

This problem could be overcome if enough people would make a firm commitment, which would govern their actions in most foreseeable circumstances. In everyday life the best sign of such a commitment is a reputation – for instance, for honest behaviour even when it might pay to cheat. Such a reputation has its rewards. Other people are willing to enter into transactions with such a reputable person without incurring the costs of intense scrutiny.

It might seem that the best of all worlds for the self-interested person is to acquire a reputation for honesty, without actually being honest, so that he would cheat when he can get away with it. Frank's principal point is that such deception is not as easy as it looks. The best way to appear honest is to be honest, and dissembling carries tell-tale signs. He interprets this in behaviourist terms as 'feeling bad' or blushing when indulging in unworthy conduct.

Frank argues that insincere professors of co-operative or trustworthy behaviour often give themselves away, and he cites a great deal of psychological evidence.

Thus people will actually satisfy their selfish interests best if they commit themselves to behaving altruistically – just as the best way to achieve happiness or spontaneity is not to strive too obviously in these directions.

Stated in this way, altruism looks like long-term enlightened self-interest of the 'honesty is the best policy' kind. Indeed there is something paradoxical about sincere concern for others as a route to a person's own well-being. Is this genuine morality, or is it higher-level prudence? And how can the two be distinguished?

In Frank's own account there is a niche for those pretending to have a good-citizen disposition without actually having it. For although insincerity tends to be detected, there are costs to detection. If the overwhelming majority of the population is honest, it might not be worth incurring the costs of guarding against the occasional dishonest person, and this allows a niche for some dishonest people. In one of his key hypothetical examples, Frank finds that the maximum gain from co-operation is achieved when 75 per cent of the population are committed co-operators, and 25 per cent are opportunistic defectors. Very illuminating, but hardly the Sermon on the Mount, or the categorical imperative. In the end Frank admits that, 'the commitment model is less a disavowal of self-interest than a friendly amendment. Without abandoning the materialist framework, it suggests how the noble strand of human nature might have emerged and prospered.'*

Recent attempts to improve on the 'tit-for-tat' strategy demonstrate even more clearly how far the suggested rules of this type are from genuine altruistic feeling for fellow human beings .

One weakness of 'tit-for-tat', already mentioned, is the danger of getting into a counterproductive feud. Suppose that for some reason player Y has defected in a previous round; then X defects in the current round and is emulated by Y, and so on to the end of time. The other weakness is that no advantage is taken of a 'sucker' who is willing to co-operate even when his partner does not.

---

* Commitment problems also come up in a very different branch of economics – namely, counter-inflationary policy. How do you prevent government from giving the economy an inflationary boost before elections, when the immediate effects are often pleasant with the inflationary costs delayed until well after polling day? There is a genuine advantage in having monetary authorities with a good reputation for avoiding such behaviour.

An ultra-rationalist might believe that electorates will see through such tactics and that prudent policies will be adopted by governments out of self-interest. Others find it helpful to envisage a commitment device by which the government binds its hands in advance. The two favourite devices are an independent central bank and an exchange rate link to a country with sound money credibility, such as Germany at least until reunification.

An independent central bank is for the moment more fashionable than the currency link. But all these devices – including a trustworthy reputation – may break down if the pressure on them is large enough. So, I imagine, would the commitment of Frank's honest man – for instance, if he were to find a sufficiently large wallet in a sufficiently lonely place, and can appease his conscience by donating a proportion of the gain to charity. So the greater credibility of an independent central bank over a government is a matter of degree.

A variant strategy, known as 'Pavlov', has been devised by Nowak and others to overcome these drawbacks. In simplified terms, it involves occasional foraying expeditions. If the tournament has degenerated into a feud, X will initiate a co-operative move, and if Y reciprocates, he will continue to co-operate in the following round. If, however, the game has settled down into continuing rounds of co-operation, X will try an occasional defection (selected by a randomising process in the computer tournament). If Y turns out to be a sucker and still co-operates, X will repeat his defection. Otherwise he will return to co-operation. Thus there will be both more appeasement and more aggression under Pavlov than under straightforward 'tit-for-tat'. But in all cases the self-interested motivation stands out clearly.

EFFECTS OF SPECIFIC RULES

I suggest that the argument about self-interested versus co-operative man has reached the point of rapidly diminishing returns. What we need is examination of specific co-operative rules to see whether they in fact improve on the results of self-interest or whether they make matters worse.

This last possibility is suggested by the original setting of the prisoner's dilemma. If both prisoners follow a co-operative strategy and remain silent, two criminals escape punishment for a serious crime. Co-operation is only beneficial from the point of view of the criminals – thus illustrating the logic of 'honour among thieves'. But from the point of view of the rest of us, it is much better that one or both prisoners should confess.

Which of the constraints on narrow self-interest are of the perverse kind - as when the two criminals escape with reduced sentences – and which are of the benign kind – as when each householder sweeps the snow from in front of their own house in the expectation that others will do the same? As there has been little systematic study, I can only enumerate a few examples.

Let me start with one case, where the drift of the analysis so far is on the side of the co-operative norm being benign. This is the well–known argument of the late Richard Titmuss that voluntary blood donation is more efficient than commercial systems, because voluntary donors have no incentive to lie about the quality of their blood. If sufficient blood is forthcoming on a voluntary basis, all well and good. But if not, some way has to be found of monitoring commercial supplies, despite the difficulties.

A clear-cut example of harmful co-operation is the operation of a collusive cartel. Here each member refrains from selling below an agreed minimum price. The successful operation of a cartel is likely to be against the public interest; first, because consumers have to pay a higher price for the product, and secondly, because too little of that product will be produced and resources will be allocated inefficiently. The last is a more subtle point which would occur mainly to economists; but it is the more fundamental because it remains true even if the members of the cartel are poorer than the rest of us or specially deserving of increased income.

A further example of a pernicious 'moral' influence – one given by Frank – concerns US operators of ski lifts. Operators' investments in both acreage and equipment are chosen with weekend peak demand in mind. Weekend visitors are thus responsible for nearly all the costs associated with the ski facilities. Moreover, a heavy differential charge at weekends would reduce queues and entice more off-peak skiers on to the slopes. Yet in practice price differentials are much too small either to reflect cost differences or to avoid long queues at peak times. Operators apparently fear to alienate the public's sense of fairness. Similar considerations explain why price differentials at barbers' shops on Saturday mornings, or popular restaurants on weekend evenings, are, when they exist at all, far too small.

Thus, the public's sense of fairness may be based on a misapprehension about facts and causes. Skiers focus on the operating costs of lifts, which are much the same at all times, without asking what determines capacity. Barbers' customers focus on the cost of the barber's time without worrying about investment in extra chairs or saloon capacity, let alone the dissatisfaction of waiting a long time for a haircut.

It might be a mistake to rush into a crusade for higher peak prices without further reflection. Both biological behaviour and evolved social institutions may serve purposes which are not immediately obvious. Traditional rules, as Hayek warns us, often contain more embodied wisdom than any individual critic can hope to have. Such respect for existing institutions can, however, provide no more than an amber light for caution. It is doubtful, for instance, if excessively low price differentials at ski resorts have any such deeper social function.

'VENGEANCE IS MINE'

There is indeed more than one way in which a seemingly good-neighbour strategy can do harm. It can be against the interests of the rest of the community – as in the prisoner's dilemma and cartel examples – or it can be counterproductive even from the point of view of the participating individuals themselves. This latter possibility arises when a strategy is selected that appears to be co-operative, but is inappropriate at a deeper level. Most real-world situations are more complicated than the simple prisoner's dilemma, and the possibility of choosing an inappropriate strategy is a real one.

This possibility arises because the way in which strategies are normally determined is via the application of widely accepted rules – whether these are obviously moral, such as 'do not kill'; conventional, such as 'drive on the left'; or habitual, such as 'do not scatter litter'.

But many widely supported moral practices and rules are distinctly double-edged. Frank cites a hypothetical Jones who sacrifices a day's earnings of $300 to prosecute Smith for stealing a $200 briefcase. The motive here can only be described as vengeance. Frank is inclined to regard Jones as a social benefactor because his action discourages theft.

Maybe. But encouraging vengeance as a general practice is playing with fire. It is vengeance for real or imagined past wrongs that stirred up the conflict in former Yugoslavia, Northern Ireland and between Israel and the Arabs. As St Paul warns: 'Vengeance is mine; I will repay saith the Lord.'

'SOCIAL RESPONSIBILITY OF BUSINESS'

In which category should one put such movements as Business in the Community? According to a manifest by Grayson, it stands for 'companies using some of their people, their expertise, their surplus product, premises and equipment, and sometimes cash to help tackle problems like urban deprivation, school-business links, job creation and environmental improvements'.

There is a systematic ambiguity here, as in nearly all the talk about socially responsible business. Do the proponents claim that these extra activities will indeed help a business's long-term profitability? Or do they assert that a business should follow different objectives?

For, as Elaine Sternberg points out: 'If, for example, a corporation looks like a business and portrays itself as a business, then it encourages the reasonable expectation that maximising long-term owners' value is its objective and guiding principle.' A corporation which makes its decisions on 'some other undisclosed criterion is a particularly dangerous sort of loose cannon, whether that other end is imperial, ideological or just personal'.

Grayson is full of *bien pensant* clichés, such as a shift away from 'me-ism' toward 'us-ism', 'value-driven companies' (all rational conduct is value-driven), 'making employees feel part of a team', 'public–private partnership', 'empowerment', 'holistic approach' and of course 'caring'. But the basic ambiguity remains. The author insists that the movement has 'a strong business rationale', but also warns 'against activities claimed to be helping the community which are really for the company's benefit'.

Socially responsible businessmen, and their slogan writers, regard any questioning of their rationale as an attack on objectives such as urban renewal, support for the arts or employee welfare facilities. And if one is not careful they will insinuate that one is to the right of Genghis Khan, not to speak of being a monetarist.

The point that the critics should be making, however, is that the corporate responsibility movement lacks the legitimacy of either the market or the political process. It is up to the individual citizen to decide how much to devote to such causes, whether individually or collectively via elected representatives. It is not for managers to set themselves up as taxing authorities over funds which belong to shareholders – who may be their own employees or other workers investing through their pension funds.

Moreover, people function best if they have specific responsibilities. If a businessman is partly responsible for government policy, and a government official sees himself as partly responsible for the profitability of companies, then everyone becomes responsible for everything in general, and no one is responsible for anything in particular.

There is a further objection to the fashionable cult of the businessman as the person to run, and advise on, everything. I often wonder how the favoured executives have time to manage their own companies if they are also supposed to sit on hospital boards, run public committees, and have a chance of normal family life and leisure. I suspect that the business leadership which both the Thatcher and the Major governments tried to introduce in many semi-governmental areas is a façade behind which the old-time professionals just carry on as before.

The constitutional liberal is not arguing that the pursuit of market objectives is enough. He is saying that if there are market failures or inadequacies, it is up to the government to set up incentives to different behaviour by taxes or subsidies, or if necessary by regulation or financing public services. Income can be redistributed via the tax and social security system. The government can intervene to improve incentives for training or for letting homes. But it is not for corporations to take on a pseudo-governmental role.

I have deliberately exaggerated. For the weakness of what I have called the constitutionalist position is that it falls into the trap I have earlier castigated of supposing that government will conform to some textbook model of optimal behaviour. But of course official programmes will be driven or distorted by interest groups, or by the providers of public services. Education, training and environmental programmes will often be very different from those which would do most to help.

As corporate executives may have dispersed local knowledge, why not make use of them? All right; so long as we recognize the limitations. Even our imperfectly enfranchised shareholders will ensure that companies do not devote more than a small proportion of their resources to non-bottom-line activities. So, both the business enthusiast and the government are deceiving themselves if they expect socially responsible businesses to carry the public policy load. My final reservation about business responsibility is that it is an attempt to achieve public policy objectives on the cheap and on the side.

CODES THAT KILL JOBS

The area where popular morality clashes most with market principles is in the labour market.

There is evidence that firms with higher profits pay higher wages to employees of any given skill level. This may appear as common sense, but anyone who has taken a course in market economics will ask why workers do not drift from low-wage firms and bid for jobs in high-wage firms until pay is roughly equalized.

Some labour economists believe that they can explain the persistence of inter-firm wage differentials by a theory called 'efficiency wages'. On this theory a profitable firm will pay above market-clearing wages to motivate employees and obtain better performance. Profitable firms will also see higher rates of pay as a rationing device to enable them to pick and choose among potential workers with equal paper qualifications. The validity of efficiency wage theory is a topic of its own. While it may help to explain why pay does not move quickly to market-clearing levels, it is less successful in explaining long-lasting differentials. I would agree with Frank that part of the explanation lies in the prevalence of 'moral' beliefs that profitable firms should share some of their surplus with workers and – equally important – the widespread toleration for less-profitable firms who can only afford to pay lower rates.

But I am less than sure that the outcome is a good one. The net effect is to retard the movement of resources from less- to more-efficient firms and thus hold down national income, without any clear distributional benefit.

Controversy becomes much fiercer when we come to a different set of practices: the minimum pay levels enforced by legislation or collective agreements – or other kinds of costs imposed on employers by measures of a 'European social charter' kind. Such policies are supported by the popular belief that it is wrong to encourage anything that smacks of undercutting by workers bidding for a job, or by employers trying to obtain workers on the cheap.

How reasonable is this anti-undercutting mentality? The one near-certainty to hold on to in the heat of debate is that, if the loosening of minimum pay laws or their equivalents increases total employment, then the income of the whole community will be higher.

There are likely to be low-income losers. Some of the workers priced into jobs may be worse off than they were on social security, taking travel costs and other add-ons into account. Even if all newly taken-on workers are no worse off, their entry is likely to worsen the pay of the less-well-paid already in work.

Thus, a reasonable condition for eliminating minimum wages is that those priced into work should not receive less than they received on social security. This can be done with the aid of an income supplement such as the present UK Family Benefit, provided it can be extended to families without children and to single people, and the conditions for claiming made less restrictive.

The more difficult people to compensate are those already in work earning above, but not too much above, the social security minimum, whose wages will fall in the new equilibrium. Complete compensation for the distributional effects of all market changes is hardly compatible with a dynamic economy. Nevertheless, some softening of the blow would be desirable. A basic or minimum guaranteed income, with a high cut-off rate, or marginal tax rate, is the most likely bet. This could be achieved by adjusting existing social security payments and need not involve a vast new scheme. The more selective social security becomes, the more generous governments can be with top-up payments.

There is a still more difficult hornets' nest, which I can only stir and not really tackle. This is the high unemployment in OECD countries and particularly in Europe that prevails over the business cycle and even in boom periods. For it is now possible that quite a big fall in average real pay would be required to price into work enough people to satisfy even a modest definition of full employment.

Let me score an own-goal here by stressing that national estimates of the responsiveness of employment to real pay changes may be over-optimistic (a typical example is that if pay costs were 1 per cent less, employment would be from $\frac{1}{2}$ to 1 per cent higher). For a large part of the hypothetical employment growth from lower real labour costs arises from gains in market share at the expense of other countries. The relevant question is: what would have to happen to real remuneration in the OECD area as a whole if, say, one-half of those presently unemployed are to be priced back into work?

Extreme neo-classical economists dodge some of the deeper questions of moral attitudes and social practices by assuming that all unemployment is ultimately voluntary, and determined mechanistically by the social security floor. They therefore avoid having to debate popular attitudes head-on. And if they cannot get away with arguing for a lower dole, they try to argue for a less attractive dole by making the conditions for drawing it more stringent or forcing people who draw it to undertake some kind of training or token performance (workfare). They therefore leave it to the less mechanistic market economists to face the popular fire by arguing with attitudes which hold pay rates well above market-clearing rates in segments of the labour market well above the social security floor.

Minimum pay rates, employment regulations and other employment add-ons have now discouraged employers from taking on workers for so long that investment has had a labour-saving bias. A shift towards more market-related pay rates and differentials, sufficient to price people back into jobs, even gradually, would still increase national income. But it is possible that more than 100 per cent of the increase would accrue to owners of capital and land. Some extra tax on capital or income from capital could surely be justified to cushion the shock, although not so much as to kill the labour-using investment required. I make the suggestion, not as a cure-all but to indicate the impasse which we have reached as a result of the collision between popular attitudes towards just rewards and the requirements of high employment.

CONCLUSIONS

The market is only one part of a well-functioning economic system; and many surrounding policies, practices and habits of mind are required to obtain good value from the market system. Yet a functioning market core is still indispensable.

Matthew Parris, in one of his excellent tongue-in-cheek newspaper columns, has reminded us that most people do not accept the market system – not even to the extent that a Labour Chancellor, Social Democrat Finance Minister or Democrat US Secretary of the Treasury would want them to.

Parris writes of an aunt of his who believes that there is such a thing as a fair price or wage that can be determined by contemplation rather than the state of the market. 'To my aunt – who votes Conservative, takes *The Daily Telegraph* and regards socialism as the work of the devil – a fair price is what will secure a reasonable profit after paying employees a decent wage.' Presumably her idea of a decent wage is her impression of the average of the last few decades corrected for inflation.

I have made a few soundings of my own among business journalists, who might be expected to have a higher degree of sophistication. But even here I find great resistance to the allocational and market-clearing functions of pay and prices.

It is not that such people are rabid egalitarians. Parris's aunt is not, and I doubt if my professional colleagues are either. They can nearly all understand the incentive role of pay and prices. They also accept – if anything too readily – the hierarchies and financial differentials of modern life. And they all operate against a background in which 'prices' mean the general level of prices, which they would like to see as stable as possible.

What still meets with blank incomprehension – even among people who can perform textbook exercises – is the role of relative prices, including pay. The elementary role of relative prices in allocating resources and reducing queues, even in a community bathed in mutual love, has little meaning even for the educated public. As Parris says, 'our morality does not mesh with our economic system; but because we need both they cohabit in an awkward marriage based on silence'.

A dialogue – suspended since the time that Dickens, Ruskin and Shaw thundered at nineteenth-century political economists – will have to resume. I am not suggesting that Parris's aunt should begin a course in either moral philosophy or economics. What is needed is more critical scrutiny, both of widely accepted moral beliefs and their role in economic activity, and of the moral implications of widely advocated economic policies. The idea of technocratic value-free economics has had its day.

REFERENCES

Axelrod, R., *The Evolution of Co-operation*, Harmondsworth, Middx: Penguin Books, 1990.
Beardsley, T., 'Never Give a Sucker an Even Break', *Scientific American*, October 1993.
Brittan, S., *A Restatement of Economic Liberalism*, London: Macmillan, 1988.
Brittan, S., 'Two Cheers for Utilitarianism', in *The Role and Limits of Government*, London: Temple Smith, 1983.
Dunkley, C., 'Ethos of Vans, Doors and Bosnia', *Financial Times*, 4 August 1993.
The Economist , 'How to be Ethical and Still Come Top', *The Economist*, 5 June 1993.
Frank, R., *Passions Within Reason*, New York and London: W.W. Norton, 1988.
Grayson, D., *Corporate Community Involvement as a Strategic Managerial Tool*, Durham: Durham University Business School, 1992.
Hausman, D.M. and M.S. McPherson, 'Taking Ethics Seriously: Economics and Contemporary Moral Philosophy', *Journal of Economic Literature*, XXXI (2), (1993).
Hume, D., 'Of the First Principles of Government', in E. Miller (ed.), *Essays Moral Political and Literary*, Indianapolis: Liberty Classics, 1777.
Johnson, H.G., *Economics and Society*, Chicago, Ill.: 1975.
Kay, J., 'How the Ethics Men Miss the Point', *Daily Telegraph*, 5 July 1993.
Nowak, M. and K. Sigmund, 'A Strategy of Win-stay, Lose–shift', *Nature*, 364, 1 July 1993.
Nozick, R., *The Nature of Rationality*, Princeton, N. J.: Princeton University Press, 1993.
Parris, M., 'It is Unhealthy ...', *The Times*, 21 December 1992.
Radnitzky, G. (ed.), *Universal Economics*, New York: Paragon House, 1993.
Russell, B., *Human Society in Ethics and Politics*, 1954; London: Routledge, 1992.
Sen, A.K., *Collective Choice and Social Welfare*, San Francisco, Cal.: Holden Day, 1970.
Smith, A., *An Inquiry into the Nature and Causes of the Wealth of Nations*, 1776; Indianapolis: Liberty Classics, 1981.
Smith, A., *The Theory of Moral Sentiments*, 1759; Indianapolis: Liberty Classics, 1982.
Sternberg, E., 'The Responsible Shareholder', *Business Ethics*, July 1992.
Stigler, G., *The Tanner Lectures on Human Values*, Cambridge: Cambridge University Press, 1981.
Titmuss, Richard M., *The Gift Relationship*, New York: Random House, 1971.
von Mises, Ludwig, in F.A. Hayek (ed.), *Collectivist Economic Planning,* London: Routledge, 1935.

2   Two cheers for self-interest[*]

The previous chapter discussed whether political economy assumed self-interest; and how far that assumption provided a good explanation of economic behaviour. In this more personal paper, written eight years earlier, the focus is normative. It is on the suggestion, to be found in some liberal economic writing, that better results will be achieved if people avowedly follow their self-interest in market transactions than if they try to follow more elevated precepts.

GOD AND MAMMON

How selfish soever man may be supposed, there are evidently some principles in his nature, which interest him in the fortune of others, and render their happiness necessary to him, though he derives nothing from it except the pleasure of seeing it.

A number of people now know that these words were uttered by Adam Smith as the opening sentence of *The Theory of Moral Sentiments*: the same Adam Smith who is much more celebrated for a very different quotation from the later *Wealth of Nations* about the individual who 'intends only his own gain', but is 'led by an invisible hand' to promote the good of society 'more effectively than when he really intends to promote it', and who added for good measure: 'I have never known much good done by those who affected to trade for the public good.'

Adam Smith scholars assure us that there is no head-on contradiction between *The Theory of Moral Sentiments* and *The Wealth of Nations*. The doctrine of 'sympathy' in the earlier volume claimed to explain the basis of moral judgement; and the doctrine of the invisible hand explains the *consequences* of one kind of human motivation, namely the pursuit of gain in the market place.

Yet even if there is no formal contradiction between the two doctrines, there is a sense of strain which Smith did not eliminate even when he went back to revise *The Theory of Moral Sentiments* near the end of his life. The two works are not a seamless web. (I cannot resist the unscholarly comment that *The Theory of Moral Sentiments* is not on a par with *The Wealth of Nations* and would

* Based on 16th Wincott Memorial Lecture, IEA Occasional Paper 73, London, 1985.

not be studied today except by a few specialists in the period if Smith had not gone on to write the later work.)

Subsequent moralists have found it difficult to reconcile market economics with most kinds of conventional good behaviour. When I studied economics in Cambridge, I shared supervisions in my first year with a fervent member of a religious group which stressed four moral absolutes: absolute purity, absolute unselfishness, absolute honesty and absolute love. My fellow pupil found these absolutes hard to put together with the economist's working assumption of profit maximization. He could not see why a virtuous person should want to equate marginal costs and marginal revenue, simply to make himself as well off as possible.

Indeed, it does not seem to me that the pursuit of personal gain, or the maximization of utility in a non-tautological sense, is at all easy to reconcile with Christian teachings taken at their source.

On any straightforward examination, many New Testament sayings seem strongly opposed both to the rationalizing, calculating aspect of market economics and to the private gain motive. For that matter, they seem equally opposed to the sort of socialism which promises widely spread material benefits here and now on this earth.

Christ's parables are full of sayings about the folly of pursuing wealth. 'Go thy way', said Jesus to a man who asked what he should do to inherit eternal life: 'Sell whatever thou hast, and give to the poor, and thou shalt have treasure in heaven.' He did not say: 'Make a fortune, float the company and give the proceeds to famine relief.' Such a rationalization could perhaps be supported by the Old Testament but scarcely by the New. Most attempts to show the compatibility of Adam Smith economics and the Bible lean heavily on the Old Testament and on sophisticated interpretation of the New, and warn against liberal quotation of the latter,

What could be more opposed to conventially rational behaviour (in either a market or a planned economy) than 'Take no thought for the morrow, for the morrow shall take thought for the things of itself. Sufficient unto the day is the evil thereof'?

Even a non-theologian can see that Christ and his followers did not dismiss material needs completely. Some verses in St Matthew just before the ones I have quoted remark: 'Your heavenly father knoweth that ye have need of food, drink and clothing. But seek ye first the Kingdom of God and his righteousness; and all these things shall be added unto you.'

The suggestion seems to be that if people raise their sights to the spiritual level, the material side of life will somehow take care of itself. But this still seems a long way from Adam Smith's self-interest in the market place.

I realize that this is a highly controversial area and that there are those who interpret some of Christ's parables (for example, that of the talents and the unjust steward) as commendations of shrewdness in material matters. (To me they seem metaphors about spiritual diligence.)

There is also the long-standing discussion on 'Religion and the Rise of Capitalism', in which scholars such as Max Weber and R.H. Tawney debated whether Protestantism provided a more favourable environment for the rising capitalist class in the sixteenth and seventeenth centuries than traditional Catholicism. Far be it for me to venture into this highly specialized debate, except to say how interesting it is that the branch of Christianity which may at one time have flirted with mercantile values was the branch that took the Old Testament most seriously.

The main weight of Christian tradition seems to me to be strongly suspicious of market economics. It is not surprising that Christians who have recoiled against a communist background, such as Pope John Paul II or Alexander Solzhenitsyn, do not find the western market economy much more to their taste. Nor is it surprising that the Church has sometimes been on the side of feudal reaction, sometimes of a vague, egalitarian socialism, occasionally on the side of corporatism, but only rarely, despite the recent valiant attempts of writers such as Michael Novak, has it had much good to say for competitive capitalism.

BEYOND TAUTOLOGY

The Christian teaching on usury and the concept of a just price formed part of the anti-market mentality against which Adam Smith had to contend. The earlier demonstration of some sixteenth-century Spanish Jesuits that the best definition of the just price corresponded to the market price prevailing in the long run is of limited help. For we have to move to the long run by a series of short-term price movements starting far away from the eventual equilibrium, the nature of which we do not know.

The tendency of some modern economic theory is to escape from such controversies by making maximizing behaviour of both households and firms a purely conventional postulate. Whether people pursue pecuniary gain, leisure, knowledge or the promotion of aesthetic endeavour, or some combination of all these, they are assumed to be engaged in maximizing their own utility subject to the constraints of their environment. This tautological form of utility maximizing may be useful for the formal analysis of some problems – but it is no help in evaluating behaviour. I am therefore assuming that terms like 'personal gain' or the 'profit motive' have a non-tautological meaning. In personal behaviour it makes sense to say that, if you sacrifice a holiday to look after a sick relative, you are subordinating what you would *like* to do to what you think you *ought* to do.

Some economists, working at a non-tautological level, might have told my fellow pupil that economic theory is purely descriptive or predictive. To analyse the consequences of pursuing Mammon is not to approve it. But this would also have been an evasion, as I would have discovered as soon as he had gone on to ask me, as he surely would have done: should we not urge people to live in a different way and not remain content to analyse the *status quo*? Moreover, one cannot brush aside two centuries of normative economic teaching – from Adam Smith to economic reformers in post-communist countries – which argues that, in *some areas and under some conditions,* the use of markets avowedly based on self-interest will prove more beneficial than an overt attempt to achieve the public good directly. This normative view was entitled by Adam Smith 'Natural Liberty', as well as the 'Invisible Hand'. It has also been called 'free-market competition', the 'profit' or 'gain' motive, and so on. Although these terms are not identical, between them they convey the main idea.

PRIMA FACIE MAXIMS

How then can one best make sense of such strange-sounding maxims of conduct as 'subject to the rules of society, follow your own self-interest in the market-place' or 'buy in the cheapest market and sell in the dearest'?

Too much current discussion is unhelpfully polarized. There are those on whom Adam Smith has made no impact whatever. For them market forces are self-evidently anti-social, vulgar, divisive and philistine. For the other side, market forces are self-evidently the best way of supplying the consumer with 'what he or she wants' and not only promote efficiency, but enlarge choice and freedom. Most people feel one way sometimes on some issues and the other way at other times on other issues, but without any real reconciliation.

The insensitivity of both views was apparent to me in my work on the Peacock Committee on the Finance of Broadcasting (described in my *Political Quarterly* article). Some of the more fanatical protagonists of the BBC were completely oblivious to the potential of the market for enlarging freedom as well as consumer satisfaction. For them, Adam Smith lived in vain. Too many of the protagonists of commercialism, on the other hand, failed to appreciate that a true broadcasting market requires a direct method of selling programmes to viewers and listeners, and a system by which the latter can register the intensity with which their preferences are held. Not all moves to *laissez-faire* are market-promoting.

It will help if I try first to summarize the logical status of the 'Invisible Hand' doctrine. I shall then mention the background conditions and implicit rules of behaviour required for the successful operation of markets. After that I shall explain the margin of discretion which remains, even where free-market doctrines apply. Finally, I shall discuss briefly how to exercise this discretion.

It is in my view easiest to explain both the strengths and limitations of the 'Invisible Hand' doctrine in terms of a system of utilitarian morality. In doing so, I want to limit my hostages to fortune. By 'utilitarianism' I mean the view that actions are to be judged by their consequences for the welfare of other people. I do not need to pre-judge the issue of whether welfare is to be seen in terms of choice or of some direct measure of satisfaction. Nor do I need to resolve all distributional issues. And I do not have to argue whether utilitarianism can provide a complete moral system or whether it should be constrained by the requirements of personal freedom or supplemented by ideals of human excellence, matters discussed in the next Chapter. Suffice it to say that the criteria of judgement usually applied to activities in the public sphere, such as business and politics, are of a utilitarian character, and it is difficult to see how they could be otherwise in our sort of society.

Contrary to popular superstition, utilitarians do not suppose it is possible to dispense with all traditional morality and work out afresh the effects of every action on fellow men and women. We do not have the knowledge to assess the effects of our actions on other human beings, especially those more remotely affected by them. For this, if for no other reason, we need *prima facie* rules of conduct such as 'Don't tell lies', 'Do not steal', 'Keep promises', or, in the public sphere, 'Observe international treaties'.

These rules have arisen from the common experience of mankind. Because of the human propensity to wishful thinking, we need to think many times before breaking any of the *prima facie* maxims of conduct. We need to assess as best we can, not only the balance on the particular occasion but the long-term effect of a particular breach of the accustomed rules of conduct in weakening their force on future occasions.

But none of these considerations excuses reflection in difficult cases. It may be unclear either how to apply the normal rules or hard to say which rule is applicable. There may be conflict between different maxims, such as not telling lies and avoiding hurting another person's feelings. Or the appropriateness of some traditional maxims – for instance, in sexual relations – may be a matter of controversy. In new areas of human activity there may be a need to develop new maxims of behaviour – for example, in respecting the privacy of other people's electronic communications. Choices are unavoidable, both about which rules of conduct to follow and whether accepted rules should be overridden in exceptional circumstances.

The Adam Smith 'Invisible Hand' doctrine is one of the more surprising *prima facie* rules to have been suggested, as it has more of a cynical than a pious flavour. The suggestion is that in matters such as buying and selling, or deciding what and how to produce, we will do others more good if we behave *as if* we are following our self-interest rather than by pursuing more altruistic purposes.

The fact that pious people find this rule-of-thumb shocking is not an argument against it. The fact that it sanctions and removes guilt-feelings about what most people do anyway is – other things equal – a positive recommendation.

The doctrine of 'natural liberty' is nevertheless more convincing as a permissive one – 'People should be allowed to follow their self-interest in the market and should not feel guilty in doing so' – than as a positive injunction: 'maximize your own self-interest'. If the maxim is converted into a positive one, it may be misinterpreted as a duty to make more profits when you would rather lie in the sun, or to make your life a misery by grasping at an uncongenial, highly paid job. The subjectivity not only of benefits, but also of costs, is a most important contribution of the neo-classical school, a hundred years after Adam Smith; and it is a great pity that it has since been developed as a branch of applied mathematics rather than as a brand of economic psychology.

Whether stated positively or negatively, even some economist supporters of the profit motive have still felt the need to apologize for it. Alfred Marshall wrote that the case for competitive markets arose from the 'imperfections which still cling to human nature' and from the need to rely for the present on the stronger rather than the higher motives of mankind.

But is the market merely a way of channelling human self-interestedness to good use? Would all need for it disappear if people became sufficiently altruistic?

Any economic system needs to:

1. co-ordinate the activities of millions of individuals, households and firms;
2. obtain information about people's desires, tastes and preferences;
3. decide which productive techniques to use; and
4. create incentives for people to act on such information.

It is only the last, incentive, role of the market, which could be abandoned in a community of saints. Even such a community would need to know how best to serve their fellow men and women. They might proceed best by behaving *as if* they were concerned with their own worldly well-being, in order to create the market signals which they could follow in their productive activities.

MARGIN OF DISCRETION

One insufficiently noted aspect of the pursuit of profit in the market is that it rarely determines a unique course of action; and for many reasons. Very often lack of information and uncertainty about the future are so great that there is little to choose between alternative courses on profit-maximizing grounds.

The applicability of strict profit maximization has itself been disputed by some economists who have experimented with slightly different interpretations of self-interest, for example, that businesses strive to grow as fast as possible subject to the constraint of earning a required return on capital. Another rather vaguer variant is 'satisficing', which has been described as looking for a course which is 'good enough', without necessarily being 'the best available'.

Even if one sticks to profit maximization, there is some ambiguity as soon as one moves from individual ownership to the joint stock company. Are the directors of a company trying to maximize their own utility and treating shareholders as creditors with certain rights? Or are they trying to maximize the present value of shareholders' capital (as in orthodox financial theory)? Even if they are doing the latter, are there one clear-cut rate of time discount and degree of risk aversion to apply?

It is also in a company's self-interest to take into account forces such as government, unions and public opinion; and there is probably room for more argument about how to respond to these than to more narrowly commercial and technological forces. The moral of these uncertainties and controversies is that, subject to overriding constraints of solvency and avoiding a hostile takeover bid, organizations often have a good deal of freedom of action in their precise interpretation of the profit motive, and are able to take other objectives into account at the margin.

A word also needs to be said about the demarcation of the profit-seeking sector. Neither Adam Smith nor any of his successors believed that the whole of public activity should be left to the market place. A functioning market presupposes a basis of trust (which is itself a form of social capital), a legal system and an apparatus of law enforcement. Smith did not believe that police and defence should be left to private armies. (A few anarcho-capitalists in the USA do so. Their arguments are more instructive than convincing.)

Smith enumerated many areas for state activity which were not to be governed by profitability calculations, of which the most famous were public works and some sorts of education. The analysis of the lighthouse, which provides benefits for which no charge can be made, has been in the textbooks for two centuries. The precise boundaries of the market sector are also the subject of controversy today. Arguments rage on whether they should include, for instance, health and education, as well as goods bought across the counter. But for my present purpose, I am accepting that in all human societies, from China to Peru, there is at least some market sector. My question is: what structure of beliefs and constraints on behaviour are required if markets are to produce a reasonable result, or even function at all? Even here the answer will not be as general as I would like.

BACKGROUND CONDITIONS

A less obvious topic than the demarcation of the market sector, but one closer to my purpose, is: what background conditions are necessary for the market to produce, not an optimum, but even reasonably satisfactory results? For instance, there needs to be a way of dealing with the more blatant spillovers or externalities – that is, costs imposed on others which do not appear as financial expenses to those who perpetrate them, or benefits for which no reward is received. The classic examples are the polluting chimney on the negative side, or the well-tended front garden on the positive side. Labour and housing markets have to be free enough to give a displaced worker a chance of early re-employment. There needs to be a social security net to look after the victims of change. At a more technical level, either exchange rates or nominal wages need to be flexible enough so that the balance of payments can take care of itself without patriotic exhortation to export more or import less.

Neither textbook writers nor advocates of the market economy devote enough attention to numerous other unstated provisos. The shooting of one's competitors is not an acceptable way of maximizing profits or even minimizing losses. Nor is the bribery of legislators. But there are less banal and obvious questions. Is it legitimate to try to monopolize a market in the absence of strong restrictive practices legislation? If there are such laws, should we co-operate actively, or merely conform? If certain markets, such as those for labour, are clearly malfunctioning, is an employer who tries as a deliberate policy objective to provide more jobs a social benefactor? Or is he meddling in matters outside his influence, and would society be better off if companies confined themselves to promoting shareholders' financial interests?

Theoretical welfare economics is too exacting in setting up impossibly perfectionist yardsticks, but not exacting enough in its silence about the rules, inhibitions and instinctive reflexes – too numerous and subtle to codify – which are the most important modifications in practice of the pursuit of uninhibited self-interest and which at their best internalize many externalities.

The two 'theorems' most often invoked in modern welfare economics, the 'basic theorem of welfare economics' and the 'converse' theorem, are well explained by Amartya Sen. The basic theorem states that every competitive equilibrium is a Pareto optimum – that is, a state of affairs where it is impossible to make any one person better off without making someone else worse off. The theorem only holds under extremely restrictive assumptions.

A Pareto optimum can, however, be extremely unsatisfactory if the initial distribution of resources is highly skewed – for example, landless labourers may be dying of starvation. This has caused some welfare economists to shift attention to the converse theorem, which states that, given the right distribution of resources, the best feasible social state is a competitive equilibrium.

This sort of approach seems to me a blind alley. The true case for the market mechanism is that it is a decentralized and non-dictatorial method of conveying information, reacting to change and fostering innovation. That is why I have made Adam Smith rather than more recent formal work my starting point. This approach to markets has been followed in recent years by both the Schumpeterian and Hayekian branches of Austrian economics, as well as by American exponents of 'workable competition'. In the last resort an empirical comparison of the prosperity and freedom achieved in collective, market-orientated and intermediate societies must provide the test.

The full set of assumptions, side-conditions and constraints required for the pursuit of market gain to yield beneficial results can never be fully written down. Many of the most important rules are not formulated explicitly until a special problem arises.

It is only very occasionally that an outside theorist is able to suggest a new maxim, as with Adam Smith's 'natural liberty', and he will usually be most successful if he can encourage some kinds of behaviour that actually exist, and perhaps discourage others. In interpreting and applying these suggestions, we still need the help of the traditions and unformulated rules which embody more knowledge than any individual can hope to have.

But to say this does not solve all problems. As these other rules and traditions are often contradictory or imperfectly formulated, we cannot escape conscious reflection about how to interpret them or decide between them. The only way we can hope to do so is to look at specific problems when difficulties and conflicts arise. It is impossible to evaluate all law, institutions and moral codes at the same time, or from scratch.

ANALOGY WITH FREE SPEECH

No real-world market economy is likely to be even approximately satisfactory in all the background conditions. What then does the businessman, who wants to be a reasonably good citizen, do?

No system of political economy can absolve him from exercising his own moral judgement. Let me take an analogy from a different sphere emphasized by Peter Jay. Freedom of the press is a good general maxim and a part of our basic freedoms that most needs defence. This serves as a warning that any justification for censorship or self-censorship needs to be examined with a jaundiced eye. The harm involved in a particular kind of censorship or self-censorship is often difficult to see because it is indirect. A large part of it is the precedent established. The immediate gain may be direct and obvious. Therefore the general assumption should be 'publish and be damn'd!'. But this general presumption does not absolve the newspaperman or television reporter from examining carefully the possibility that a particular act of publication could be so damaging to specific human beings – for example, information that would interfere with a hi-jack rescue – that the general presumption must be overthrown.

A similar story applies to the pursuit of profit maximization or personal gain in a competitive market economy. The absence of effective legislation should not excuse a chemical company for polluting the air – although the competitive advantage gained by an unscrupulous firm over others suggests that the law should be put right soon, so that the public-spirited firms are not forced out of business.

Market economists are often, for instance, ill at ease when faced with 'professional' ideals. A great musician will have a strong sense of vocation and not just play for the money. A doctor or teacher should have some responsibility to his patient and pupil over and above the search for fees, and so on.

Several different ideas are involved in professionalism. The first is that of side-constraints and background conditions. These confine the pursuit of self-interest more closely in the professions than in other occupations.

Secondly, there is the subjectivity of benefits and costs. Many people – not just professionals – earn economic rent (that is, a surplus over and above the minimum required to induce them to do their jobs). The rent may be larger or more obvious to the great musician who would be determined to play or compose even for a pittance. But a bricklayer or tourist guide, who would, if necessary, perform his or her job for less, also earns rent. Market rates of pay have their effects at the margin. They bring in the less-dedicated who might otherwise have chosen a different field of endeavour, and they affect even the dedicated in their choice at the margin between work and leisure. (X might be a surgeon even if he were not paid for it. But he would perform fewer operations.)

There is a third and more interesting element involved. Amartya Sen has said that the immediate motive even of Adam Smith's baker is to supply bread rather than to make money. There is surely a spectrum of cases. At one extreme there is the commodity trader or property dealer, whose daily purchases or sales are closely linked with the profit motive, so clearly that it becomes pedantic to insist that his immediate motive is to buy land or sell copper. At the other extreme is the surgeon or orchestral conductor. Such a person might be affected by the gain motive in his choice of career or country or sphere of operation. But having made these decisions he is expected to give his attention to the operation or symphony in front of him, and keep cash well in the background. In between are the butcher and the baker, who may at the moment concentrate on providing meat or bread, but would switch their activities pretty quickly if faced with a change in financial opportunities.

There is a fourth element, too, which adds to the economist's unease. 'Professions' are not confined to noble aims, but are often drawn into restrictive

practices, whether fixing minimum fees, restricting entry, or insisting on artificially high standards to reduce supply. There is no sharp dividing line between
these interest group activities and the nobler aims. The safe maxim is to
minimize the legal privileges accorded to particular groups, whether professional
or not.

HOW TO BE AN ALTRUIST

These complications do not destroy the presumption that by following the
profit motive, subject to the written and unwritten rules of the society in which
he lives, a normal business practitioner will also best serve the interests of his
followers.

Nor is there any presumption that the altruist, who has an exceptionally
strong concern for the welfare of others, should strive less hard for income and
wealth. Indeed, he should probably strive harder. The difference between the
altruist and the average selfish citizen is surely in what the former does with
his gains.

It is true that the best-known single sentence in political economy is probably
Adam Smith's: 'It is not from the benevolence of the butcher, the brewer or the
baker that we expect our dinner, but from their regard to their own interest.'
Yet this sentiment can be misleading without amplification of the term 'interest'.
It is not necessary for the functioning of the market that the butcher and baker
be selfish, callous or indifferent to other people. Indeed, they are likely to be
more enterprising butchers and bakers if they are concerned for the welfare of
their family and friends and wish to accumulate enough to help good causes
and endow charitable institutions.

An innocent altruist might suppose that he should never increase prices in a
period of scarcity, but should aim at some kind of 'just price' which merely
covers costs. But here political economy tells him that he would often be wrong.
Prices have a role in allocating resources. It would have been the height of social
folly to have sold oil or coal at artificially *low* prices in the energy crises of the
1970s. Within limits the altruist should play to win; and if he dislikes benefiting
from scarcity, he should devote his windfall gains to good works, not to profit
minimization. In normal circumstances a businessman does not serve his
fellows, least of all the poorest of them, by selling a product at a price well below
what the market will bear.

If he were to do so, the most likely result would be a misallocation of scarce
resources, which is likely to make the community worse off, with no presumption that the poor will escape the effects. Even the apparent direct transfer
from the altruist's own pocket to the community will be spread across the

board to rich and poor, deserving and undeserving, whereas under conventional pricing the altruist-owner could transfer his profits to those whom he believes most in need or in other ways deserving.

'CLEAR AND PRESENT DANGER'

Can we say anything in general terms about the qualifications and exceptions to the maxim that business enterprise should act 'as if' motivated by the desire for financial gain?

I would suggest that the nearer home are the supposed benefits from deviation, the more specific they are, and the more clearly they affect identifiable individuals, the stronger the case is likely to be.

David Hume observed that 'the generosity of men seldom extends beyond their friends and family, at most beyond their native country'. Even where their generosity does extend further, their *knowledge* is not likely to do so. The analogy with press freedom applies here too. A local reporter is much more likely to be able to judge whether the distress caused to a bereaved individual from a probing interview outweighs the public's 'right to know' than his colleagues on the international desk will be to judge whether any net harm will come from publishing a story about secret treaty negotiations or likely currency upheavals. The international writers should need much stronger evidence before they succumb to self-censorship.

Similarly, the takeover tycoon who shows the faithful old retainer the door, without asking what is to become of him, deserves all the obloquy he is likely to receive. But he does not have the knowledge to estimate the remoter consequences of supposedly patriotic, grandiose deviations from self-interest, such as 'buying British' when the overseas product gives better value for money. Nor is such knowledge available to Ministers who suggest he should, or to their Permanent Secretaries or even their economic advisers.

But just as there are some rare occasions when a journalist dealing with great diplomatic, military or financial issues should waive his rules and censor himself, there may just occasionally be a 'clear and present' economic danger, where the businessman should re-interpret the rules of the profit game. Even when this arises, the modifications can be in different elements. They can be within the margin of discretion in interpreting profit-seeking, described above. They can also be modifications in the background rules and conventions which normally *restrain* the pursuit of profit. For instance, it is possible to disregard conventions about going pay rates, thus *removing an inhibition on profit-making,* while at the same time shifting the emphasis to concepts of profit-seeking likely to result in the employment of more rather than fewer people.

The catch-all term 'corporate responsibility' is sometimes used to describe any and every departure from narrowly conceived profit maximization. Anyone who has followed me thus far will understand my reluctance to give a generalized 'Yes' or 'No' to the concept. The appropriate response should be wariness and suspicion.

ROLE OF OPINION

Examples of a 'clear and present danger', suggesting modifications of the pursuit of self-interest, will be given in later chapters of this book. The more general point to emphasize here is that the normal citizen or business leader cannot just pick and choose where he follows self-interest axioms and where he departs from them. Certain ways of following self-interest are effectively ruled out if he wishes to retain the regard and co-operation of his fellows, irrespective of his own opinion or moral goals. Moreover, some apparently altruistic departures stand little chance of being understood, followed by others, or making their intended impact if the general climate of opinion is against them.

Like language, law, money and other human phenomena, opinion is more the result of evolution than of conscious attempts to influence it. The evolution takes place mainly when existing opinion throws up contradictions, controversies and unsolved problems to which political economy is entitled to make a modest contribution.

It was David Hume who first demonstrated that 'ought' cannot be derived from 'is'. It did not prevent him from discussing, with scepticism and good humour, but with underlying seriousness, how nations, governments and individuals could improve their notions about appropriate behaviour.

REFERENCES

Acton, H.B., *The Morals of Markets*, London: IEA with Longman, 1971.
Brittan, S., *The Economic Consequences of Democracy*, London: Temple Smith, 1977, ch. 24.
Brittan, S., 'The Fight for Freedom in Broadcasting', *Political Quarterly*, Jan–March 1987.
Brittan, S., *The Role and Limits of Government*, London: Temple Smith, 1983.
Buchanan, J.M., *The Limits of Liberty*, Chicago, Ill.: Chicago University Press, 1975.
Griffiths, Brian, *Morality in the Market Place*, London: Hodder & Stoughton, 1985.
Hume, David, *Treatise on Human Nature*, 1739–40; Book III, Part III, section 3.
Jay, P., 'What is News?' in *The Crisis for Western Political Economy*, London: Andre Deutsch, 1985.
Kristol, Irving, *Reflections of a Neo-conservative*, New York: Basic Books, 1983.

Novak, Michael, *The Spirit of Democratic Capitalism*, New York: Simon & Schuster, 1983.

Rawls, J., *A Theory of Justice*, Cambridge, Mass.: Harvard University Press, 1972.

Sacks, Jonathan, *Wealth and Poverty*, London: IEA Social Affairs Unit, 1985.

Schwartz, Pedro, *The New Political Economy of J. S. Mill*, London: Weidenfeld & Nicolson, 1972.

Sen, Amartya, 'The Moral Standing of the Market', *Social Philosophy and Policy*, Spring 1985 (Bowling Green State University, Ohio).

Smith, Adam, *An Inquiry into the Nature and Causes of the Wealth of Nations*, 1776; Indianapolis: Liberty Classics, 1985.

Smith, Adam, *The Theory of Moral Sentiments*, 1759; Indianapolis: Liberty Classics, 1976.

Wilson, T. and A.S. Skinner (eds), *The Market and the State*, Oxford: Oxford University Press, 1976.

3   Choice and utility[*]

The ghost that has been stalking the previous chapters is that of utilitarianism. Various beliefs, including the common-sense pursuit of self-interest in the market place, have been defended in terms of a qualified utilitarianism. But what do I understand by this term and how is it to be qualified? The following essay is my attempt at an answer.

It has had a long gestation period. It was originally sparked off by a book of essays edited by Amartya Sen and Bernard Williams (1982); and my own reaction appeared both in a previous collection of essays and in an academic journal, published in 1983. I then thought that I had taken the subject as far as I could. But my interpretation of utility in terms of satisfaction of personal choice was challenged by some British political theorists, who found the emphasis on choice too reminiscent of the supposed doctrines of the Thatcher government. Thus I was under pressure to elucidate my position further, and produced the new version which appears here. I welcome the opportunity to do so, particularly because of the section entitled 'A Weighting System'. Whether valid or not, it embodies the earliest insights I have had into the ethics of public policy, going back to near-undergraduate days and is the one thing in this book which may be even slightly original.

THE APPEAL OF UTILITARIANISM

It is impossible to make decisions on public policy, or in any other sphere of human affairs, without some general principles of evaluation. It is impossible to take decisions entirely 'on their merits' or 'on the facts', because without some principles of evaluation we do not know what their merits are or where the facts point. It is just the self-styled pragmatists whose principles of evaluation are most likely to change with the fashions or pressures of the moment and whose decisions are least likely to be related to 'the facts' in any stable or predictable way.

On the other hand, virtually all substantive principles of evaluation suggested by moral and political philosophers have been found on closer examination to be highly unsatisfactory. They are either ambiguous or internally contradictory

* This chapter is based on my contribution to *The Utilitarian Response* (ed. Lincoln Allison, London: Sage Publications, 1990). Earlier versions entitled 'Two Cheers for Utilitarianism' were published in *Oxford Economic Papers*, 35 (1983) and as Chapter 2 of *The Role and Limits of Government: Essays in Political Economy* (London: Wildwood House, 1983, 1987).

in important instances; or they lead to conclusions which people find they cannot in practice accept. Thus we are unable to do without doctrine, yet should be on the lookout for snags in any doctrines we adopt. It is best to bring out into the open – rather than to suppress or keep implicit – the doctrines we cannot help using, but to appreciate that they are no more than broad presumptions in continual need of reformulation.

Controversial as it still is, utilitarianism is one of the most strongly established of the suggested systems of evaluation. Although it is in principle applicable to all human conduct, it has always been regarded as having special application to public policy. It has provided most economists with their policy yardsticks, although the more down-to-earth 'applied' practitioners have not always been conscious of the fact. It is the starting point for much of the current theorizing on 'ought' questions, even on the part of those who reject it or wish to modify it drastically. Above all, it has a great attraction for thinkers of a 'liberal' variety, who have, like John Stuart Mill, agonized and puzzled over it but found it difficult to reject or replace.

The thesis of this chapter is that some form of utilitarianism is a partial but indispensable guide to action, especially in the public sphere. But it cannot be adequate on its own and needs to be qualified and supplemented – or best of all placed in a broader framework which would indicate its sphere of applicability.

The attractions of utilitarianism include (a) its humanity, (b) its individualistic methodology and (c) its ability to provide an attractive combination of freedom, choice and welfare. Its defects include (a) that it is nevertheless an inadequate guarantee of reasonable personal freedom, (b) that unqualified, it gives free reign to illiberal satisfactions or preferences, and (c) it lacks a principle of distribution. To assess utilitarianism in this (or most other) ways reveals that one's own ultimate yardsticks are not utilitarian.

To understand both the appeal and the problems of utilitarianism, it is helpful to go back to the formulation of one of its best-known fathers, the British jurist and political theorist, Jeremy Bentham:

> By the principle of utility is meant that principle which approves or disapproves of every action whatsoever, according to the tendency which it appears to have to augment or diminish the happiness of the party whose interest is in question.... if that party be the community in general, then the happiness of the community: if a particular individual, then the happiness of that individual...
>
> The interest of the community then is, what? – the sum of the interest of the several members who compose it.

These sentences from the opening of the *Introduction to the Principles of Morals and Legislation* show that utilitarianism was from its early days, and still remains, a challenging assertion, rather than the grey or platitudinous doctrine which it is often popularly supposed to be.

An ambiguity in the word 'utilitarian' has fostered this misunderstanding. For it has a common-or-garden meaning of 'narrowly functional'. If a building or article of furniture is described as strictly utilitarian, we expect it to be adequate for its purpose but without any attempt to make it attractive or pleasing. The wartime 'utility scheme' was designed to save resources by concentrating on a minimum number of functional designs. Thus it becomes all too easy to present utilitarians as opposed to all colour, variety or fun – whereas a true utilitarian values everything that makes people satisfied, no matter how frivolous or 'inessential' it may appear to the man in Whitehall. Bentham himself became aware of how unattractive and misleading the label could be, and in the 1822 edition of the *Principles* canvassed the substitution of a term such as 'the greatest happiness' or 'greatest felicity'.

Since Bentham's time a vast literature has developed and there are almost as many varieties of utilitarianism as there are writers. This essay will have to be very selective, concentrating on a few points which I think *ought* to be of interest to the non-specialist or where I have something special to say. (An example of the kind of omission is whether utilitarianism is best stated as the promotion of pleasure or the prevention of pain, or whether the two can be assimilated in a common formulation.) Nor will there be any discussion of the vast mathematical literature on the measurement, comparison and assessment of utility levels produced mainly by economists of an abstract bent. More seriously, it will not be possible to discuss adequately metaethics – the logic of moral judgements and the logical status of utilitarianism or other normative systems.

Utilitarianism is compatible with many different metaethical views and utilitarians come from many different philosophical stables. In my view, the best starting point is to treat the principle of utility as neither a mysterious institution nor a deduction from some theory about the nature of moral discourse, but as a *proposed standard* for judging actions. It is thus not capable of strict proof; but it can be suggested by asking people to reflect on their basic judgements. If further justification is insisted upon, the most promising avenue is contractarianism – that is by thinking about the criteria that could, after reflection, command general assent among a group of people who did not know what their own personal circumstances were likely to be. It is worth putting up this flag here, because contractarianism will return at the end of the chapter, not only as a method of justifying a partial utilitarianism, but as a way of suggesting the role and limits of utilitarian thinking and institutions in a wider framework.

Consider, for instance: 'International aggression should always be punished.' Many people who assert such propositions have never reflected on whether this is a basic judgement, beyond which no argument is possible, or whether it is part of a vaguely articulated view of world politics in which unopposed aggression is deemed likely to lead to greater long-term suffering than the effort to resist. If it is the latter, it is necessary to ask about the cost of either any particular act of resistance or such resistance in general, and its likely benefits. If people are prepared to assess the costs and benefits by their effects on individual – not necessarily identifiable – human beings, their 'principles of foreign policy' stand revealed as subordinate to a principle like that of utility, to which direct reference may have to be made in case of difficulty.

The original doctrine has been analysed by Amartya Sen (1982) into three components:

1. *Consequentialism* – judging actions or policies in terms of their consequences for individual human beings.
2. *Welfare* – judging states of affairs or policies in terms of the level of satisfaction achieved, which is identified with utility.
3. *Sum-ranking* – the technical term for the summation of everyone's satisfaction to give a global utility total.

Thus utilitarianism is a member of the family of moral doctrines which judge actions neither by their motives nor their intrinsic qualities, but by their consequences. It is a form of what used to be called teleological ethics and is occasionally known today by the ungainly term 'consequentialism'. The contrast is with 'deontological' systems which judge actions exclusively by their conformity to some law or rule. It is possible to accept the consequential aspects of utilitarianism without accepting, or accepting in a very qualified form, the other two aspects.

Many people have instinctive deontological views and are shocked by consequentialist morality of any kind. An age-old objection to utilitarianism is that it runs counter to common ideas of good behaviour embodied in maxims such as 'Do not punish the innocent', 'Keep promises', 'Do not break treaties' or 'Do not invade other countries' territory'.

In one sense this criticism is unfair, and was already rebutted in John Stuart Mill's *Utilitarianism* (first published in 1861). Utilitarians are not so foolish as to imagine that they have either the knowledge or the disinterestedness to assess directly the utility consequences of alternative courses in either private or public life. The maxims of commonsense morality embody the accumulated (if imperfect) wisdom of generations; and their observance may do more to promote utility than any attempt to pursue it directly.

THE TWO LEVELS

Richard Hare has thrown light on the role of normal behaviour in a utilitarian system by drawing attention to two different levels of thinking, the first or 'intuitive' level and the second or 'critical' level. At the intuitive level we take for granted the maxims of popular morality and their public-policy counterparts. *Prima facie* rules are necessary, as it is quite impractical to make a direct calculation of the utility effects of every decision; and the attempt to do so would probably be clouded by self-interest and prejudice as well as insufficient knowledge. As Mill long ago pointed out, utilitarianism is not only consistent with, but requires, the 'intermediate generalizations' of popular morality.

The second 'critical' level of thinking is needed (a) when the generally accepted principles appear to conflict (e.g. truth-telling versus preventing suffering); (b) in determining exceptional cases when there seems to be an argument for waiving the rules; and above all (c) in the critical reflection required for the choice of the first-level *prima facie* rules, their elaboration and development.

It is the failure to move to this second critical level, when it is clearly required, which makes so many policy arguments merely a heated exchange of slogans. If debate on an issue such as the 1982 Argentinian invasion of the Falklands remains stuck at the level of 'They have invaded our territory!', 'Britain has been knocked around enough' – or on the other side 'Do nothing without the UN', 'You will alienate world opinion' – no rational discussion is possible.

Because of the emphasis on *prima facie* everyday rules of behaviour at the first intuitive level, Mill and Hare may be regarded as rule-utilitarians (in one special sense of that rather ambivalent term).* In considering whether to disregard some rules of everyday morality in an exceptional case, a utilitarian of this type will not stop at the direct effects of observance and non-observance. He will have to ask about the effects of his actions in weakening valuable rules and institutions. He is never on this interpretation content just to ask: 'Will telling a lie to save the feelings of a terminally ill patient' or 'Will breaking a treaty

---

* Rule-utilitarianism was invented to reduce the clash between the Principle of Utility and the rules of ordinary morality. It comes in many forms, but it is worth distinguishing two important types, 'primitive rule-utilitarianism' and 'ideal rule-utilitarianism'. According to the primitive variety, 'an act is right if, and only if, it conforms to a set of rules, conformity to which would maximize utility'. In other words, if weighing up the evidence and trying to allow for personal prejudices, someone is convinced that breaking a rule of conduct would promote more utility or less disutility than observing it, the rule should be broken. Under 'ideal rule-utilitarianism', on the other hand, 'an act is right if, and only if, it conforms to a set of rules *general acceptance* of which would maximize utility'.

As David Lyons, from whom these definitions are taken, has shown, primitive rule-utilitarianism is theoretically equivalent to act-utilitarianism (*The Forms and Limits of Utilitarianism*, Oxford: Clarendon Press, 1965). The everyday rules are simply practical aids (which may differ very much from one society to another). 'Ideal rule-utilitarianism' would, however, sometimes prescribe a different conduct to that of act-utilitarianism. Where the two systems diverge, the ideal rule-utilitarian would knowingly be departing from the Principle of Utility.

Hare fully accepts that his form of rule-utilitarianism is not ultimately distinguishable from act-utilitarianism. The distinctions between the two levels of thinking and the respect paid to popular morality are best regarded, not as a new kind of utilitarianism, but as a prudential way of applying the old kind.

to avoid a bloody war' cause more happiness or pain in this particular situation? He must also ask whether the comfort of the patient or the avoidance of bloodshed will outweigh the cost in future human suffering of the marginal weakening of the practice of truth-telling and treaty-keeping, which do in general promote human well-being and thus have a high acceptance utility. Even if he can act secretly, he has to consider the effect of his breach of the rule on his own future dispositions and character.

WELFARE, CHOICE AND FREEDOM

So much for the apparent contrast between consequentialism and the apparently deontological maxims of commonsense morality. It is time to turn to the second aspect of utilitarianism summarized earlier – judging actions, policies or states of affairs in terms of happiness and satisfaction.

By happiness Bentham meant the kind of satisfaction which would show up on a happiness meter – a primitive example being a cat purring. Aldous Huxley's *soma* pills in *Brave New World*, which made the taker happy, would be the ideal. Since Bentham's time there has been a shift, inaugurated mainly by economists, from satisfaction as such, to the maximization of individual opportunities for choice. The economists concerned had no conscious intention of revising moral philosophy. They interpreted satisfaction in terms of the opportunity to satisfy desires; and the only way they knew of examining these desires operationally was in terms of actual choices as revealed in the market and elsewhere: a doctrine known as revealed preference.

The newer type of utilitarianism treats people *as if* they are the best judges of their own interest. Some, but far from all, philosophers follow a similar route. In any case the term *choice-utilitarianism* is useful to demarcate this modern form from Bentham's happiness meter.

The key role assigned to the individual and his choice in choice-utilitarianism seems to offer an attractive combination of welfare and freedom. Policies are chosen which open up the maximum of opportunities and the minimum of restriction in making use of them. Opportunities depend on real income and wealth, defined quite subtly to take account of leisure, the quality of the working environment and the satisfaction gained from it; but they also depend on people's health, the physical environment and other amenities of a public goods kind. Restrictions on the exercise of choice are condemned, except when this exercise has harmful effects on other people. Thus choice-utilitarianism will often help the campaigner against restrictions on personal freedom, ranging from the Scottish sabbath to compulsory military service and censorship. Thus the doctrine *looks* like one of giving as much opportunity as possible to satisfy their choices to as many people as possible. It would seem to be at the opposite pole from authoritarian or paternalistic systems which either attempt to tell us our own good or subordinate individual freedom and happiness to some higher collective or metaphysical goal.

The choice-utilitarian goal lends itself to representation in economists' jargon as putting each person on the highest possible indifference curve. (An indifference curve represents combinations of goods and services with which a person is equally content, e.g., four oranges and five bananas, two oranges and eight bananas.) Improvements which make at least one person better off and no one worse off are known as 'Pareto-improvements' and are unequivocally to be welcomed. If, as is usually the case, some people gain and some lose, a distributional judgement has to be applied. But even then it is still a helpful first step in judgement to ask if a change is a potential Pareto-improvement – i.e., if the gainers could compensate the losers and still be better off. As can be imagined, a vast academic industry has arisen to develop the mathematics of all this, with the name of welfare economics – most of it far too rarefied to be of help to any practical economist concerned with actual welfare issues.

In positive economic theory it is customary, in the words of Armen Alchian, 'to postulate that an individual seeks to maximize something subject to some constraints. All that counts is that we can assign numbers to entities or conditions which a person can strive to realize.' Thus individual utility maximization is made true by definition. Everyone tries to maximize utility; and utility is whatever he or she is trying to maximize. This is not as silly as it sounds as a working axiom, provided it is used in conjunction with empirical information to produce results that are not tautological. An economist can use the utility-maximizing assumption without any commitment to any particular normative doctrine. He is only a 'choice-utilitarian' if he insists that people should have every chance of satisfying as many of their preferences as possible to the maximum feasible extent and wishes to see social institutions which will further these aims.

At this stage in the argument – in practice long before – some people's patience runs out and the question is put: What are you really interested in: maximizing satisfaction or pleasure (for which choice has to be a proxy because of the difficulty of assessing satisfaction)? Or are you advocating (or accepting) the replacement of satisfaction by choice as an alternative form of consequentialism, consciously different to classical utilitarianism? What I have actually been doing is observing the evolution of utilitarian doctrine from the happiness meter towards observed choice, under the operational necessities of disciplines such as economics, with a quiet satisfaction.

'What is so wonderful about choice?' asks Andrew Reeve, a British political theorist. The value lies in the absence of coercion or man-made obstacles to the exercise of people's powers and capacities. This value is part of the western tradition; and, although it can be defended (as I have tried to do throughout this volume and elsewhere), it cannot in the final analysis be rigorously demonstrated against those with incompatible different values. Nor, of course, can traditional utilitarianism or any other values – as Hume argued convincingly in the eighteenth century.

What has caused all the excitement and demands for impossible standards of rigour in defining or defending 'choice'? One should have guessed. For as Reeve admits, it was the invocation of choice by the Thatcher government in defence of its policies towards education, health care, housing and trade unions. At the mere mention of Margaret Thatcher too many otherwise level-headed academics lose all sense of proportion.

To answer the original question put to me: Yes, I am content to replace the opportunity to satisfy preferences for the direct happiness assessment of Benthamite utilitarianism. But as there are no happiness meters and no *soma* pills without unpleasant after-effects, there is little option. The conflicts between Benthamite utilitarianism and the choice variety are minimal if one believes adults are normally the best judges of what will bring them satisfaction; and that if they make mistakes, wise men acting on their behalf will make even more. But because of the absence of an actual happiness meter, there will always be a subjective element in the assessment.

Consider, moreover, the following. If X makes a mistake in assessing what will bring him satisfaction, that is one misfortune. But if Y decides for him there is a double misfortune: X has his satisfaction lowered and in addition there has been an act of coercion – X has been made subject to the will of Y, and has had his freedom diminished, which, according to widely held and defensible values, is an evil in itself.

Consider some of the ways in which people's pursuit of their own choices or preferences may differ from the pursuit of satisfaction. People may make simple mistakes. If they knew what they now know about the consequences of certain actions, they would not have embarked upon them. The presumption, from the point of view of both liberty and satisfaction, is that they should be free to make their own mistakes. But a value pluralist will occasionally allow a presumption to be overthrown. To give a specific example: a liberal should be instinctively suspicious of anti-drugs legislation. But unless his thought is monomaniac he will want at least to look at the evidence before campaigning for the legalization of hard drugs.

There are other examples of possible conflicts between choice and satisfaction. The act of choice, at certain times for certain people and beyond a certain limit, may be painful. Sometimes, too, people will knowingly sacrifice their own well-being for altruistic reasons. Or they may wish to become martyrs, or heroes or saints. It is only if these are defined tautologically as pursuing satisfaction in a particular way that then the distinction between choice-utilitarianism and the Benthamite variety collapses.

The distinction between choice-utilitarianism and the satisfaction variety is nevertheless much less important in relation to many of the virtues and defects of utilitarianism listed at the beginning of this chapter than one might suppose, and to which I can now return.

Prima facie, utilitarianism should be a highly humane doctrine. It accepts the need to deter wrong-doers who could bring misery on society; but punishment – as the infliction of suffering on human beings – is always an evil, even if a necessary one. In the words of an early utilitarian jurist, Beccaria, punishment must be 'public, prompt, necessary, *the least possible in the given circumstances*, proportionate to the crimes, dictated by the laws'. (It is indeed the words I have italicized which create an unbridgeable gap between it and either the New Right or the Old Right.)

But not only is it humanitarian, it is also – as the opening quotation from Bentham brings out – highly individualist in its methodology. Statements about nations or about large abstractions such as the 'morale of the country' or 'the health of the economy' must be translatable into statements about individual human beings and their well-being before a judgement can be made. The translation of policies into effects of individual satisfaction can lead us to pose such useful questions as: How much suffering is justified by the gratification of my feelings of national price? How much less take-home pay is my psychic satisfaction in Ruritanian ownership of Ruritanian resources worth? Analysis along these lines would be likely to make people more self-conscious than they would otherwise be. It might even lead to a weakening of unreflective willingness to 'die for one's country' and to a waning of nationalist and ideological enthusiasm in general.

To move on from the matters of war and peace to other aspects of utilitarianism is inevitably a descent. But we must persist. The value of choice-utilitarianism in promoting a mixture of welfare and choice has already been discussed. But as was noted at the beginning, utilitarianism, even in its choice variety, may be insufficient as a guarantee of a minimal area of basic personal freedom. This is because, although there is a large overlap and marked mutual support between freedom and choice, the two values can conflict, especially when the imperative 'maximize' is put in front of choice. An example is the frequent suggestion of some form of compulsory peacetime national service. Let us grant hypothetically – which I would not grant in practice – that such a scheme would broaden the horizons of many young people and provide them with a greater range of choice in the future, both by enlarging their earning power and by broadening their cultural horizons. Even then, national service is a complete negation of the freedom to lead one's life in one's own way. For a liberal, this potential conflict with freedom is a defect of choice-utilitarianism as well as the Benthamite variety.

ILLIBERAL PREFERENCES

A better-known case of conflict between either variety of utilitarianism and freedom is that of illiberal preferences. Amartya Sen is well known for his demonstration that free choice in personal matters can easily conflict with utilitarian principles. His best-known illustration is that of two people, 'Prude' and 'Lewd', deciding who should read *Lady Chatterley's Lover*. Clearly the liberal solution is for Lewd to read it and Prude not to. But it so happens Prude would rather read it himself, however reluctantly, than allow Lewd to indulge his 'depraved tastes'. Lewd, on the other hand, given that only one of them can do so, would like it even more if Prude were forced to read it to shake him out of his stuffiness. Thus Prude reading *Lady Chatterley* has a higher utility ranking for both men and would be said in the jargon to be 'Pareto-optimal', in contrast to the libertarian solution of allowing Lewd to get on with his reading himself.

The Sen paradox is but one example of many potential conflicts. A fully fledged utilitarian would take into account the desires of some mature citizens for compulsory haircuts for long-haired youths. He would also take account of the desires of other citizens for restrictions on the number of overseas villas or yachts the wealthy can possess. (This is not a question of the distribution of income and wealth but of the freedom of people to spend whatever wealth they have.) These linkages of one person's well-being to the behaviour of others, whether reflecting envy or aesthetic or 'moral' views, are labelled 'interdependence effects' in the economics literature, and it is their recognition which can make utilitarianism an illiberal doctrine. If negative interdependence effects are taken into account in public policy, people will be penalized for carrying out private personal acts which affect others only because thinking makes it so.

Anyone with liberal value judgements will therefore have to qualify his utilitarianism by the exclusion of some interdependence effects. Wants arising from non-benign interdependence effects are a disguised form of coercion which arise from a desire to regulate the way other people spend their lives or from envy of their well-being or success. Many utilitarian writers are willing to make this qualification. According to one typical formulation due to Harsanyi, 'All clearly antisocial preferences, such as sadism, envy, resentment and malice should be excluded from the social utility function.'

Once such qualifications are made it is admitted that other principles are being used to qualify utilitarianism, which thus loses its status as a single ultimate guide to moral conduct in favour of a tacit pluralism. Critics have remarked on the amount of 'doctoring or idealization' of choice-based preferences in which utilitarian writers indulge.

Utilitarians often go too far in their attempts to demonstrate that it is only the principle of utility that is being used. Hare considers cases where total utility might, it seems, be increased by allowing a sadist his way, or a Nazi to free himself of the presence of Jews. He dismisses these cases as 'fantastic' examples, factually highly unlikely. But why is it important to show that perverse results would not occur? Either the expositor is using some yardstick other than utility with which to evaluate utilitarianism, or he is saying that current 'humanitarian' rules happen to be justified as a practical application of the principle of utility, but if they proved not to be so, they should be abandoned. We should not be ashamed of using some other notion, such as that of human dignity, to supplement the principle of utility and we do not need to attempt to govern our behaviour by one principle, whether utilitarian or otherwise. Utility can remain important in a pluralist set of values.

CHANGES OF TASTE

Another difficult problem for the utilitarian relates to the effects of changes in tastes. Even a spontaneous change of tastes may be welfare-reducing on a strict utilitarian view. If demand for commodity X is replaced by demand for a novel commodity Y, capital used to produce X becomes obsolescent. New investment which could have been used to produce more of X and raise living standards has to be diverted to the production of Y merely to maintain the existing level of satisfaction. *A fortiori*, activity designed to make people dissatisfied with their lot so that they try out new products, services or ways of life, risks being utility-destroying.

This applies not only to advertising (which has always attracted the ire of utilitarian economists) but to political propaganda, imaginative literature, the dissemination of new technical knowledge and most cultural activity. The result of social innovation on the level of well-being is in fact indeterminate. If total capacity of satisfaction has increased, because human imagination has been stimulated, then a person may be better off with a smaller proportion of his new desires satisfied than with a larger proportion of his old. On the other hand, cultural change and exposure to new habits and methods may make a person restless and disturbed, and less satisfied than if he had been left alone.

Let us consider a stylized historical example. Suppose that for a certain group of workers the changes brought about by the Industrial Revolution are, from the standpoint of their initial tastes and preferences, changes for the worse. Nevertheless, as a result of the Industrial Revolution these workers may acquire a greater desire for manufactured goods, become more tolerant of factory conditions and less prepared to put up with their earlier rural privations; so they would be worse off still if they return to their old life. Their attitude is characterized by Elster: 'We were happier before we got these fancy new things, although we would now be miserable without them.' But why should we not assert that the loss of satisfaction is offset by the increase in choices or opportunities resulting from industrialization?

The more liberal view would regard the enlargement of opportunities as good in itself (or at least not so bad as to be prevented by state action). So long as people are allowed to do the best for themselves (as they interpret best at any particular time), the liberal will not busy himself with sorrowful comparisons about how much better off people might have felt themselves to be if culture, circumstances and tastes had not changed.

DISTRIBUTION

Finally, there is the question of distribution which many commentators regard as the most important issue raised by utilitarianism. On the contrary, I think that the problems of distribution are something of a diversion from more profound issues.

Whose satisfaction should be promoted when the interests of different people and groups come into conflict? For purposes of public policy it is necessary to assume that an evil affecting two million people is worse than a comparable evil affecting one million (e.g., a missile attack on a smaller or larger city). A benefit of given size for two million people has to be regarded as better than the same benefit for only one million. These are judgements on which most people can agree even though they are unlikely to agree on the reasons for them, if 'reasons' be required at all.

Sometimes it is necessary to go further. If the amount of harm likely to be suffered by a representative member of the one-million community is clearly far greater than that suffered by a representative member of the two-million community, most people would want to reverse their initial decision as they would regard the suffering of the larger community as the lesser evil. However vague and imprecise the comparisons, they cannot be avoided; and the necessary estimates typically involve units such as real income, casualty numbers, accident risks and so on. Some kinds of decision (e.g., military expenditure versus social services or take-home pay) can only be rationalized if there is some way of converting these units into each other.

It is tempting, therefore, to think in terms of units of utility and say that we are maximising either total utility or, more sensibly, utility per head. This does no harm as a piece of mathematical shorthand, so long as we are clear that we are dealing with a fictitious entity which corresponds to nothing which actually exists.

The mistake of many utilitarians has been to conceive of something called 'total utility' as one great total of which each individual's utility is a part. The concept can be likened to a 'national petroleum tank' representing the total stock of petroleum to which each individual petrol tank contributes. It is known technically as 'sum-ranking', the third of the components of utilitarianism mentioned earlier.

The concept of one huge utility tank, if it makes any sense at all, suggests a giant collective consciousness of which each individual consciousness is part. If the object of moral conduct is to maximize some utility total, then each individual is important only as a utility carrier contributing to the total stock. This seems to me not only objectionable, but factually wrong. Two patients in hospital may each be suffering to roughly the same degree, which we may call x. But two patients, each suffering x, are by no means equivalent to one patient suffering $2x$. Utility or satisfaction belongs to individuals. Satisfaction, or pain, can be compared,* but I can attach no meaning to the aggregate of everyone's satisfaction and pain. Who is supposed to experience it? It is either obfuscatory metaphysics, or it pre-supposes some giant Hegelian collective consciousness of which each consciousness is but a subordinate part. Total utility may be a computational convenience, but it is not something which actually exists, like the joy of one human being or the suffering of another.

Utilitarians need a principle of distribution which they cannot derive from their own system. Many utilitarian economists have tried to derive egalitarian conclusions from the principle of diminishing marginal utility, which asserts that each additional unit of income or wealth leads to a continually diminishing increment of satisfaction. Thus, other things being equal, an extra pound or dollar is worth more to a poor man than to a rich one.

This reasoning has led many utilitarian economists to a qualified egalitarianism. A typical formulation, still held by many mainstream economists, is that equalization should be pushed to the point where further redistribution would

* The objections given here to the tank concept of total utility are entirely different from those usually advanced by those economists (such as Lionel Robbins in the 1930s) who 'denied the validity' of interpersonal comparisons. This seems to me misconceived. We can and do say 'A is slightly better off than B but much worse off than C'. Such statements cannot be made with great precision and are prone to error. But they are neither meaningless nor pure value judgements, as they have a factual component.

Doubts expressed about the legitimacy of interpersonal comparisons of satisfaction probably represent the intrusion of the epistemological doubts about the 'existence of other mind' into a sphere where they do not belong. For when we engage in discussions on ethics, political philosophy or economic policy, we necessarily have to assume that other minds exist. The best discussion of the topic is still to be found in Chapter 4 of I.M.D. Little's *Critique of Welfare Economics*, rev. edn, Oxford: Oxford University Press, 1957.

reduce total utility by its effects on incentives. Its application should, of course, take into account other qualifications such as Hume's observation that 'It would be greater cruelty to dispossess a man of anything than not to give it to him.'

To build a justification for redistribution on the principle of diminishing marginal utility involves, however, extremely questionable value judgements. For many policy purposes people have to be treated in broad categories. Policy-makers can reasonably assume that a representative individual earning £5,000 per annum will value an additional pound more than a representative person earning £100,000. (The rich are different. They have more money.) But once we have knowledge of individual cases, it would be no surprise at all to find a particular poor man so physically handicapped or dispirited, and with so little power of enjoyment, that his welfare is little affected by changes in income over a considerable range. A particular rich man may be, on the other hand, a riotous liver with a huge unsatisfied capacity for enjoyment. Do we then make a reverse transfer from poor to rich?

Almost certainly not. Most people, whether egalitarians or not, who are concerned with the level of the poorest and most disadvantaged, would not find, even after critical reflection, that their concern is derived from some beliefs about the shape of the individual utility curve. We would not be in favour of taxing the poor and handicapped to benefit the rich and healthy, even if some utility meter showed that 'total utility' had thereby been increased.

The conclusion to which I am leading is that the common practice of analysing utilitarianism largely in terms of its distributional implications has shunted discussion onto the wrong track. Utilitarians have often been attacked by radicals for being insufficiently egalitarian, and occasionally by conservatives for being too much so, and they have been tempted to reply. In my view the principle of utility does not have much to contribute to the distributional question, one way or the other. The main utilitarian contribution is the assertion that actions should be guided by their effects on the welfare of individual persons. Anyone who thinks this trite or obvious need only reflect on the variety of reasons for which wars have been fought and punishments inflicted. It is much less use as a guide to whose welfare should be raised where there is a choice.

A WEIGHTING SYSTEM

There is one question which cannot, however, be avoided; and its implications particularly affect matters of war and peace and foreign policy. Utilitarians, along with many other moral philosophers, endorse a general impartiality towards all our fellow human beings. How do we square this requirement with the greater sympathy which most people instinctively feel towards their family, friends and fellow countrymen compared with the unknown millions of the Third World?

Utilitarian moralists are not so foolish as to condemn these very natural human feelings. They tend, however, to regard them as being no more than useful rule-of-thumb maxims at the first or intuitive level. Richard Hare defends them as being in practice the best way to promote the interests of all the inhabitants of the world. For instance, if mothers were expected to care equally for all children, and not just their own, then children in general would almost certainly be less well provided for than they are now. Loyalty to country is a virtue only to the extent that it happens to promote the interests of all human beings.

Let us look a little further. Take the case of the person who consciously attaches more weight to his family and friends than to unknown millions in the Third World or even to the mass of his fellow countrymen, and insists that this is a perfectly moral course. He may say that this is how he believes everyone else in the world ought to behave too (subject, perhaps, to certain exceptions statable in general terms – e.g., unless he is working as a minister, official, judge or recruitment officer). On the other hand he may reply that these are the standards he expects from the people with whom he is likely to come into contact, but that he is either completely indifferent to, or cares much less about, how people in the forests of the Amazon do or should behave. If asked whether he would be prepared to accept this dictum if he lived in the Amazon basin himself, he can reply, without making a logical mistake, that he is not prescribing for the inhabitants of Amazonia, but only for the more restricted groups with which he can identify, and that he is not worried if one school of academics chooses to label him as 'amoral'. (As some readers will see, I am trying to avoid discussing the thesis that all moral judgements are necessarily universal as well as prescriptive. If, as usually maintained, universalism is a logical thesis about the use of the moral terms, then nothing follows about how much weight we ought to give the interests of the different inhabitants of the world.)

The reader should also ask whether on critical reflection he really does give equal weight to the interests of creatures with partially human characteristics who may be found on other planets; or to animals on this planet; or to some link in the evolutionary chain between primordial ape and man who might one day be discovered still existing in some corner of the world.

An impartially benevolent utilitarian will try to justify giving more weight to family and friends than to unknown millions in the Third World, by saying that we can do more for them. But this is not self-evident. It is conceivable that we could do more to promote human satisfaction ('we' being those above a certain level in the world income scale) if we gave every minute of our non-working time to Oxfam.

Too many moralists have paid lip-service to the idea of the whole human race counting equally (sometimes including generations yet unborn), and have then gone on to concentrate on policies affecting exclusively their own communities. Ordinary people are then presented with the false choice of either giving equal value to every inhabitant of the earth or giving no value at all to those outside their immediate circle or country. The result of paying lip-service to impartial benevolence is too often in practice the total neglect of those outside their own group.

There would have been no way of persuading many of the most pacific Englishmen or Israelis in recent conflicts that an Argentinian or Lebanese life was of equal value to that of an Englishman or an Israeli. But he would, one hopes, have accepted that they were of *some* value. If I may quote from an essay I wrote in the aftermath of the Suez Crisis, a weighting system under which different people counted in different degrees 'designed to fit these successive circles of feelings of obligation (which people actually have) might appear to some less exalted than an equal concern for all human beings; but surely it would be preferable to a narrow nationalism which arbitrarily rules out the small but existent sympathies that most people have for their fellow men of different nationalities?'

The weights are measures of relative concern in the minds of the individuals making the assessment. Utilitarianism cannot supply the weights. The weights are a precondition of applying utilitarian-type principles.

CONCLUSION: A RIGHTS FRAMEWORK

The preceding argument suggests that any utilitarian system, which could both serve as a practical guide to action and respect individual liberty and autonomy, has to be heavily circumscribed and heavily supplemented if it is to be acceptable to liberals. Utilitarianism, despite its claim to the contrary, needs distributional criteria which it cannot itself provide. The desires it aims to satisfy must be people's desires for themselves, not their wishes for others, especially when the latter are affected by envy, malice or disapproval. Comparisons of satisfaction should, moreover, be made with extreme caution over a period when tastes have changed in important ways, partly as a result of utilitarian policies and institutions.

Is there another system which will provide more directly the goals of a qualified utilitarianism without the need for such a large protective belt of explanations, exceptions and disclaimers? The main alternatives on offer, likely to win liberal converts from utilitarianism, are some modern versions of individual rights theory.

The main characteristics of rights-based theories are (a) that some preferences or choices are treated much more favourably than others, and (b) that the concentration is on the opportunities open to people rather than the use they make of these opportunities and their resulting psychic states. Many systems of rights have their origin in 'contractarianism' (or 'contractualism'). A contractarian regards an action as wrong if it would be disallowed by any system of regulation which, as Scanlon puts it, 'no one could reasonably reject as a basis for informed, unforced general agreement'. Contractarianism is, however, only a method of assessing principles of conduct. There is no guarantee that it will lead to one unique system.

Conversely, not all personal-rights theories are based on contractarian reasoning. The most widely discussed non-contractarian theory of personal rights is that of Robert Nozick's 'entitlement system'. This maintained (the past tense is used because Nozick is no longer committed to these principles) that property holdings are just if they have been justly transferred by gifts or fee exchange or if they have been justly acquired in the first place. The only legitimate state in this scheme is the night-watchman version, confined to protection of the person and property and to the enforcement of contracts. The community has no right to interfere with property rights in even as general a way as redistributive taxation to help the very poorest.

Nozick did not in fact even claim to have given us a theory of 'just acquisition'. His ingenious and illuminating treatise is mainly preoccupied with deriving the implications of such rights, assuming that a justification will eventually be forthcoming, and with exhibiting the drawbacks of the 'end-state view' of some other writers. Nozick gives no reason for the prohibition of state-enforced transfers which will persuade those who do not accept his minimal state at the outset. We badly need a conception of liberty and individual rights which will provide protection against the proclivities of a temporary majority for trampling over the rights and liberties of the rest of us in the name of a debased kind of act-utilitarianism. Unfortunately, all the well-known variations of libertarianism and limited state conservatism – Nozick, Hayek, Oakeshott *et al.* – lack a theory of legitimate property rights, without which they are powerless to provide a comprehensive theoretical defence against collectivism, and we have to fall back on vaguer notions of a sufficiently large 'protected area' for the individual.

The leading fully developed contractarian theory of personal rights is still that embodied in John Rawls's system of 'justice as fairness'. The idea is to work out the principles on which free and rational people concerned to further their own interests would desire their community to be run if they did not know their own social or economic place, the market value of their own talents, and many other key features of their real situation. If one excludes knowledge of one's own actual position, there is some chance of working out the principles on a disinterested basis.

The results which Rawls derives are summarized as follows:

1. Equal rights to the most extensive scheme of equal basic liberties compatible
    with a similar scheme of liberties for all.
2. Social and economic inequalities must:
    (a) work to the benefit of the least advantaged and
    (b) be attached to offices open to all.

Principle 1 has priority over 2, and 2(b) over 2(a).

It is possible to accept the method – 'the veil of ignorance' – without accepting
the principles which Rawls derives. Indeed, some have argued that people
would, behind the 'veil of ignorance', choose to be governed by utilitarianism.
Rawls's own two principles have been subject to widely varying interpretations.
Rawls has been attacked for being everything from a Gladstonian free-market
liberal to a ruthless egalitarian – and both extremes of criticism find sustenance.
'Equal liberties' can mean different things according to whether the emphasis
is on 'liberties' or on 'equal'. The system is also much less collectivist if it is
regarded as a guide to basic institutions than to current government policy.

My own first desire under the 'veil of ignorance' would be to make sure that
everyone had a basic minimum, defined not in absolute terms but in relation to
the wealth of my society. This would be a safeguard in case I drew the unfortunate card and found myself at the bottom of the pack. Secondly, I should want
to ensure a large area of personal freedom where I could make my own decisions,
and to ensure political, social, cultural and economic opportunities which could
not be literally 'equal' all round, but could be free of barriers of privilege and
irrelevant entry qualifications.

Would I carry redistribution beyond the idea of a basis minimum? I should
be tempted to turn round Rawls's principle 2(a) and say that *redistribution* is
only justified if it improves the position of the least well off, instead of saying
that inequalities are so justified. The inversion shifts the onus of proof where
knowledge is imperfect and leaves at least a shadow of the entitlement principle,
by giving the benefit of the doubt to the incomes or holdings which people have
acquired through their own efforts or from gifts and bequests.

It is also worth remarking that the 'liberties' postulated in systems such as
Rawls's First Principle (and emphasized by many less-formal theorists of
democracy for over a century) consist partly of negative freedom as defined in
Berlin's words: 'I am normally said to be free to the degree to which no man
or body of men interferes with my activity'. But they also contain certain 'participatory rights' – the right to vote, to stand for office on the same terms as
other citizens, to be consulted on decisions, and in many formulations, to
receive education enabling one to play a full role as a citizen. These rights, however
valuable, have to do with ideals of participatory democracy. They may and often
do enlarge choice, but it only confuses the issue to associate them with freedom,
which is not quite the same value.

Leaving aside the distributional principle 2(a), a great deal of further elaboration is required of principles 1 and 2(b) about equal rights and liberties, and offices open to all. One worry is that certain devices such as representative democracy, which are convenient ways of changing governments peacefully and indicating where the shoe pinches for particular societies at a particular time, are given a universal status they do not deserve. We are all aware of the sentiment: 'You've got to be an active, informed citizen or else.' Rawls himself nowhere says it; but many enthusiasts for participatory democracy give this impression.

It may be that the Rawlsian primary goods could be stated in a way which did not attract such worries. Even then they would still have a much more limited domain of application than the principle of utility. There are many issues – war and peace, foreign policy, crime and punishment, even the 'management of the economy' – which have a moral dimension and where principles of the Rawlsian type shed little light, but where utilitarianism has something to contribute.

There are thus attractions in trying to combine a system of personal rights or primary goods and the principle of utility in a hierarchy. An improved Rawlsian system of personal rights based on contractarian reasoning might be most suitable for the basic constitutional and structural features of a society, and utilitarianism may be a better basis for everyday policy. Such a synthesis would require an operational method of separating structural and constitutional changes from everyday policy, which would be far from easy to establish.

No synthesis yet exists; and it is extremely doubtful whether there will ever be any organized hierarchy of principles which will not occasionally come into conflict with some moral judgements not incorporated in them and which, after the most extensive critical reasoning, we are still not willing to drop. It is indeed possible to improve on utilitarianism; but it is also possible to fall short of it. My own suspicion is that in the majority of cases where we fail to take a utilitarian stance, it is because we fall short of it rather than because we improve upon it.

REFERENCES

Alchian, Armen, 'The Meaning of Utility Measurement', in Harry E. Townsend (ed.), *Price Theory*, Harmondsworth, Middx: Penguin, 1971, pp. 123–54.

Beccaria, Cesare, *Dei Delitti e delle Penne*, first published 1764; quoted by Anthony Quinton in *Utilitarian Ethics*, London: Macmillan, 1973, p. 23.

Bentham, Jeremy, *Introduction to the Principles of Morals and Legislation*, ed. Wilfrid Harrison, Oxford: Basil Blackwell, 1948.

Berlin, Isaiah, 'Two Concepts of Liberty', reprinted in Berlin, *Four Essays on Liberty*, Oxford, 1969.

Brittan, S., 'Morality and Foreign Policy', reprinted as the Appendix to *A Restatement of Economic Liberalism*, London: Macmillan, 1978.

Elster, John, in *Utilitarianism and Beyond*, Cambridge: Cambridge University Press, 1982.

Hare, R.M., *Moral Thinking*, Oxford: Clarendon Press, 1981.

Harsanyi, John, in A. Sen and B. Williams (eds) *Utilitarianism and Beyond*, Cambridge: Cambridge University Press, 1982.

Mill, John Stuart, *Utilitarianism*, 1861; London: J.M. Dent, 1948.

Nozick, Robert, *Anarchy, State and Utopia*, Oxford: Basil Blackwell, 1974.

Rawls, John, *A Theory of Justice*, Oxford: Oxford University Press, 1972.

Reeve, Andrew, 'Individual Choice and the Retreat from Utilitarianism', in L. Allison (ed.), *The Utilitarian Response*, London: Sage, 1990.

Scanlon, T., in A. Sen and B. Williams, *Utilitarianism and Beyond*, Cambridge: Cambridge University Press, 1982.

Sen, Amartya, *Choice, Welfare and Measurement*, Oxford, 1982.

Sen, A. and B. Williams, (eds), *Utilitarianism and Beyond*, Cambridge: Cambridge University Press, 1982.

4 'There is no such thing as society'*

All I have is a voice
To undo the folded lie,
The romantic lie in the brain
Of the sensual man-in-the-street,
And the lie of Authority
Whose buildings grope the sky;
There is no such thing as the State
And no one exists alone;
Hunger allows no choice
To the citizen or the police;
We must love one another or die.

W.H. Auden, *September 1, 1939*

The qualified welcome given in previous essays both to utilitarianism and to the pursuit of self-interest in markets suggests the need for a statement of what I really *do* wholeheartedly believe. A lecture invitation in 1992 provided an irresistible invitation for such a statement.

I used as a peg Lady Thatcher's celebrated statement, made in 1987, although my interpretation of it may differ considerably from the ex-Prime Minister's. I merely mean that the interests, feelings and welfare of individual human beings should be the ultimate yardstick for public policy, and that the collective wholes dealt with by social scientists and administrators need to be anchored to actual people. The quotation from Auden should dispel misunderstanding except among the wilfully blind and deaf.

INTRODUCTION

The prospect for a liberal with a small 'l', who attaches a special importance to personal and political freedom, does not look good. We liked to suppose that freedom and prosperity went together and could indulge in the luxury of asking how the two were best interpreted and promoted.

* This essay is based on the 1992 J.C. Rees Lecture at University College, Swansea, published by the College, and reissued in slightly revised form by the Social Market Foundation, London, 1993. I am extremely grateful to Dr James A. Davies of the Swansea Department of English for locating the lines from Auden, which the poet himself had perversely expurgated from later editions of his published work.

The early 1990s have seen the collapse of the greatest experiment in state direction in world history in the former Soviet Union, which now faces hyper-inflation and possible collapse. They have also seen the disintegration of the much-vaunted Swedish 'third way'. At the same time western capitalism looks in bad shape. Among the major powers only China, which combines emergent capitalism with a ruthless dictatorship, and openly models itself on Pinochet's Chile, seems to be experiencing satisfactory progress – hardly a model for those of us who believe that man does not live by bread alone.

Nearer home – and indeed in my own profession – a conflict has emerged between one aspect of John Stuart Mill's ideal, namely an open vigorous press, and another aspect, the individual's right to lead his own life unmolested. The tensions between free speech and the right to privacy could no doubt be put into the language of John Stuart Mill or Jeremy Bentham (not of course the same); but my back of the envelope attempts to do so have turned out to be merely translations; and I am not sure how far the political theory helps us to resolve them.

Indeed I sometimes wonder whether even discussing such objects is not simply a way of taking refuge from the crude inhumanities of groups of people to each other. We must all have had the experience of tuning into a news bulletin part of the way through, hearing of ghastly killings and mutilations of innocent civilians, often children, and not knowing whether the event is in Northern Ireland, Bosnia, the West Bank, Cambodia, Somalia, South Africa, some of the former Soviet republics or in numbers of other trouble spots, including disturbances in the main urban centres of the west. Indeed in pessimistic moods I find it difficult to add anything to the statement of Immanuel Kant: 'Out of the crooked timber of humanity no straight thing was ever made.'

But life goes on; and I have decided to take refuge in discussing a modern political statement which may not be very congenial to all of my readers, but which is worth pursuing if we are interested in the value of the individual human being and therefore in his or her well-being and freedom.

MARGARET THATCHER'S VIEW

One of the most famous utterances of Margaret Thatcher was: 'There's no such thing as Society. There are individual men and women, and there are families.'

I got into trouble by supporting Lady Thatcher's assertion at a joint meeting held in 1991 by the Tory Reform Group and the Social Market Foundation, especially as I also expressed mild scepticism about John Major's Citizen's Charter. It was the Tory Reform element who regarded me as a hard-hearted cynic; and it was left to the Social Market element, who were mostly Owenite-SDP by background, to explain, as Bryan Magee put it, that I was merely expounding Methodological Individualism.

The incident was typical. Lady Thatcher's remark achieved notoriety and was far more often repeated by her detractors than by her supporters. Most of the latter were put on the defensive by words which, taken out of context, seemed to be the epitome of an uncaring pursuit of personal self-interest.

The view I want to put forward is the opposite: namely that this is one of the best things the former Prime Minister has said. The Thatcher proposition is obviously not literally correct. Philosophers rightly warn against assertions about what does or does not exist. There is no point in denying the existence of complex wholes, such as society, nations, social classes and so on, any more than there is in denying the existence of herds of cattle or flocks of sheep. Lady Thatcher was reminding us that society consists of individuals, just as herds and flocks consist of individual cows and sheep.

This is an obvious truth of which we need reminding and which is disputed by some supposedly higher-level thinkers. It was not of course original, having been uttered before by many political theorists, philosophers and even poets of widely varying ideological colours. Whatever you may think of Lady Thatcher's views on 'not bucking the market', or on any other characteristic subject, they do not follow from her remarks about society and individuals.

HISTORICAL ANTECEDENTS

There are numerous antecedents to the Thatcher view of society and individuals coming from writers in the empirical, sceptical, analytical and utilitarian traditions. In the first paragraph of the Part of *Leviathan* dealing with the Commonwealth, Hobbes remarked that it is set up by men 'for their own preservation and for a more contented life'. Jeremy Bentham proclaimed in the opening of his Introduction to the *Principles of Morals and Legislation* (published in 1789): 'The interest of the community then is: What? The sum of the interests of the several members who compose it.' Earlier on, David Hume remarked, 'A nation is nothing but a collection of individuals.' It would have been better without the 'nothing but'. A nation is a particular kind of collection of individuals, just as a company is another kind.

David Hume's remark was made *en passant* in the context of a slightly whimsical essay on national character. He said there that the manners of individuals were frequently determined by 'moral' conditions – which he used in the eighteenth-century manner to cover any kind of general influence, such as the political system or economic conditions. Since individual manners are frequently determined by these influences, so are so-called national characteristics, 'since a nation is nothing but a collection of individuals'. He regards the assertion as obvious, treating it as a link in an argument, and does not bother to justify it.

The two formulations – 'There is no such thing as society...' and 'A nation is a collection of individuals' – amount to pretty much the same, but appeal to different segments of public opinion when uttered today. The Thatcherite formulation appeals to the free-market radicals who are anxious to proclaim economic self-interest as legitimate and important. David Hume's formulation would appeal to those on the Foreign Policy Left, A.J.P. Taylor's dissenters: those who were not usually Christian pacifists but who were highly suspicious of overseas military ventures leading to death and injury for many individual human beings for the sake of some problematic national goal. Nevertheless, the two formulations belong very much to the same way of looking at collective entities; and I belong to the minority happy with both formulations.

None of the writers I have mentioned – despite Hume's two careless words – were guilty of the primitive confusion of supposing that a nation or society is only a collection of individuals. It is a set of individuals who have certain relationships to each other and may have other characteristics in common: territorial, linguistic and so on. You could even use the words 'nation' or 'society' to describe these relationships (words have no fixed or 'essential' meanings). Nevertheless the relations are between individuals.

A forest is not *just* a collection of trees. The trees have to be close together; and to talk sensibly about forests we should have to say something about the influence of climate, soil and the interrelation of the trees with each other in terms of light, shade and so on. We should nevertheless still be very suspicious about profound statements about forests which were not a function of possible statements about the trees of which they were composed. (Anyone who is worried that trees may not be sentient beings can substitute herds or flocks.)

'... AND FAMILIES'

There is one difference between Margaret Thatcher and the philosophers quoted. They all spoke of individuals; she added 'and their families'. This addition obviously dilutes the logical force of her statement. Brian Barry says it is like someone saying: there is no such thing as a forest; there are only trees and copses.

Whatever else you may think of Margaret Thatcher she is not intellectually stupid. The insertion of the words 'and families' suggests that she was not intending to make a philosophical (still less ontological) statement at all. If you look at the full context of her remarks, you will see that, so far from being an apology for selfishness, they were a prelude to a homily on people's duties and obligations. Her actual words were:

> I think we've been through a period where too many people have been given to understand that if they have a problem, it's the Government's job to cope with it. 'I have a problem, I'll get a grant.' 'I'm homeless, the Government must house me.' They're casting their problems on society. And you know, there's no such thing as society. There are individual men and women, and there are families. And no government can do anything except through people, and people must look to themselves first. It's our duty to look after ourselves and then, also, to look after our neighbours. People have got their entitlements too much in mind, without the obligations. There is no such thing as entitlement, unless someone has first met an obligation.

She meant, I believe, that people should first try to solve their own problems, then to help their families, friends and neighbours, and only as a last resort rely on government. The one logical point she did stress is that there is no Father Christmas or Good King Wenceslas in Whitehall who can help people. Government is simply a mechanism through which people can help each other and (although she would not have put it like that) force would-be free-riders to make a contribution. If she had wanted to be more conceptual, she could have added that many on the left use 'society' as a misleading synonym for government.

METHODOLOGICAL INDIVIDUALISM

Stress on the fact that a nation is composed of individuals and that the national interest is a shorthand way of referring to the interests of these individuals is, as I have already noted, often known as 'methodological individualism'. Had it not been for the storm unleashed by Lady Thatcher's remark, I would not have dared to add to the forests of paper already consumed by philosophers and theoretical social scientists in discussing the pros and cons of this position.

A methodological individualist insists that any satisfactory explanation of the working of complex wholes must be capable of being expressed in terms of the actions of individual members. He or she will not be so foolish as to believe that we can in practice get along without convenient collective nouns referring to groups. But when there is acute controversy, tension, difficulty or ambiguity he will want to analyse what is being said by translating it into possible statements about individual men and women.

Another label often used for methodological individualism is 'reductionism', because of the desire to look through complex entities to their individual components. (Of course, a reductionist in political or social theory does not need to be a reductionist on other philosophical issues, although he often is.)

Karl Popper illustrates methodological individualism in relation to such familiar ideas as 'the war', or 'the army'. These are, he writes, 'abstract concepts, strange as this may sound to some. What is concrete is the many who are killed; or the men and women in uniform etc.' He believes that the task of social theory is to analyse such terms 'carefully in descriptive nominalist terms, that is to say *in terms of individuals* [his italics], of their attitudes, expectations, relations etc. – a postulate which may be called methodological individualism'.

Let me take another example. In his justly famous book on *The Concept of Law*, Herbert Hart describes how many people see the law. 'It forbids things ordinary citizens want to do, and they know that they may be arrested by a policeman and sentenced to prison by a judge if they disobey.' Hart presents this as a deliberate caricature before presenting his own more subtle conception of the law, seen from within, as a structure resulting 'from the combination of primary rules of obligation together with the secondary rules of change and adjudication'. It is an interpretation from which I have learned a lot.

But in the last analysis the structure must be founded on primitive facts about frightened would-be wrongdoers, policemen, judges, wigs, ushers and all the rest. Not only as a matter of method, but because the more primitive statements remind one of where the shoe pinches.

The opposing idea that collective entities are in some logical, scientific or moral sense prior to the individuals who compose them used to be known by the dreadful name of 'holism'. I do not think anyone has yet found a better word for the whole family of attitudes it describes. But I shall ring the changes by sometimes describing it as collectivism, in one of the many meanings of the latter word.

ANTHROPOMORPHISM AND FOREIGN POLICY

I have been a methodological individualist since I was in short trousers, long before I became aware of the words. It was in foreign rather than economic policy that I first became aware of it.

When we were schoolboys my brother and I used to find very comic the practice of some bombastic Central Europeans we knew who showed their contempt for the ineptitude of western foreign policy by saying things like 'Russia is laughing' or 'Germany will gobble them up'. They failed to appreciate that entities like Russia, Germany or Britain are complex entities, not superbeings.

The issue entered more seriously into my thinking with the Suez expedition of 1956 in which the British government colluded with the French and the Israelis to find a pretext for invading Egypt, whose government had just nationalized the Suez Canal. It seemed to many of us that the British government's action flouted both international law and international morality. The people who got under my skin, however, were not those who took a contrary view of the moral or legal issues or who argued (erroneously) that the nationalization of the canal would inflict such great damage on the welfare of British citizens that normal rules would have to be flouted.

The view that I found most insidious was that expressed in numerous letters to the press stating that 'moral considerations are out of place in foreign policy' or words to that effect. Count Cavour put it more elegantly when he said, 'What scoundrels we would be if we did for ourselves what we stand ready to do for Italy.' (He wrote this in French!) It was also at about this time that I had come into contact with people who had studied linguistic philosophy at Oxford and who I hoped would help me to clarify the confusion. Vain hope. I had largely to labour by myself.

So what is meant by the assertion that 'moral considerations are out of place in foreign policy'? It is often enunciated as if it were a fact of life which those experienced in international affairs have empirically established and which we therefore have to accept: or, still worse, it is presented as a conclusion which political thinkers are supposed to have reached by profound *a priori* reasoning.

There are perfectly sound reasons why a naturally humane person may on occasions decide to support a 'tough' foreign policy; he may, for example, believe that in the end fewer lives will be lost thereby. But it is also likely that in many cases people are misled into supporting policies at variance with their own beliefs about right or wrong because they suppose that there is something 'in the nature of' politics or foreign affairs that makes these beliefs irrelevant.

PITFALLS OF TAUTOLOGY

Methodological individualism recommends a particular language and method of analysis to investigate all sorts of collectivist and nationalist claims. Is it not therefore empty? Is it not possible that the subordination of the individuals to the collective that so upset in their different ways Leonard Hobhouse, Bertrand Russell and Margaret Thatcher may simply re-emerge in different language if translated into more individualist terms?

A well-known economist, the late Professor Harry Johnson, once argued that, although the policies of economic nationalism adopted by new nations caused material loss, they also conveyed psychical satisfaction to individuals in their countries by 'gratifying the taste for nationalism'. He went so far as to write that

> the psychic enjoyment that the mass of the population derives from the collective consumption aspects of nationalism suffices to compensate them for the loss of material income imposed on them by nationalist economic policies, so that nationalistic policies arrive at a quite acceptable result from the point of view of maximising satisfaction.

I hope that these remarks were tongue in cheek, but they do suggest that the pure logic of individual choice could justify the most destructive behaviour. Costly wars, involving much human suffering and little tangible reward, can be rationalized by saying that the psychic satisfaction from the thought of a certain disputed area being administered by people of one's own ethnic group, outweighs all the miseries involved.

It thus must be admitted that even if people habitually spoke of foreign policy in individualist terms, many extreme nationalist positions could still be logically upheld, although they would be expressed in terms of people's feelings towards other people of the same nationality and towards foreigners, and in terms of their feelings towards patches of soil, flags, buildings and other symbolic objects. Nevertheless, assessment in such terms would bring a new perspective to many issues. Decisions involving loss of prestige – frontier adjustments, evacuation of territory – might well take a different turn if the material cost and human sacrifices of a hardline policy were weighed against the benefits to actual citizens, the swelling of patriotic breasts included among the benefits.

The making of this translation has thus a point. For it forces people who take it to be more self-conscious than they would otherwise be and ask: How much suffering is worth the gratification of my feelings of national pride? How much less take-home money pay is worth my psychic satisfaction in the Ruritanian ownership of Ruritanian resources? Self-consciousness about these issues might lead to policies of a less nationalistic blood-and-soil kind than simple reiteration of Horace's *Dulce et decorum est pro patria mori* (It is sweet and honourable to die for one's country').

Recognition of these rather obvious points in practice would have far-reaching implications. Take the question of armed conflict. If one sincerely believes that it is wrong to kill any human beings, except in literal self-defence or in defence of one's family, then calling the killing a war does not make it justifiable. Most people who are not complete pacifists would, under pressure, make some exceptions to the rule against killing. But even they may be misled into condoning killing and being killed through the uncritical use of clichés about 'national interest', 'duty to one's country' and 'military action'.

Nations and national interests are convenient portmanteau terms with which we could not easily dispense. But as complex entities we are likely, if we are not careful, to talk of them in a confused and misleading way. It is quite probable that profound unconscious conflicts and objectives are a more potent influence than the perverse use of collectivist language. All I suggest is that the unanalysed use of concepts such as 'nation' or 'society' can make a difference, and often for the worse.

THE METAPHYSICAL THEORY OF THE STATE

At the opposite extreme from any kind of methodological individualism is the metaphysical theory of the state. The term 'the state' is altogether heavier than either the nation or society. I normally use the 'state' in as downbeat a way as possible to refer to the machinery of government which remains irrespective of the names of the politicians supposedly at the top. Cabinets come and go; but a large apparatus remains endowed with legally constituted coercive power: the law courts, the police, the civil service, health officials, sanitary inspectors and numerous others. People learn about the reality of these lower officers of state very early. It does not take them long to realize that it is much easier to get away with mocking the Prime Minister than the village policeman, postman or headmistress.

But there have of course been so-called thinkers who, by cunningly playing with words, have tried to fuse together the idea of a nation with that of the government apparatus into a mystical entity, superior to us all. To cite a summary by the early twentieth-century liberal political philosopher, Leonard Hobhouse: 'The state system' is seen by such thinkers as 'part of an order which is inherently rational and good, an order to which the lives of individuals are clearly subordinate'.

This is in Hobhouse's words the 'metaphysical theory of the state ... the endeavour to exhibit the fabric of society as something very great and glorious indeed'. Or as Hegel put it: 'All the worth which the human being possesses in all spiritual reality, he possesses only through the state.' The 'highest duty of an individual is to be a member of the state'. I am no Hegel scholar; life is too short. But I assure you he did say these things, and much more in the same vein.

Hobhouse believed that the Hegelian doctrine mattered. In the dedication inscribed during the First World War he writes: 'in the bombing of London I have just witnessed the visible and tangible outcome of a false and wicked doctrine'. His own book was dedicated to his son, Lieutenant R.O.F. Hobhouse RAF, fighting in a war which, his father believed, had been at least partly caused by 'the metaphysical theory of the God State'.

It is worth recalling that Hobhouse was not an extreme individualist in either the economic or the anti-war sense. He was an active New Liberal, intent on weaning the Liberal Party away from Gladstonian free markets to a degree of support for state intervention and backing for trade unions which, with the wisdom of hindsight, seems excessive. He was moreover fully committed to winning the First World War, rather than to Russellian pacifism, excusing his own book as 'such part in the fight that the physical disabilities of middle age allow'.

COLLECTIVE ENTITIES

Many people will think that the idealist theory of the state is a straw man to fight at the turn of the twentieth century. I wonder. Is it more than an intense form of the common error of attributing to collective entities an identity over and above, and supposedly superior to, the individuals of which they are composed?

I went to a rather mild sort of grammar school in north-west London, which tried only weakly to ape public school customs. One of these ways was a slogan: 'School first, house second, self last'. I cannot claim that any major atrocities were committed in its name. It was not emblazoned on the walls or even recited at assembly, but was mainly used in exasperation at particularly selfish or irresponsible conduct. But it did worry me. How could a school or a house have a superior existence to the individuals of which it was composed?

These are not just verbal quibbles. Take something like 'regional policy' which is supposed to improve the position of poorer or declining regions. It is relatively uncontroversial to say that help should be given to the victims of economic change. But how much meaning are we to attach to averages over particular geographical areas? No real world unmetaphysical political authority, whether in Brussels, London or Cardiff, has an unlimited pot of gold. There is always at the margin a choice between regional policy and, for instance, social security payments targeted to individual need. Help for regions may do less to help people who most need it than increased well-targeted social security payments, irrespective of whether the beneficiaries live in the poorer or the richer parts of Europe.

In my own sphere I am tempted to say that there is no such thing as 'the economy'. There are people, what they produce, the prices at which they exchange, and many other features which are not easily quantified, such as the difficulty of obtaining a job. It is puzzling that in some opinion polls voters say that one party is better at running the economy but another better for living standards, jobs, prices and so on. Either the respondents are confused; or they are trying to hint at aspects of performances – such as business confidence – ignored in the more specific questions. Alternatively they may have a dim sense of long term versus short term, 'the economy' qualifying as long term.

POPPER VERSUS WINCH

In our own day the most influential argument for the primacy of the group over the individual purports to come from one school of linguistic analysis. One of the best-known assertions that the institutions and modes of behaviour are the starting point comes from Peter Winch. He takes issue with Popper's example of war and says:

> It is an idea which provides the criteria of what is appropriate in the behaviour of members of the conflicting societies. Because my country is at war there are certain things that I must and certain things that I must not do. My behaviour is governed, one could say, by my concept of myself as a member of a belligerent country. The concept of war belongs essentially to my behaviour.

Winch believes that it is such concepts which explain the attitudes, expectations and relations of individuals rather than the other way round.

The original battle between Popper and Winch was on the most fruitful method of pursuing social science (although Winch may be saying that there can be no such thing). But my real reason for siding with Popper's approach is that it seems to me to lead to more probing questions. Or to put my cards further on the table: it enables a person to step outside the institution of war, or any other group activity, and make evaluative judgements about whether or when it is justified. The problem with starting from social institutions and the language they embody is that one can never get outside them and raise objections to the whole shooting match.

Let me try to move the argument to basics. Those who say that society is prior to the individual often mean that a person's desires, preferences and habits are not entirely innate (or given, in the economist's sense), but depend on the history of his or her society, geographical location, family background, local traditions, and all the other things Hume had in mind when he spoke of 'moral influences'.

To which my response is: So what? To come back to the forest, it is a collection of trees, whatever the influence of climate, soil or the interrelation of the trees with each other. And we should be very suspicious about profound statements about forests which are not a function of possible statements about the trees of which they are composed.

THE DISSOLUTION OF THE SELF

A much more interesting attack on individualism comes from the opposite direction: the doubt thrown over the idea of a unique individual self. So far from combining separate selves into larger unities, the tendency of some modern philosophers, drawing on the data of brain surgery, is to break the individual self up into smaller units on the grounds that the popular notion of personal identity is profoundly mistaken. The best summary I know is given by Jonathan Glover:

> Our natural belief that a person has an indivisible unity is mistaken. This will be supported by considering psychiatric and neurological syndromes in which, in various ways, people seem to divide. Some of these cases show how the unity of a person depends on neural links, which can be severed. Consciousness can be divided. And there is at least the theoretical possibility of a much greater degree of fragmentation.
>   … The idea of degrees of survival does not in the real world apply only to bizarre pathology. I can expect only partial survival over a long stretch of my life. The psychological unity of a life is not all-or-none. Memories or intentions can fade or disappear. I can be linked psychologically to other stages of my life to a greater or lesser degree. If I am hit in old age by senile dementia, perhaps nearly all my present self will have faded out. And perhaps there is very little of my five-year-old self left in me now.

Many philosophy graduates have been taught to think of the self in terms of spatio-temporal identity, plus continuing consciousness. The more recent work suggests that this criterion might be impossible to apply in certain situations.

One of the philosophers who has done most to break down the concept of the self or the ego is Derek Parfit. But Parfit manages to draw curiously collectivist conclusions from his ultra-reductionist analysis. He writes that it 'makes me care less about my own future and the fact that I shall die. In comparison I now care more about the lives of others. I welcome these effects'. Having disposed of the individual self, he starts again putting all experiences together into a single collective utility basket, which is one of the most dubious aspects of traditional utilitarianism. I can see no connection between his analysis and his high-minded collectivist conclusions.

My own reaction is the opposite. It is that we should look at more experiencing subjects rather than less: myself at 15, myself now, my several future selves, my double on Mars and so on. It is certainly not to throw all experiences into some super-collective utility basket.

It was some relief to discover, again after I had drafted this section, that Glover shared my doubts about Parfit's collectivist conclusions. Glover says that he does not find the proposed way of thinking about death particularly consoling. He also takes issue with the collective utility basket. We still, in Glover's words, have no warrant for 'adding up gains and losses across different lives, as though who gains or loses makes no difference. It is as if utilitarians treat different people as part of one super-person', which was certainly not Bentham's original intention.

THE NEED TO BELONG

The strongest opposition I expect to meet will come, however, not from those interested in dividing up the ego but from those who think in terms of linking it up with more and more other egos.

Sometimes those who think in terms of collective entities go beyond linguistic logic-chopping and make statements like: 'Being a miner, a Welshman, a supporter of a particular rugby club, and so on *define* a person's identity. Take away those and you have taken away everything of importance.' Such statements are a closer approximation to the truth for a miner in a pit dispute or a soldier in a state of patriotic fervour in the early stages of a war than for a suburban London family. They are characteristics of what John Goldthorpe once described as morally intense situations.

Of course there are such situations; and even in less-pressurized circumstances feelings of belonging are important to most people at most times. *But in the last analysis, even in the most embattled 'us versus them' situations, it is individuals, not collectives, who feel, exult, triumph or despair. It is this which distinguishes individual people from trees and makes the individual person the ultimate end of political and moral discourse.*

So in the last resort my form of individualism is ethical rather than methodological. There have been many attempts to ground the study of collective behaviour in the behaviour of individuals. For instance, macroeconomists are trying, so far without conspicuous success, to rebuild their shattered subject by basing it more firmly on the behaviour of rational maximizing individuals. Similarly, there are those who want to reduce individual behaviour to biology, and biology in turn to chemistry and physics.

Such attempts are a useful precaution against pretentious nonsense. But suppose that they are unsuccessful: that the best explanations of business cycles turn out to be in terms of moods and expectations not easily grounded in micro theory? Or that human behaviour is ultimately best explained at the level neither of individual people nor of molecules and atoms, but of the genes transmitted from one generation to the next, a concept that Richard Dawkins has popularized in *The Selfish Gene*.

The result may have some bearing on Methodological Individualism, or at least on the level to which we should take reductionist explanations. But it has little relevance to ethical individualism. This rests on the virtually indisputable fact that it is individual people – or at least human selves at particular times – who feel pain, experience pleasure and all the other states to which people are prone. Ethical individualism also avoids ontological debates about whether collective wholes exist or not.

Ethical propositions are not of course entailed by any factual proposition. What ethical individualism does, however, is to take as its starting point certain facts of human experience which can be doubted only in a mood of epistemological doubt about everything. From these facts the logical jump to the 'ought' proposition follows from pretty widespread value judgements. (I accept that the label 'individualist' could be misleading because of its associations with Herbert Spencer and certain specific political positions. The only other terms I can think of are 'liberal', 'utilitarian' or 'choice utilitarian', which also stir up hornets' nests of problems, some of which have been discussed in previous chapters.)

The French writer Romain Roland wrote to Sigmund Freud of an 'oceanic' feeling when he felt he was in some way one with the world as a whole. Freud replied that he had no experience of this feeling. However, he suggested that it might be a residue of early infancy before a child has learned to distinguish between itself and the rest of the world.

The last thing I wish to do is to sneer at such experiences. I may not be Welsh, but I am not a cold-hearted Anglo-Saxon. One of the most moving experiences I ever had was watching the much-lamented Sir Geraint Evans in a farewell performance in Wales, leading the audience in singing *Mae Hen Wlad fy Nhadau* (Land of my Fathers). Even watching it on a television set in London with bad acoustics brought tears. But however 'together' we all felt, it was still individual people having the feeling. Even if a few in the audience really did experience the oceanic feeling, this would not have lasted when they got home and woke up next morning, perhaps with a toothache or headache. If such feelings lasted long enough for enough people, we would need entirely different languages and concepts which we can hardly even imagine from inside our own.

What we really feel on such occasions was well stated by one of the greatest hymns to human fraternity, Schiller's 'Ode to Joy': *Alle Menschen werden Brüder* ('All men will be brothers'). Brothers, not units in a cosmic whole or parts of some pantheistic utility tank.

THE CONCEPT OF FRATERNITY

Indeed, I can best tie up a few of the many loose ends of this paper by saying a few words about fraternity.

In discussing the possible objections to Lady Thatcher's remarks about society Brian Barry talks about a general obligation to provide for the well-being of our fellows, which he thinks the former Prime Minister would reject. (Barry actually uses the word 'solidarism', but fraternity will do, and it is more familiar.) He cites the following argument in support of various kinds of collective provision:

> We think of it as natural and proper for the members of a family to accept some responsibility for one another. A family that had the collective resources to care for all its

members but let some of them go without food, shelter, clothing, medical care or education would rightly be condemned. But, in exactly the same way, the members of a society should accept responsibility for one another. And a society that had the resources to care for all its members but neglected some should be condemned.

This is not the argument for which Barry settles himself, but it is one he cites.

This enables us to set out more clearly the argument between the real Margaret Thatcher and her more reflective opponents. The former Prime Minister implicitly accepted as a positive doctrine the tough-minded version of the economic approach: that people are mostly moved by the gain motive. But she moralized it by broadening self-interest to cover family and close friends and by emphasis on the various non-egotistical ways in which wealth can be spent. And as a matter of public policy, she believes that the state will function best and be least over-burdened if people rely first on self-help and then on family, friends and neighbours, leaving nationwide collective provision by government as a last resort. In other words, charity begins at home.

The collectivist reply would be to say that both Margaret Thatcher and mainstream (or rather US-trained) economists underplay the professional and public-spirited elements in conduct; that people might be encouraged to look beyond their own circle – to be patriotic if they are right-wing collectivists and to be community-minded if they are on the left. As a matter of public policy, collectivists would say there are so many examples of market failure and of the shortcomings of private good works that the free-market doctrines are system-atically misleading.

Who is right on the last issue is partly an empirical matter, but not entirely. It is also a matter of where you place the onus of proof and also what you fear most: the excesses of authority or the defects of commercialism and, perhaps most relevant for this paper: are you more worried about the horrors inflicted in the name of social morality – re-read the Grand Inquisitor scene in *Don Carlos* – or the evils of private greed? From some points of view they have a lot in common. Wagner's *Ring* is intended as a warning against putting both power and money above love. But in many contexts there is some difference between power and money; and the practical individualist would be inclined to agree with Dr Johnson: 'men are seldom so harmlessly employed as in making money'.

The objection to the arguments of this paper from supporters of the real Margaret Thatcher is likely to be that 'society' and 'the nation' are not as similar as I have made them out to be and that the same analysis should not be applied to both. Similarities and differences are largely in the eye of the beholder. But I do find that the territories covered by these words overlap to a very large extent. Both words apply to large numbers of people linked together by political boundaries or ethnic affinities. Both are extremely vague. Both are subject to perverse ambiguity. Just as society is often confused with the government so is the nation with the state. Both nation and society consist of individuals and both are wrongly elevated into collective beings.

FALSE UNIVERSALISM

Whether we prefer to talk about a nation or the community, is the choice between private and collective virtues correctly posed? Do we really have to choose between a special concern for our immediate circle and an equal concern for others? And what is the moral value of sticking to national frontiers? The quotation from Barry would sound more 'moral' but less realistic if the word 'world' was substituted for 'society' in the last two sentences. Yet, is it not putting too great a burden on people to expect them to have an equal concern for all the inhabitants of this earth, including those yet unborn?

My preferred picture is that of the successive circles of obligation expounded in Chapter 3, in which it is acceptable to have more concern for our nearest and dearest than for our fellow countrymen in general, and more concern for the latter than for people in distant lands. On this view we should have some concern for future generations, but more for our own. The successive circles concept also allows for individual variations – some of us may feel a special affinity for a fellow-professional or for European neighbours or speakers of the English or Welsh languages.

It is at a public policy level that I arrived at this successive circles view. It is reasonable to give more weight to the life of a British than an Iraqi soldier, but not to give the Iraqi no weight at all. We need not on this view be ashamed of identifying more with the inhabitants of the former Yugoslav republics who are on the edges of Western Europe, where many people have been on holiday and with whom they can identify, than with those involved in remoter tragedies.

I find this weighting concept helpful in dealing with the puzzles of Benthamite utilitarianism, under which people are described as following their own self-interest, but are assumed to espouse a public policy of universal benevolence. Strangers do and should count. Other countries should count in public policy, but we need not be ashamed to give most weight to those closest to us.

Too many moralists have paid lip service to the idea of the whole human race counting equally and have then gone on to concentrate on policies affecting exclusively their own communities. Ordinary people are then presented with the false choice of either giving equal value to every inhabitant of the earth or giving no value at all to those outside their immediate circle or country. The result of paying lip service to impartial benevolence is too often in practice the total neglect of those outside our own group.

CONCLUSION

This paper has been an abstract assertion of the need to ground public policy in the experiences of individuals who alone feel, think, suffer and rejoice. Even as I put down my pen, people are being tortured in the name of a higher truth or a higher concept of nationality. Let us at least deprive their persecutors of their rationalizations.

Envoi

> If in some smothering dreams, you too could pace
> Behind the wagon that we flung him in,
> And watch the white eyes writhing in his face,
> His hanging face, like a devil's sick of sin;
> If you could hear, at every jolt, the blood
> Come gargling from the froth-corrupted lungs,
> Bitter as the cud
> Of vile, incurable sores on innocent tongues,
> My friend, you would not tell with such high zest
> To children ardent for some desperate glory,
> The old Lie: *Dulce et decorum est*
> *Pro patria mori.*
>
> Wilfred Owen, *'Dulce et Decorum Est'*

REFERENCES

Barry, Brian, *Does Society Exist?*, London: Fabian Society, 1989.
Brittan, Samuel, *A Restatement of Economic Liberalism*, London: Macmillan, 1988.
Brittan, Samuel, *The Role and Limits of Government*, London: Temple Smith, 1983.
Dawkins, Richard, *The Selfish Gene*, Oxford: Oxford University Press, 1976.
Glover, Jonathan, *The Philosophy and Psychology of Personal Identity*, Harmondsworth, Middx: Penguin, 1989.
Hart, Herbert, *The Concept of Laws*, Oxford: Oxford University Press, 1961, p. 63.
Hobhouse, L.T., *The Metaphysical Theory of the State*, 1918; London: Allen & Unwin, 1938.
Hume, David, 'Of National Character', in *Essays, Moral Political and Literary*, 1741.
Johnson, H.G. (ed.), *Nationalism in New and Old States*, London: Allen & Unwin, 1968.
Parfit, Derek, *Reasons and Persons*, Oxford: Oxford University Press, 1984.
Popper, K.R., *The Poverty of Historicism*, London: Routledge & Kegan Paul, 1957.
Radnitzky, Gerard, *Universal Economics*, New York: Paragon House, 1992.
Taylor, A.J.P., *The Trouble-makers: Dissent over Foreign Policy, 1792-1939*, Oxford: Oxford University Press, 1957.
Thatcher, Margaret, Interview in *Woman's Own*, 31 October 1987.
Winch, Peter, *The Idea of a Social Science*, 1958; 2nd edn, London: Routledge, 1990.

PART TWO

Keynes and Hayek

5 Can democracy manage an economy?[*]

This essay is by far the oldest in the book. It is not intended as an appraisal of Keynesian economics, to which Chapter 7 is more relevant, but of the political assumptions of Keynes the man. His belief that democracy would be guided by an enlightened intellectual elite appears as the most vulnerable aspect of his outlook. Much of the essay, however, is devoted to Schumpeter's alternative theory of democracy as a competitive struggle for votes, which itself depends on certain preconditions too often overlooked by today's number-crunching political economists. One detail, which gives away the origin of this essay in the 1970s, is its attitude to monetarism as a new challenge, instead of as yet another oversold quick-fix. A much more important qualification is that the search for constitutional-type rules, to lessen the reliance on government discretion, has itself proved difficult and elusive, although it is still well worth pursuing.

RULES VERSUS DISCRETION

One of the great growth industries of the English-speaking world is the exegesis of the writings of John Maynard Keynes. What exactly did Keynes say? When did he say it? Who were his precursors? What did he really mean? What should he have meant? What would he be saying if he were alive today? Anyone who finds these questions too arid will be able to find relief in the stream of new insights and revelations into the life of the great man and his significance for the era in which he lived. As a twentieth-century subject for life-and-times hagiography, he joins the select company of Freud, Mahler, Wittgenstein and a very few others. (All these others were, remarkably, of Austrian origin, as were Hayek, Popper and Schumpeter, whose names come up in similar contexts.)

I enjoy a good wallow as much as anyone else. But it is an interesting reflection on the would-be scientific standing of economics that exponents of rival theories think it important to find chapter and verse for their views in Keynes – which they always can, for like most such figures he said a great many different things. Can one imagine the protagonists in a controversy in modern physics trying to advance their views by showing that they were implicit in some obscure passage in Einstein, and their opponents replying either that this was a misunderstanding or that it was all really said much better by Isaac Newton?

[*] From Robert Skidelsky (ed.), *The End of the Keynesian Era*, London: Macmillan, 1977.

If there is, however, one aspect of Keynes which unquestionably dates him, it is his attitude to the democratic process. In his economic writings he was concerned with the extent to which the pursuit of self-interest in the market place did or did not promote the general interest. Yet it never occurred to him to see the political process as a market place, governed by the self-interest of politicians, officials and voters. He took it for granted that decision would ultimately be made by a small group of the educated bourgeoisie, who were inspired by a disinterested concern for the public good. He assumed that wrong decisions were taken out of intellectual error or, at worst, narrowness of vision; and that if the correct ideas were promulgated with sufficient clarity and vigour they would eventually win the day.

These characteristics can be illustrated by the present-day arguments between those economists who call themselves Keynesian and those who call themselves monetarists. The first, most highly publicized is the importance of changes in the money supply in influencing the economy. Keynes himself avoided an entrenched position on this issue and would almost certainly have been prepared to adjust his views in the light of evidence and logical argument. He would surely have seen (indeed, probably did see somewhere in his writings) the absurdity of regarding nominal interest rates as a guide to monetary policy in an era of chronic inflation such as the 1970s, when the high interest rates about which the business community, the Tribune Group and the home-owners lobby joined forces to complain, were heavily negative in real terms.

But a second and much more fundamental argument is whether discretionary demand management of any kind, whether through monetary means or through the budget, is destabilizing and actually aggravates the booms and slumps it is meant to cure. The issue is only in part technical. Those monetarists who follow Milton Friedman believe that we should have a much more stable economic environment if government did not adjust the controls so often and contented themselves with a moderate steady annual growth of the money supply and a budget calculated to balance at high-employment levels of business activity.

This approach is not in the spirit of Keynes at all. It is easy to imagine Keynes pointing out the perverse effect of would-be stabilization measures. Yet the idea of abandoning discretionary management and going by fixed, pre-ordained rules was entirely foreign to his temperament. Both in personal and in public life he had an unquenchable faith in men's ability to work out directly the effect of each of their actions and behave in good faith. In contrast to David Hume, he was an 'act utilitarian' rather than a 'rule utilitarian'.

It is, however, a third argument between Keynes and the monetarists which most directly challenges Keynesian political assumptions. Friedman's most central challenge to the prevailing orthodoxy has little to do with the technicalities of monetary policy. It is on whether it is possible to achieve a target level of full employment by manipulating total spending – whether through the budget, monetary policy, the exchange rate or import controls. Friedman returns to an earlier tradition in insisting that the minimum sustainable level of unemployment – the so-called 'natural rate' (later rechristened the NAIRU, see Chapter 7) – is determined by underlying economic forces such as the speed of industrial change, training and mobility, union and other monopolistic restrictions, and a host of other influences. Any attempt to run the economy persistently below the sustainable level will need to be supported by an ever-increasing rate of monetary expansion and the end result will be not merely inflation, but accelerating inflation.

The Friedmanites have not simply gone back to the old orthodoxy. They fully accept that a Keynesian boost to demand can reduce unemployment below the sustainable level for a temporary period. 'Temporary' might have been a decade or even more in the 1950s, when people still thought that a pound was a pound and a dollar was a dollar. Today, when 'money illusion' has practically gone and people bargain in real terms, a 'temporary' boost will, with good fortune, last for two or three years at most.

It is this temporary success, but ultimate futility, of so-called 'Keynesian' spending boosts that is such a trap for a democracy. Not only do such episodes bring no lasting benefit to employment; on the contrary, unemployment will subsequently have to be abnormally high if governments wish to reverse the ensuing inflation, or perhaps just prevent it accelerating.

Although it would be absurd to press the question 'On whose side would Keynes have been?', the idea of a sustainable level of unemployment, which could not be reduced further by 'a boost from the centre', occurs several times in Keynes's own papers. He put this level at 800,000 for the UK for the pre-war period, when the total labour force was much smaller and social security benefits were far more restricted than now. The post-war economic models geared exclusively to real output and employment, in which wages and prices depended entirely on the mood of the unions and incomes policy and in which any increase in the money supply was treated as a minor by-product, would have been foreign to the spirit of anyone as obsessively interested in money and financial flows as Keynes was. The difficulties that the 'natural rate' doctrine would have posed for Keynes relate more to his discretionary approach to policy than to fundamental theory.

SCHUMPETER'S ALTERNATIVE

To understand the political threat posed by short-term temptations of money creation and excessive deficit spending, it is helpful to turn to the analysis of democracy of one of Keynes's contemporaries, the Austrian-American economist

Joseph Schumpeter in his *Capitalism, Socialism and Democracy.* One is not surprised to find that the two thinkers had very little understanding of each other.

Schumpeter's analysis starts with the truism that democracy in a large country cannot be – as the literal-minded see it – the rule of all the people by all the people. There are, at least for the foreseeable future, limits to the ability of technological progress in communications which make continual consultation of all the people all the time impossible. Even if it were possible, most people might well prefer a less inconvenient and burdensome system of organization. In any case, there would be the difficulty of weighting the importance of different views on issues where people's interests, knowledge and feelings are involved to very different degrees.

A more realistic definition of democracy, which would include the essential characteristics of many of the systems of government in the western hemisphere, was provided by Schumpeter. He conceived of democratic representatives as akin to other economic agents: they deal in votes as steelmen deal in steel or oilmen in oil. The democratic character of their behaviour results from the competition between different politicians and parties for votes. To gain or to retain power, they must offer policies or, more characteristically, promise results that will attract votes away from other potential governments. To this extent, the views of at least part of the electorate will influence the way in which the country is governed.

The electors are assumed to act according to their own self-interest. This does not imply any view of their motives; as individuals, or within small groups, people can display great generosity. In larger groups, however, any individual who does not look after his own interests is likely to suffer in comparison with those who do. It seems realistic, therefore, to assume that voters will, at least at the margin, vote according to their perceived interests.

The commercial market place is characterized by the *individual* pursuit of self-interest. This is unlikely to cause irresistible demands for more than the economy can provide. Individuals in their own lives are subject to budget constraints; they cannot spend more than they can earn or borrow.

The political market place is characterized by the pursuit of self-interest by large groups, where these personal budget constraints are absent. Electors can rather more easily demand an increased slice of the cake without any agreement on the part of those who are supposed to have the thinner slices. The costs of the handouts, whether met through taxation or inflation, will not necessarily accrue to the groups who benefit from them. In each individual case, whether a subsidy is paid to council-house dwellers, cheese producers or car makers, there is a strong incentive for the interest group to press its demands as forcefully as possible without any real discipline on the sum total of interest group demands.

Even with fixed rules on public finance, the process will induce a bias toward public expenditure. Nevertheless, because taxpayers or borrowers have votes, an increase in public expenditure which requires an increase in taxation or high interest rates is likely to be somewhat less attractive to a government than an increase which can be financed effectively by printing money. With traditional rules such as the balanced-budget principle, or gold-standard limits on money creation, the bias towards government overspending is likely to have some limits placed on it by opposition from taxpayers.

If, on the other hand, the government is permitted to boost aggregate demand by extra expenditure without either levying extra taxes or paying long-term market interest rates, its trade-off is different. One alternative is to lose votes by failing to offer an interest group as much as other parties offer. The other is to join the competitive bidding and offer as much.

If the effects on inflation of printing money were immediate, the government might have some qualms about substituting, say, temporary job-preservation for stable prices. But, as the inflationary effects are delayed, the government is presented with a choice between a certain benefit in increased electoral support in the short run and the uncertain cost of some very unpleasant choices between a slump and runaway inflation in some years' time. It is not surprising that governments, conscious of Keynes's view of long-run mortality, accept the inflationary alternative.

In short, therefore, there are two reasons why governments are liable to overstimulate demand, or attempt to promote unsustainably high employment: the benefits are short run, while the costs are long run; and the benefits are specific and easily attributable to the government, while the costs are general and less easily attributed to any single cause.

DEMOCRATIC SELF-RESTRAINT

Schumpeter himself was less of a Cassandra than a present-day adherent of his analysis would tend to be. He put forward three main preconditions for the insulation of liberal representative democracy against the internally generated economic forces that would tend to destroy it. It is interesting that these conditions were also part of Keynes's implicit view of the political world. But because of the latter's underlying optimism about the political process, he did not bother to spell them out himself or consider the circumstances in which they might be endangered.

Schumpeter's three conditions were the limitation of the area of effectively political decision-making, the existence of a well-trained bureaucracy and the exercise of political self-restraint. If these were fulfilled, there would be a greater chance of achieving the Keynesian ideal of a policy in which rational ideas and rational men held sway. It is under these conditions that one could realistically assert, as Keynes did in the most widely quoted single passage of his *General Theory* (p. 387) that 'The power of vested interests is vastly exaggerated compared with the gradual encroachment of ideas.'

Government by rational men and rational ideas is possible, if at all, only if there are limits to the incursions of vote-seeking politicians. In the UK there have existed a number of special agencies whose non-political nature has been constantly stressed, both by themselves and by the government of the day. The pre-1914 Bank of England was a leading example. Keynes may well have envisaged an entire government operating in this fashion. However obscurantist those running such an institution might be, mortality and the permeation of ideas could be relied upon to disseminate enlightened thinking after, at worst, a lag of a generation. Macroeconomic debate in such a society would be confined largely to the technical problem of how to manage demand optimally to face existing and expected states of nature, with no danger that demand management would become the tool of competing political teams.

Thus Keynes almost certainly believed that the second Schumpeterian condition, the need for a powerful well-entrenched bureaucracy, was also fulfilled and could keep government in the hands of 'experts'. A government that could, for reasons of prestige or dogma, choose to go back to the pre-1914 gold parity in 1925 at the expense of considerable unemployment, would surely be able to resist popular pressures when it was pursuing better ideas which really would promote the public interest.

Besides the evidence that governments could resist democratic pressure if the experts thought it necessary, the theory of government by experts was reinforced in Keynes's era by the class composition and attitudes of politicians and civil servants. Politicians of all main parties were, to some extent, enlightened amateurs with sufficient means and independence to resist democratic pressures, while many bureaucrats were for similar reasons able to resist the pressure of politicians. Members of neither group were under financial pressure to continue at their posts carrying out tasks in which they no longer believed. There was a division of labour between the politicians, who were professionals at dealing in votes, and the bureaucrats, who were professionals at policy analysis. Since economic policy-making clearly fell into the domain of the second group, demand management could be insulated from the political process.

The existence of a large sector of government that could be insulated to some extent from democratic pressures was both made possible and further reinforced by Schumpeter's third condition for the success of democracy: the existence of tolerance and democratic self-control. In the UK in the earlier part of the twentieth century, electorates were able to exercise this self-restraint partly because they were slow to realize their power; and partly because of a series of *ad hoc* events, such as the First World War, which produced an external threat and a patriotic myth to override sectional conflicts or the Great Depression, which weakened the pressure which could be exerted by unions on industry and government alike.

THE WANING MORAL LEGACY

Yet just as important was an ethic, which took a long time to erode, which limited the demands on the sharing-out functions of the state. Personal success was seen by nineteenth-century defenders of capitalism as having a firm connection with duty performed. In a society permeated by a Puritan ethic it was agreed that there was a strong correlation between certain personal virtues – frugality, industry, sobriety, reliability, piety – and the way in which power, privilege and property were distributed.

This partly spurious correlation was mistakenly taken to be the sign of a just – not merely a free – society. The public morality of capitalist bourgeois society was, however, inevitably a transitional one. On its own grounds it could not hope to stand up to serious analysis. Luck was always as important as merit in the gaining of awards; and merit is inherently a subjective concept in the eye of the beholder. Society was living on the moral heritage of the feudal system. A mediaeval king was expected to 'do justice and to render each his due'. It was not a matter of what the king thought a subject ought to have, or what the subject thought best for himself, but what belonged to him according to custom, which in turn was supported by theological sanctions.

For a long time capitalist civilization was able to live on this feudal legacy, and the aura of legitimacy was transferred from the feudal lord to the employer, from the mediaeval hierarchy of position to that derived from the luck of the market place. But this feudal legacy was bound to be extinguished by the torchlight of secular and rationalistic inquiry, which was itself so closely associated with the rise of capitalism. The personal qualities of middle-class leaders did not help to kindle that affection for the social order which is probably necessary if it is not to be blamed for the inevitable tribulations and disappointments of most people's lives. Modern politicians and business chiefs lack the glamour of an aristocracy. With neither the trappings of tradition nor the heroic qualities of great war leaders or generals, they cannot excite the identification or hero worship which previously reconciled people to much greater differences of wealth and position than exist today.

Yet without the self-restraint of the electorate, the other two preconditions for the successful combination of democracy with demand management – the limitation of political decision and the key role of the mandarin class – have inevitably crumbled. The area of effective political decision-making has been vastly enlarged from its size in the inter-war period, while the independence of the bureaucracy from political pressure has declined. Moreover, in so far as the bureaucracy has been able to promote its own interests, it has itself come to operate in the same direction as other interest groups rather than as an elite which does not have to lobby for jobs and privilege. It thus tends to stimulate rather than discourage the excessive expectations of the electorate. The public sector has itself become an important lobby for increased public expenditure.

Keynes died in 1946 and we do not have the benefit of his observations on the new social and political environment (which could hardly have failed to distress him aesthetically, whatever his final judgement). Unfortunately, a system of economic thinking was developed in his name which rationalized the most self-destructive tendencies of democracy, instead of acting as a bulwark against them. To escape from our predicament we need not another revolution in economic theory, but a revolution in constitutional and political ideas which will save us from the snare of unlimited democracy, before we find ourselves with no democracy – and very little freedom – left. The widespread call for 'a new Keynes' reflects the worst aspect of the great man's legacy: the belief that we can make deep-seated problems go away by a few tactical gimmicks which can be applied costlessly by a few clever men in an office.

REFERENCES

Keynes, J.M., *The General Theory of Employment, Interest and Money*, 1936; London: Macmillan, 1973.
Schumpeter, J.A., *Capitalism, Socialism and Democracy*, 4th edn, London: Allen & Unwin, 1952.
Skidelsky, Robert, *John Maynard Keynes*, vol. I: *1883–1920: Hopes Betrayed*, London: Macmillan, 1983; vol. II: *1920–37: The Economist as Saviour*, London: Macmillan, 1993.
Skidelsky, Robert (ed.), *The End of the Keynesian Era*, London: Macmillan, 1977.

6   Hayek's 'spontaneous social order'*

The waning of belief in the 1970s and 1980s in Keynesian economic management brought back to prominence the writings of Friedrich Hayek, who came to see economics as part of a much wider study of spontaneous social order. Like Keynes, Hayek has suffered both from sycophantic admirers and from scoffers, unwilling to make the effort to see what he was getting at. The following informal remarks differ, however, from the previous chapters on Keynes, in trying to take a more comprehensive view of Hayek's work, which – outside limited circles – is still far less well known than that of Keynes.

POLITICAL AND INTELLECTUAL FASHION

Friedrich August von Hayek was born in Vienna on 8 May 1899. His father was a professor while the imperial city was enjoying its celebrated sunset. The composer Brahms had only recently died and Freud had yet to publish his major works. Hayek's own career began in the Austrian Civil Service and, after holding academic posts in Vienna, he came to the London School of Economics in 1931.

Recording his arrival, Lionel Robbins subsequently wrote: 'I can still see the door of my room opening to admit the tall, powerful, reserved figure which announced itself quietly and firmly as "Hayek".' His lectures were so successful that the LSE's director, William Beveridge, suggested that he remain as Tooke Professor, a post he held until 1950. Hayek brought a whole host of cosmopolitan contacts to the LSE. He was, for instance, instrumental in the appointment of Karl Popper, the philosopher and author of *The Open Society*.

Although Hayek's later career took him first to Chicago and then back to Austria and Germany (his last years were spent in Freiburg, in Breisgau), he retained his British nationality (acquired in 1938), and he remained a close observer of the British scene. He soon dropped the 'von' in front of his name, although sneering critics often insisted on re-inserting it.

Hayek's fortunes teach us a great deal about intellectual fashion. During the 1930s he was mainly known for technical economic studies, which were at the time overshadowed by the new Keynesian theories on unemployment and

* Based on a talk given in 1984, supplemented by material from my obituary of Hayek, which appeared in the *Financial Times* of 22 March 1992.

economic policy. One conclusion from that period, which had to be disinterred several decades later, is that market institutions cannot be just grafted on to state socialism, as mainstream economists long believed was possible.

His greatest intellectual regret, looking back on those years, was that he never wrote a full-scale critique of Keynes's *General Theory*. He had previously written a long review of the first volume of Keynes's earlier *Treatise on Money* – only to be told by Keynes that the latter had changed his views. This experience led Hayek to suppose that the *General Theory* was just another 'tract for the times'.

In the 1940s, Hayek became a hate figure to some on the political Left because of his onslaught on centralized economic planning and his insistence on the links between political and economic freedom in his best-selling *Road to Serfdom*: the book is said to have influenced Winston Churchill's controversial 1945 election broadcast about the threat of a 'Gestapo' under socialism. It is less well-known that Keynes sent Hayek a letter expressing his 'deeply-felt agreement' with a good deal of the argument.

Hayek was not a charismatic public figure. His brief post-war notoriety was followed by decades of neglect, during which he treated economics as part of a much wider study of spontaneous social order of a kind which was later to become familiar from cybernetics. Finally, following his Nobel Prize in 1974, he emerged as a cult figure of the Radical Right – which did neither side too much good. For there was far more to Hayek than the demolition of socialism and the standard case for free markets. In presenting him as a revered thinker with a complete system, his followers may have made his work neater, simpler and less interesting than it really was.

Although Hayek was too shrewd to overrate the Nobel award he received in 1974, for one reason or another the years following it witnessed a personal rejuvenation. Among political theorists and sociologists critical of the New Right, he was studied more seriously than were the more fashionable economic technicians. But he took this adulation with a large pinch of salt and was no more a Hayekian than Keynes was a Keynesian.

Hayek was unfashionable in the 1950s and 1960s as much for academic as for political reasons. At a time when most go-ahead economists were rearing to equip themselves with forecasting models and computer printouts, Hayek seemed an armchair thinker preoccupied with out-of-date ideas, such as the limitations of human knowledge and the difficulties that economists would have if they tried to ape the natural scientist. An essay by Hayek was more likely to attract the attention of political theorists or (though Hayek would have hated the term) of 'sociologists', than of economists.

The contrast does not necessarily tell, however, against Hayek. A disadvantage of current methodological orthodoxy is that many economists have acquired a vested interest in the existence of stable, discoverable numerical relationships between phenomena such as income and consumption, or short-run changes in the money supply and the price level. One cannot rule out the successful discovery of relationships of this kind; but equally one cannot guarantee it; and it is Hayek who pointed out that scientific method can still be applied to predict certain general features of interacting systems in the absence of specific numerical relationships. Such procedures are commonplace, for example, in biology and linguistics.

Milton Friedman, by contrast, fitted the contemporary mood exactly. Despite the unfashionable nature of his policy views, he spoke the same language as the post-war Keynesians, fitted equations to time series and provided a wide new field for economists in the investigation of 'demand for money functions', which multiplied enormously their employment opportunities. Indeed, Friedman's contribution was essential. For if age-old verities about the relations between money and prices, or the futility of nations trying to spend themselves into full employment, were to be rehabilitated, it had to be in modern statistical dress.

Yet the very modernity of Friedman has meant that he has been vulnerable to new researchers claiming to refute his work by still more up-to-date statistical methods. By contrast, Hayek's insistence that, while inflation is a monetary phenomenon, there is no such thing as *the* quantity of money and no sharp boundary between money and other financial assets has stood the test of time much better. The experience of the Thatcher government, which overshot its monetary targets by miles but, nevertheless, presided over a sharp fall in the inflation rate in its first few years, was much less puzzling to a Hayekian than a Friedmanite. So, too, was the high unemployment cost of the reduction in inflation, which Hayek always insisted would be inevitable while labour markets were dominated by the collective bargaining mentality, whose influence the Friedmanities have usually played down.

A DIFFERENT DEFENCE OF MARKETS

Hayek's defence of markets is also subtly different from that of many other economists. Whereas mainstream economists have been preoccupied with the optimal allocation of resources in given conditions, Hayek has been concerned with the effect of the market system on the evolution and stability of society. He has been interested in markets as examples of human institutions, like language or law, which have evolved without any conscious plan on anyone's part. This is all right so long as we are free in the last resort to judge the outcome and do not feel bound to welcome institutions simply because they have survived. The evolutionary analysis of markets is a useful instrument of

political economy, provided it is not subordinate to some more far-ranging conservative evolutionism of the kind with which Hayek became associated in his
later years.

Hayek the political economist approaches his subject from the standpoint (rare
in mainstream Angle-Saxon economics) that wants, techniques and resources
are not given. They are constantly changing – in part due to the activities of
entrepreneurs who open up possibilities which people did not know existed before.
The market system is a 'discovery technique' rather than a way of allocating
known resources among known wants with known techniques. The latter
problem could, in principle at least, be solved by computers on the assumption
that people's preferences should be satisfied to the maximum possible extent
for any given distribution of income. No computer can predict, however, the
emergence of new knowledge, original ideas or commercial innovations – and
people's reactions to them.

The market also provides a method of co-ordinating the activities of millions
of people and of solving problems without a vast apparatus of political decision
and of governmental enforcement. The very existence of this self-regulating
system is quite unsuspected by 99 per cent of the population, who assume that
we must have a national or international 'policy' for energy, jobs, productivity, or whatever other problem hits the newspaper headlines.

The Hayekian approach does not solve all problems. Hayek sees the market
network as a gradually evolving social system rather than as a mathematical
solution to the problem of resource allocation on the basis of known, certain
and unchanging information. But, like language and law, the transmission and
incentive mechanism of the market can be improved. So shifting attention from
the static allocation of resources to 'the market as a discovery procedure' does
not remove the issue of intervention, but may help us to make progress with it.

One suggestion I have made myself is that we should try to map out the areas
where the 'invisible hand' prevails and those where the 'prisoner's dilemma'
does (Chapter 1). The former principle explains how private self-interest
promotes the public good, the latter how it undermines it. As 'invisible hand'
mechanisms require less coercion, it is worth investigating the conditions
under which prisoner's dilemma situations can be transformed into invisible
hand ones.

THE 'RULE OF LAW'

Hayek has not, in fact, provided any easily recognizable criterion for identifying state intervention of the harmful type. The free-market arguments in *The
Road to Serfdom* were based on the incompatibility of central planning with

personal liberty. In subsequent years Hayek approached the issue indirectly. He argued, especially in *The Constitution of Liberty,* that the main condition for a free society is what he calls the 'rule of law'. He certainly does not mean that the mere observance by rulers of constitutionally enacted laws is enough. On the contrary he would condemn many perfectly valid legislative acts for being arbitrary, discriminatory, and giving far too much discretion to politicians and officials. By 'the rule of law', he means a presumption in favour of general rules and against discretionary power. Hayek attempts to derive, not only the fundamental political and legal basis, but also the economic policies of a free society, from this conception.

Hayek is right to emphasize that general rules are an important protection – perhaps the most important single protection – for freedom. But he often argues as if general laws are a *sufficient* condition for a free society; and this is mistaken. Many policies involving a high degree of coercion could be imposed by general rules – such as a ban on the teaching of evolution in the southern states of America, or on any literature or music which flouted the principles of Marxist-Leninism in the former Soviet Union. There is no one philosopher's stone for minimizing coercion in society.

Moreover, neither Hayek nor anyone else has been able to give a statement of the doctrine of the rule of general laws which will make clear what it implies in particular cases. To say that 'laws must not single out named individuals' would not be controversial even among collectivists, and would not be enough to protect us against a great deal of arbitrary legislation. On the other hand, general rules must mention categories: traffic laws deal with motorists, sales taxes make traders liable and so on. Once this is admitted, it is very difficult to see how rules can be prevented from singling out occupations or industries: nor is it necessarily always desirable that they should be prevented from doing so. But once we have gone along this road, a supposedly general law may well pick out for especially severe treatment a group or even a single individual.

A further restriction is required, but is extremely difficult to formulate. Hayek's proposal – that a general rule should be acceptable to a majority of both those whom it benefits and those whom it harms – is much too strong, because it gives a veto to any minority in any circumstances, for instance to the Mafia in a proposal for a new law against banditry. His illustration of progressive taxation as contrary to the rule of law, because it is not acceptable to high-rate payers, hardly helps his case. There are many arguments against high marginal tax rates: but the objections of those who pay them are hardly conclusive.

The quest for a foolproof definition of just general rules is most unlikely to succeed, but this is not an argument for throwing out the notion. Once the idea has been outlined, we can readily see its importance, even though, like most key concepts in many disciplines, it is extremely difficult to define satisfactorily.

THE MYTH OF JUST REWARD

An outstanding example of how far Hayek was from believing the conventional bourgeois pieties is his attitude to the idea of 'just reward'. He denied that there was such a thing or that people's relative pay should reflect their supposed merit. This view has often been interpreted as an attack on measures to improve the wages of the poorly paid or reduce high salaries and profits. In fact, Hayek's attack is directed just as much at conventional defenders of free enterprise who believe that the market wage for a person's services represents his marginal value to society and is, therefore, just.

So far from being just, market rewards depend, he argues, on an unpredictable mixture of effort, ability and luck. A person is not responsible for his genetic inheritance. Still less is he responsible for the vagaries of the market, which can cause a collapse of the demand for an occupation for which someone has had a life of training. It is fruitless to debate whether truck drivers should receive less than junior college professors, as they did before the Second World War, or more, as they do in contemporary America. It is the market, not the merit, that has changed.

Hayek has two main arguments against attempting to reward merit. First, it is highly inexpedient. For, if the merit awards of some incomes policy tribunal were different from market valuations, there would be shortages of some workers and unemployment among others – thus aggravating present job shortages which are, as he rightly argues, due to union and other institutional forces pricing workers out of employment. Secondly, quite apart from the adverse economic consequences, it is not even desirable for governmental authorities to try to reward merit, which would involve supposing that some authority can decide between how much pain and effort a task has cost and how much of a person's achievement is due to outside circumstances. Hayek does not even think it rational to strive to be meritorious but rather 'to achieve a minimum of pain and sacrifice and, therefore, a minimum of merit'.

Yet, characteristically, he spoils a splendid and heretical contribution to understanding by extending the denial of just occupational reward to the much more sweeping assertion that there is no such thing as 'social justice'. The value, or otherwise, of distinguishing a special kind of justice from justice in general is not the issue; and it is a semantic problem whether people's ethical views on the distribution of wealth and income should come under 'justice', or under some other heading. The substantive point is that Hayek (in striking contrast to John Rawls) insists that *any* public policy towards the distribution of income and property (beyond the provision of a basic social security minimum) is incompatible with a free society and the rule of law. In this he performs a disservice to market economists, who have tried for generations to convey to uncomprehending politicians that it is quite possible to change the distribution of income and wealth without interfering with market relativities. A combined progressive and negative income tax reduces absolute rewards at the top and increases them at the bottom, *without* attempting to evaluate jobs or merit and without interfering with market rankings.

But how far should we go in these directions? And would it not be better to look at the distribution of property and the laws of inheritance instead of relying entirely on fiscal and social security transfers? Despite the efforts of Rawls and Nozick, market liberalism still lacks a theory – not of the just wage, which is a chimera – but of the just distribution of property rights. Neither evolutionism nor any other intellectual strategy can avoid the need for a normative theory of just transfer and just holdings.

HAYEK'S SOCIAL PHILOSOPHY

It should be obvious from what has already been said that Hayek tried, much more explicitly than Keynes ever did, to embed his economic teachings in a wider view of Man in Society. It is not surprising that there were gaps and contradictions in his wider social philosophy, as in that of everyone else who has tried to construct such an edifice.

He was in fact attracted to three different political philosophies:

1. *Classical liberalism:* that is, liberalism in the old English rather than in the modern American sense, with a strong emphasis on the rule of law, competitive markets and limited government;
2. *Burkean conservatism:* that is, an emphasis on the superior wisdom of institutions which have developed with time; and a belief that changes should be based on reducing 'incoherences' in current traditions and practices, which themselves supply hints about adaptation to changing circumstances;
3. *Evolutionary ethics:* this later addition to Hayek's scheme emphasizes the survival of the human race, and its development to higher levels, and judges institutions and ideas in terms of their supposed contribution to human survival and evolution.

Occasionally these three different approaches, as in the nostalgic view of Gladstonian England, may point in a similar direction. Usually, however, they are in conflict. In the pre-Gorbachev USSR, dictatorship and state control embodied the traditional wisdom; and the proponents of free elections or free markets there could be accused of just that kind of 'constructivist rationalism' with which Hayek charges radicals in the West.

SURVIVAL OF THE FITTEST

The modern political theorist who did most to explain the traditionalist and evolutionist side of Hayek's work in sympathetic terms is John Gray (who
subsequently made a well-advertised shift in position). Gray finds the key in a
work entitled *The Sensory Order,* dating back to Hayek's student days. For even
then, Hayek was as much concerned with philosophy and psychology as with
economics. He insisted that our most important knowledge was not of propositions or theories, but of practical skills and dispositions governed by rules which
we may imperfectly discover afterwards, but not formulate in advance. He
regarded economic and social theory as the working out of patterns rather than
the formulation of easily testable numerical relations.

There are great ultimate differences between Hayek and others who may share
similar policy positions. Unlike most libertarians, Hayek avoids evaluating
social institutions by reference to preferred principles of morality, but instead
assesses them in terms of their capacity to generate, transmit and use knowledge.
Moreover, Hayek does not accept the Chicago economic approach characterized as 'maximising behaviour, market equilibrium and stable preferences,
used relentlessly and unflinchingly' – nor even the methodological individualism of most mainstream economists, 'which terminate in the acts, decisions
and intentions of individual agents'. For Hayek, the key to human institution
is the natural selection among competing traditions, and the terminal level of
explanation is not individual choice but 'genetic replication'.

Hayek regards the cardinal error of our times as something known by the
ungainly label of 'constructivism'. This is closely akin to what Michael Oakeshott
called 'rationalism' and is the error of believing that any order we find in
society – capitalism, socialism, feudalism or whatever – has been put there by
a designing mind, and can be accordingly redesigned from scratch. Any reflective
journalist will see the point. For he will be familiar with the combination of
naive rationalism and superficial moralism, which prompts many of his profession
to wade in with ill-thought schemes for salvation, whenever they fail to discover
immediately an obvious justification for any institution, practice or event. He
will also be familiar with the frequent neglect of the long-range and unintended
consequences of human activities and interventions.

Hayek's evolutionist yardstick differs from many kinds of conservatism
because *it is not based on any reverence for the past.* On the contrary, any artificial
attempt to restore past ways is regarded as just as bad a constructivist heresy
as the projects of the most utopian socialists; and his best work shrewdly reveals
the deep affinities between these two types of criticism of the market order.

So far so good. Nevertheless, it does not seem to me that the evolutionist
yardstick allows one to prefer or to criticise *any* social order which is not
visibly dying out. A Hayekian evolutionist would say that the Webbs did not

have the knowledge of inarticulate traditions to reform nineteenth-century capitalism. But must he not also insist that a 1980s Russian dissident was in no position to reform Soviet communism, and that a British 'radical reactionary' does not have the deep-seated knowledge of traditions and practices to roll back the welfare-state?

This lands Hayek in problems. For he is more than an evolutionist. He (rightly) has a strong preference for a society which maximizes individual freedom, which is governed by impartial general rules and in which the state may provide many services, but in which the bulk of human interactions will be either voluntary or through the market.

Competition between social systems may lead neither to liberal results nor even to the survival of the fittest, unless 'fit' is defined in terms of ability to capture the coercive powers of the state. So, as Gray puts it, one may have to choose between Hayek's 'evolutionaly endorsement of man's random walk in space' and his critical analysis of twentieth-century thought and practice.

My own choice is unhesitatingly for the latter. I was first attracted to Hayek by his concern, voiced in *The Constitution of Liberty*, 'of that condition of man in which coercion of some by others is reduced as much as possible'. Hayek's writings have asserted the case for general rules over discretionary authority. They have exposed the misleading identification of a liberal democracy with the divine right of a temporary majority. They have shown that the domination of both the political and economic market place by interest-group struggles is a source of evil and instability. They have explained why pecuniary rewards neither can, nor should, reflect merit. These important and controversial assertions were made before Hayek became so taken with evolutionism; and for a great deal of the time one can forget the unsatisfactory evolutionist or instrumentalist roots of his concern for liberty

INTEREST GROUPS

Hayek's later writings dealt not so much with socialist economic planning, by then out of fashion, as with the degeneration of democracy into a struggle for spoils among competing groups. Instead of laying down the ground-rules under which citizens should live, and providing certain common activities, the modern state has come to be seen as a feeding trough at which rival groups kick and jostle for position.

The pork-barrel view of politics was always defective, but did little harm when government activities and popular expectations from them were modest. Today, it has set up a series of exaggerated and incompatible expectations which constitutes a threat to liberal democracy itself. Hayek does not believe that mere technical solutions to stagflation, via monetary policy, or even union law reform, will suffice until we have rethought the basis of our political system.

Hayek sees the source of interest-group domination in what he calls majoritarian or unlimited democracy. This is known more popularly as 'the mandate doctrine' – the belief that a government elected by a majority of voters (in fact usually a plurality) should be able to enact what it likes without any check, a belief which Lord Hailsham has termed elective dictatorship. These excessive pretensions can only destroy the real value of democracy as the best way we know of changing government without force and making rulers accountable to their citizens.

CONSTITUTIONAL REFORM

Hayek's own constitutional proposals provided a field-day for his opponents. He advocated two assemblies: one elected on a conventional basis, concerned with the day-to-day management activities of government; and a superior legislative assembly concerned with the general rules of 'just conduct', whose members would come from a restricted age-group and who would serve for a very long time. Hayek did not develop the demarcation between the two assemblies in the kind of detail, and with the specific examples, which would be required before anyone could take it up in the political arena.

Nevertheless, if we step back from his particular proposals, it is clear that Hayek was trying to recover an older idea of a state, which has no purposes of its own, but provides a framework of rules and arrangements under which people can pursue their own individual aims without getting in each other's way. This has been labelled by Michael Oakeshott as a 'civil association', as opposed to the more usual idea of the state as an 'enterprise association' with its own aims and purposes. (The close similarity of the later work of both Hayek and Oakeshott, pursued in almost complete isolation from each other, is a theme which deserves a study of its own.)

The object of Hayek's superior assembly is to make sure that the activities of the day-to-day rulers are confined by certain principles. More conventional reformist suggestions, such as a written constitution, a constitutional court, a Bill of Rights, or electoral reform, might, in combination, help to apply the brakes to elective dictatorship. Limitations on majority rule might help to prevent an attempted sudden demolition of the welfare state, just as much as the confiscation of property or high incomes: and the British Left's failure to see this is characteristically superficial.

A Hayekian government of rules, rather than of men, is a long way removed from the practice of any modern government, even if its leaders claim to be members of the Radical Right and quote Hayek to their purpose. The extreme activism of even a Thatcherite Conservative administration, ever eager to promote British exports by hook or by crook, and to intervene *ad hoc* in local government, was far removed from the ideal of a civil association which leaves its members to carry on their own affairs.

However sceptical we are about the mechanics of Hayek's own proposals, they are at least a response to clear and present dangers. Political auctioneering, interest group pressure, and the combination of excessive expectations from collective action with excessive contempt for governmental and legal institutions, are a threat not merely to some pure imaginary *laissez-faire* dream, but also to a functioning mixed economy – and for that reason a threat to individual freedom and popular government. If we are ever to reconstruct our politics, some of the key Hayekian doctrines – such as preference for rules over discretionary authority; the lack of divine right in a temporary majority; the connection between markets and freedom; the realization that rewards in this world neither can, nor should, reflect merit; and that a healthy political system is not a horse-trough at which interest groups drink – will have to come into their own. In all these matters Hayek – like Keynes or Friedman or Rawls or other such seminal figures – is best seen as a stimulus rather than a guru.

REFERENCES

Just as in the case of Keynes, it is impracticable to list here all the key works of Hayek, let alone those of commentators on him. The works listed here are confined to those referred to in the chapter or strictly relevant to it.

Brittan, S., 'Hayek, Freedom and Interest Groups', in *The Role and Limits of Government*, London: Temple Smith, 1983.
Gray, John, *Hayek on Liberty*, Oxford: Basil Blackwell, 1984.
Gray, John, *Liberalisms*, London: Routledge, 1989.
Hayek, F.A., *The Constitution of Liberty*, London: Routledge & Kegan Paul, 1960.
Hayek, F.A., *Law, Legislation and Liberty*, 3 vols, London: Routledge & Kegan Paul, 1973–9.
Hayek, F.A., *The Road to Serfdom*, 1944; London: Routledge & Kegan Paul, 1976.
Hayek, F.A., *The Sensory Order*, Chicago, Ill.: Chicago University Press, 1952.
Hayek, F.A., *Studies in Philosophy, Politics and Economics*, London: Routledge & Kegan Paul, 1967.
Oakeshott, Michael, *On Human Conduct*, Oxford: Clarendon Press, 1975.
Robbins, Lionel, *Autobiography of an Economist*, London: Macmillan, 1965.

PART THREE

Jobs, Inflation and Economic Management

7 What remains of the monetarist counter-revolution?*

This chapter is devoted to macroeconomic policy: in other words the ways in which output, jobs and prices can be affected by such matters as the government's budgetary stance, money supply and interest rates or, in some cases, exchange rate movements. The handling of these aspects of policy is sometimes known (not all that happily) as 'economic management' or 'demand management'.

A CONFUSION OF ISSUES

Unfortunately, public discussion of macroeconomic questions has been bedevilled by the political symbolism acquired by that accursed word 'monetarism' and by the professional difficulty economists (like all other specialists) experience in distinguishing the wood from the trees. The campaign of vilification has been at times so successful that many educated citizens have believed the principal tenet of 'monetarism' to be support for Latin American dictatorships employing torture. Those of a more charitable disposition have supposed it to be a label for hardships deliberately imposed on peoples by governments to punish them for laziness or poor productivity.

Nor has understanding been helped by official explanations of economic policy. Questions of broad principle, about which every interested citizen has a right to be informed, have been hopelessly mixed up with highly technical questions of strictly specialist interest. At times it has even looked as if the choice of which political party to support, and which wing within that party to adhere to, has depended on the quirks of banking figures understood only by a handful of financial experts, if by them.

The preoccupation with technical means rather than basic objectives can perhaps be explained by the way in which the 'monetarist' counter-revolution came to both the USA and Britain. Until the late 1960s demand management had been seen in both countries largely in terms of fiscal policy. A minority of economists

---

* This chapter is a condensed version of *How to End the Monetarist Controversy*, London: Institute of Economic Affairs, 1981. It was originally published as Chapter 4 of *The Role and Limits of Government*, London: Temple Smith, 1983.

had always thought this a mistaken emphasis and maintained that the neglect of monetary policy was a grave error. These contentions achieved headline status as a result of two events. In the USA a tax increase, won from Congress by President Johnson to offset the inflationary forces set off by the Vietnam War, took effect in 1968, and there was a large swing out of deficit in the Federal Budget. The fiscal tightening failed, however, to have its expected restraining effect until the Federal Reserve Board responded by sharply reducing the rate of monetary expansion at the end of the year.

The second event was in the UK when, despite a highly restrictive fiscal policy, the 1967 devaluation proved slow to work and domestic consumption rose more than forecast. Partly on IMF insistence, monetary policy was tightened and the last year and a half of the Chancellorship of Roy Jenkins saw a firmer conscious control of monetary magnitudes than in any previous period of British history. The balance of payments soon swung round into surplus and inflation dropped slightly in 1970.

Subsequently concern with monetary magnitudes first came back to Britain in the latter part of the reign of Denis Healey (who was Labour Chancellor from 1974 to 1979) and even more under the Thatcher government which took office in 1979. But the most interesting test was in the USA in 1980–2, when a tight monetary policy pursued by the Fed under Paul Volcker coincided with national and international alarm over rapidly escalating budget deficits. In crude terms, the monetary forces once again 'beat' the fiscal ones. For the US experienced all the effects – both severe recession and a sharp fall in inflation – normally associated with a large contraction in the growth of demand.

Nevertheless these later experiences were not all that satisfactory for the more technical sort of monetarist. Put simply, the contraction in demand growth in both countries in the early 1980s was greater than intended and far greater than would have been expected from the rather moderate decline in the growth of the money supply as officially measured.

THE DEMISE OF THE POST-WAR WISDOM

There was nothing in the switch of emphasis from fiscal to monetary instruments which necessitated the abandonment of post-war full employment policies. The essence of post-war wisdom, often known as 'Keynesian demand management', was the attempt by governments and central banks to achieve full employment through actions to regulate demand. These actions took the form of variations in the budget balance or in the ease or tightness of money (and occasionally in the exchange rate). It will always remain an open question how far such policies and the doctrines behind them truly reflected the teachings of John Maynard Keynes, a great economist of subtle and frequently changing views, who died in 1946. But we are stuck with the label 'Keynesian' (or 'unre-constructed Keynesian' to hint at this doubt) as we are with 'monetarist'.

The key 'Keynesian' belief was that increases in total spending – whether brought about by monetary or fiscal policy, or occurring spontaneously – had their main effects on output and employment, at least until unemployment reached extremely low levels. If unemployment was forecast to rise above the target, demand was supposed to be boosted by tax cuts, higher spending, credit relaxations, and so on. That such boosts tended to take a budgetary form, with the money supply responding passively, was a secondary matter. The same underlying philosophy could just as well have been allied with planned changes in the money supply if that had been thought the appropriate weapon. The belief was that a sufficient boost to demand would raise output and reduce unem-ployment until the target was reached. If unemployment threatened to fall too low ('overfull employment') the government would restrain demand; but it usually required a sterling crisis before it would restrain it in a major way.

Despite the official doctrines, British governments did not always boost demand when unemployment rose above the chosen target; and they sometimes took restrictive measures even when recession loomed and unemployment was expected to rise. The alibi was invariably the threat of an overseas payments deficit or a run on the pound. Thus it came to look as if the fixed exchange rate for sterling was the main constraint on the growth of output. It was rarely suggested, even by the 'sound-money men' of the time, that there were any obstacles, apart from the balance of payments, to achieving chosen output and employment levels. Together the main industrial countries were in current payments balance or surplus. Thus it seemed, according to this philosophy, that if they expanded together they could spend themselves into chosen levels of economic activity.

The big blank in orthodox Keynesian doctrine was that it said very little about the price level. Many Keynesian economists, especially of the older generation, believed that domestic prices were mainly determined by wage costs, which were themselves dependent on largely non-economic institutional forces such as the attitudes of union leaders. Inflation was sometimes, according to this view, aggravated by import prices; but an individual industrial country had little control over these, and fluctuations in commodity prices were in both directions over a period of years. The main weapon proposed for combating inflation was incomes policy. This meant either wage and price controls or a government deal (misleadingly known as a 'social contract') with union leaders, as I have described in my book on the Treasury.

Not all 'orthodox Keynesians' washed their professional hands of wages and prices to this extent. Some believed there was a trade-off, known as the 'Phillips curve', between unemployment and inflation, with more of one bringing less of the other.

According to the first or purely institutional version of the traditional Keynesian doctrine, governments could more or less ignore inflation in their attempts to raise demand to full-employment levels. Inflation, if it was a problem, had to be tackled by non-financial means. The second version accepted that a price might have to be paid for full employment in terms of *some* inflation; but in neither version was there any suggestion that demand management aiming at full employment might be *entirely* dissipated in higher prices.

THE 'MISERY INDEX' RISES

After two decades of apparent success, orthodox Keynesian economics demonstrated an increasing failure to deliver the advertised benefits. Not only did inflation begin to rise to alarming proportions but so also did unemployment – a combination of events which completely contradicted the notion of a simple trade-off between them. Trouble was apparent in the late 1960s when the 'Misery Index' (the sum of the inflation and unemployment rates) began rising in country after country. Internationally, the deterioration was reflected in the growing difficulty of maintaining the post-war Bretton Woods system of fixed exchange rates against the dollar and the fixed dollar price for gold. The system finally broke down in 1971 when President Nixon formally suspended the last remaining vestiges of dollar convertibility into gold.

The next turn of the screw for all industrial countries was the fourfold increase in world oil prices at the end of 1973. Although the Yom Kippur War of that year set off the oil price explosion, an important underlying influence was the world-wide inflation resulting from the synchronized attempts of industrial countries to spend their way out of an earlier recession.

After 1973 unemployment was on a strongly rising trend throughout the industrialized world. The increase went on, both when inflation soared and when it began to decline. Until the late 1960s, '500,000 unemployed' (or less than $2\frac{1}{2}$ per cent of the working population) was a crisis level in the UK leading to policy reversals and the sacking of cabinet ministers. In the early 1970s, the alarm bells rang at one million; in the late 1970s, at one and a half million. In the early 1990s unemployment hovered just below three million (or 10 per cent). The deterioration in Britain was but an example of a trend in evidence throughout the industrialized world. Unemployment in the main industrial countries which make up the Organization for Economic Co-operation and Development (OECD) rose from 10 million in 1970 to nearly 35 million two decades later.

After the 1973 oil crisis some countries, including the UK, did try for a time to spend their way back to prosperity, but their efforts collapsed amidst currency crises and IMF rescues. The USA made a similar attempt under President Carter in 1977–8; but he too had to put on the brakes sharply and reverse course when the dollar plunged; and the last part of his presidency was marked by the ascendency of Paul Volcker, the Fed chairman who adopted a monetary policy geared to reducing inflation.

After the second (1979–80) oil price explosion no major country attempted to expand its way out of recession. The French Socialist Party under François Mitterand and the British Labour Party were in principle committed to massive demand boosting. But the Mitterand government, elected in 1981, called a halt to steps in that direction and introduced severe restrictive packages following the franc devaluations of 1982 and 1983.

In Britain the total stimulus required in the early 1980s to restore post-war levels of full employment would, on the traditional Keynesian arithmetic, have amounted to well over 10 per cent of the national income (or over £70 billion in 1990s values) in public expenditure increases and tax cuts plus a very aggressive cheap money policy to try to prevent interest rates from rising as a result. There was no chance of any government successfully administering a stimulus approaching this size. But there was little public understanding of why these measures – even if approached in steps – would be likely to turn out to be counterproductive. Many politicians, officials and economists throughout the world basically still saw demand management in unreconstructed traditional post-war Keynesian terms. They saw various 'hideous obstacles' ranging from the former OPEC surpluses to markets mistakenly obsessed with public-sector borrowing requirements and monetary figures. These factors were treated as chance misfortunes; and if only they could be circumvented governments could, it was supposed, go back to demand management in real terms aimed at chosen levels of output and employment. The intellectual basis of the counter-revolution was still far from widely understood.

THE MONETARIST COUNTER-ATTACK

The crisis in orthodox Keynesian economic policy provided, however, a hearing for all sorts of groups outside the previously reigning establishment who had never believed in that orthodoxy in the first place. The most prominent, and the ones whose teachings seemed most relevant, were the 'monetarists' associated with Milton Friedman. Their counter-revolution was based on three main propositions:

1. Governments cannot spend their way to target levels of output and employment. The long-run effect of boosting monetary demand (i.e., total spending) is therefore on the price level. Both the beneficial effects of demand stimulation on output and employment and the adverse effects of demand restriction on these variables are transitional.

2. The key long-running influence on monetary demand, and thus the main determinant of the nominal national product of national income, is the quantity of money. ('Nominal' means measured in cash terms and not adjusted by a prices index.)

3. More specifically, there is a clear-cut division between money and other financial assets; the supply of money can be readily controlled by central banks, and the relationship between the quantity of money and the national income is predictable and stable. Advocates of this final set of propositions can be called 'technical monetarists', in a descriptive and non-pejorative sense.

If variations in the quantity of money are the main long-run influences on demand, and if demand movements ultimately affect prices rather than output or employment, there is a clear link between changes in the amount of money and changes in the price level. Such a link is the main assertion of the *Quantity Theory of Money*, arrived at by combining propositions 1 and 2 above.

The evidence linking major historical inflations with monetary disturbances is inescapable. It requires perverse ingenuity to deny the connection between the inflation of Imperial Rome and the debasement of the denarius, or between the sixteenth-century inflation and the inflow of precious metals from the New World, or between the post-First World War German inflation and the billion-fold increase in the quantity of Reichsmarks. Whatever the ultimate initiating force, such as the burden of defending Imperial Rome or of German reparation payments, a necessary condition on all such occasions was an increase in the quantity of currency. If the quantity of anything is increased then, other things being equal, its value will drop; and this applies to money as to other commodities even though money may be especially difficult to define.

The 'technical' monetarists who embrace proposition 3 go, however, a good deal further. They assert not merely that inflation is a monetary phenomenon but that the effective quantity of money in a modern paper currency regime can be readily defined and measured – or, alternatively, that its exact definition does not matter so long as a single aggregate is chosen and monitored. Moreover, they believe that the control of the quantity of money is a relatively straight-forward technical question. They also set more store than other classical economists or quantity theorists by the claimed short-term stability of the relation between the quantity of money and the nominal national income. (Thus 'fine tuning' is neither feasible nor necessary, a matter discussed later.)

It was unfortunate for the course of the debate that more technical propositions about money gained public attention before the wider proposition about the futility of governments trying to spend themselves into full employment. To make matters worse, there was an excessive emphasis both by the Keynesian and the monetarist camps on the performance of rival short-term forecasts, whereas the real debate related to the longer term. Thus public debate became hopelessly confused between (a) issues on which every citizen has a right to be informed, (b) questions of general economic theory, and (c) highly technical questions best left to specialists.

Some of the technical monetarists were scarcely helpful to the clarity of the debate. They often spoke as if hope of salvation depended on their own particular definition of money being adopted; and since different monetarists looked at different measures which moved in conflicting ways, they helped to turn off patience and support. In any case, in country after country velocity in crucial periods moved outside the range implicit in the monetary targets. Some of the most vociferous monetarists insisted that nothing would come right until central banks controlled the money supply by operating directly on the reserves of the banking system (a method known as 'monetary base control') instead of indirectly via interest rates. When the US Federal Reserve Board made a change in this direction in November 1979, the attack shifted to even more technical matters such as lagged accounting by member banks of the Fed. The Duke of Wellington's remark about his troops – I don't know what effect they have on the enemy, but by God they frighten me' – could have been applied to monetarist economists by a critical sympathizer.

NO LONG-TERM TRADE-OFF

The point of a theory is in what it denies. The essence of the changed thinking, which explains the political heat of the debate, is contained in the first proposition about the inability of demand management to achieve target levels of employment. This key proposition says nothing specifically about money and can be accepted independently of belief in the other more technical contentions.

The doctrine of the long-run impotence of demand management may be labelled 'counter-revolutionary'; for that is the relationship in which it stands towards the earlier post-war revolution which brought in 'Keynesian' demand management. The doctrine can be regarded as a revival of the classical tradition, which emphasized the role of real forces, rather than monetary or fiscal policy, in determining real variables such as output and employment.

The proposition that governments cannot 'spend their way' into chosen levels of employment for more than a transitory period was first enunciated – or rather revived – in 1967 by Professor Friedman (and another US economist,

Professor Edmund Phelps, who was working independently). Nevertheless, it is in no way tied to Friedman's detailed views about the role of the money supply as an instrument for controlling aggregate expenditure. Nor has it anything to do with a belief in *laissez-faire* or most of the characteristic policies of US Republican or British Conservative governments.

A stable trade-off between unemployment and inflation, of the kind shown in the traditional Phillips curve, can exist only if wage earners continue to believe 'a pound is a pound' irrespective of inflation. The short-term trade-off is mainly between unemployment and *unanticipated* inflation. Once, however, 'money illusion' vanishes – that is, inflation is taken into account - wage earners who formerly settled for, say, 3 per cent annual pay increases will insist on 3 per cent plus an inflation premium; and, if governments pursue sufficiently accommodating financial policies, they will be able to obtain it. But, with the same policy assumptions, the higher wage increases will be passed on in still higher price rises, which will stimulate still more rapid wage increases, and so on *ad infinitum*.

The newly revived classical doctrine does not say that stable prices are more important than full employment. The proposition is one about cause and effect. It gives notice that there is no stable trade-off between unemployment and inflation. An attempt to keep unemployment low and labour markets tight by financial policy risks not merely inflation but accelerating inflation. Since no country can live with accelerating inflation, the experiment will eventually have to be brought to a halt with a painful stabilization crisis, accompanied for a time by more unemployment than if governments had not been so ambitious.

The rate of unemployment at which inflation neither rises nor falls was originally labelled the 'natural rate'. There is in fact nothing natural about it; it reflects all kinds of highly imperfect labour markets and other institutions. It is now more usually called by the colourless but accurate name NAIRU – 'non-accelerating inflation rate of unemployment'. It is the lowest rate of unemployment which can be achieved by financial policy, however high or low the rate of inflation. To avoid excessive use of an ungainly acronym, I shall sometimes paraphrase it as the 'minimum sustainable level of unemployment' or just the 'underlying' rate. A further way of putting it might be the 'inflation takeoff threshold'. For if attempts are made by demand-boosting to reduce unemployment beyond that point, inflation will soar higher and higher so long as the attempts are continued.

Further reflection on the consequences of rapid inflation suggests that any long-run relation between inflation and unemployment may be in the opposite direction to that suggested by the Phillips curve. Double-digit inflation is in practice never steady or predictable in its speed. The resulting instability distorts the signalling functions of the price system, making it more difficult for markets to work effectively; employment is therefore likely to suffer.

THE END OF THE DOLLAR STANDARD

One question is often asked: If fashionable strictures on demand management directly aimed at full employment are true, why did such policies work so well for two or three post-war decades? Those who ask it rarely wait for an answer.

The truth is that, for most of this period, neither the UK nor most other countries pursued demand management policies directed to full employment. The language of such policies was often used, but so long as the Bretton Woods system of exchange rates fixed against the dollar prevailed, the overriding aim was to maintain the currency parity.

Full-employment demand management policies did not come to the United States until well into the 1960s. For most of the post-war period American administrations and the Federal Reserve followed non-inflationary policies; and other countries, if they were to avoid devaluing against the dollar, had to imitate them. Thus, until the breakdown of the post-war system in the late 1960s and early 1970s, most countries followed sound-money policies, although some of them did not know it; and sound-money policies proved compatible with full employment. The balance of payments crises I referred to earlier, seen at the time as irritating obstacles to further growth, were in fact the way in which inflationary policies became visible under fixed exchange rate regimes. In the words of Nigel Lawson, written before he became UK Chancellor of the Exchequer: 'During this period foreign exchange crises served as a proxy for monetary disciplines.' In the late 1960s and early 1970s, demand was boosted more vigorously both in the United States and elsewhere and inflation accelerated; but 'unsound' policies failed none the less to prevent unemployment from rising sharply.

The policy of counter-inflation by proxy had one unfortunate legacy in the realm of ideas. It induced many people in Britain and other European countries to suppose that the main obstacle to more expansionary demand policies was something called the 'balance-of-payments constraint' which, if it could be surmounted, would enable demand to be expanded to stimulate more real growth. That it would stimulate inflation instead was revealed to British governments only when the decision to float sterling taken by Edward Heath's administration in 1972 was accompanied by over-indulgence in deficit spending and monetary expansion, with results that any Friedmanite – or, indeed, anyone schooled in the older classical tradition – would have foreseen.

The moral seems to be that when underlying forces in the economy are making for low unemployment and satisfactory economic growth there is no need to embark on traditional Keynesian demand management. Indeed, during the 1950s and 1960s, because of the overriding financial constraint of the exchange rate, policy was devoted to keeping British inflation rates in line with those of other countries; but because underlying unemployment was low, it was difficult to distinguish it in practice from Keynesian orthodoxy. When, on the other hand, underlying forces are making for a low level of growth or high unemployment, Keynesian policies will be very clearly distinguishable from sound money, but they will then tend to break down.

NOMINAL VERSUS REAL

The reason why demand management was discredited is that policymakers in the post-war period focused not on *nominal* but on *real* demand – or, in terms of the published figures, not on 'nominal GDP' but on 'GDP at constant prices'. The reader has only to consult a typical economic forecast to see that most magnitudes are still valued at constant prices.

The emphasis on 'real demand' was a fatal error, for it begged the question of how far a boost to spending raised output and how far it was dissipated in an inflationary increase of prices and wages.* A little reflection (always easier after the event) should have shown that all that governments and central banks can hope to regulate directly by demand management consists of flows of money. The error of most post-war demand management was to assume that real things, such as output and employment, could invariably, and as a matter of course, be affected permanently by financial manipulation.

Governments were slow to realize this limitation of their powers. When accustomed injections of monetary demand no longer yielded the expected result in output and employment, but were largely dissipated in inflation, the dose was stepped up once the Bretton Woods restraints were out of the way. This is a common experience among drug addicts who need stronger and stronger doses to regain the old 'kicks'. But in contrast to drug addicts, governments did not always realize what they were doing. They thought they were stimulating or at least bolstering output and employment, when they were in practice boosting money GDP, with the main effects on the price component.

The dissipation in rising prices of past demand increases in the UK is shown clearly in Figure 7.1. During the first quinquennium, 1959–64, nominal demand, as measured by nominal GDP, grew by nearly 40 per cent; slightly over half of the growth was reflected in increased output and slightly less than half in higher prices. The expansion of nominal demand was stepped up in successive periods, but more and more of the growth was reflected in inflation and less and less in higher output. By the time of the expansionary period, 1974–9, the rise in nominal demand of nearly 130 per cent was reflected almost entirely in

---

* It would be pleasant to exculpate Keynes himself from this misjudgement, but I am afraid that he encouraged bad habits by writing much of the *General Theory* in terms of a particular kind of funny money known as 'wage units'. Not all Keynesians have followed this bad habit. In the USA in particular the Council of Economic Advisers often examined past and prospective changes in *nominal* national product before estimating the breakdown between changes in price and changes in quantity.

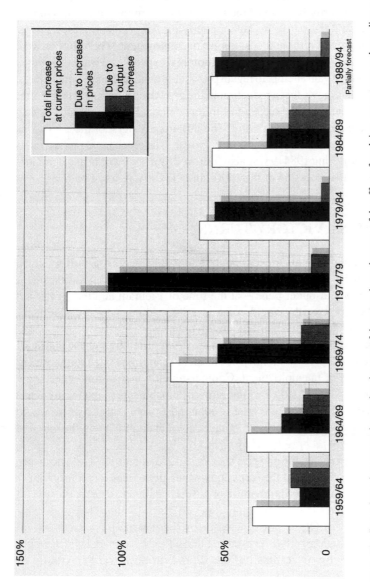

Note: The first column is not exactly equal to the sum of the second two, because of the effect of applying percentages and rounding approximations.

Source: Central Statistical Office.

Figure 7.1   The growth of nominal GDP in the UK: GDP at current market prices, expenditure-based

higher prices, while output growth was less than half its rate during the first quinquennium.

The figures in the chart are neither a tautology nor a statement of the obvious, as hasty critics have suggested. As a matter of arithmetic, successively larger demand boosts *could* have been reflected in a faster rise in output. They *were* reflected in more rapid inflation and slower real growth than ever before. The events occurred partly because of the puncturing of 'money illusion' (further discussed below) and partly because underlying *non-monetary* forces were pulling down growth rates and pushing up unemployment. These forces were misinterpreted as demand deficiency, and nominal expenditure was encouraged to gallop ahead in a vain attempt to regain previous growth and employment rates.

Figure 7.1 also shows that a reduction in the growth of nominal demand after an inflationary period still exacts a toll in lost output. There continues to be a price to be paid for reducing inflation. The inflationary burst of the 1970s was followed by a quinquennium of nearly zero growth. The much more modest inflationary upsurge during 1984–9 was also followed by a period of near stagnation, taking together the recession of the 1990s and the early years of recovery.

MONETARIST VICTORY TURNS SOUR

The counter-revolutionary or classical school thus scored a bull's eye in predicting, well before the event, that demand-boosting policies such as President Johnson's 'guns-and-butter policy' at the time of Vietnam and the Heath and Carter 'dashes for growth' would come to grief, ending with an inflationary explosion and no ultimate benefit to employment.

But just as the orthodox Keynesians were discomfited by the escalation of inflation, the counter-revolutionary or classical school has been embarrassed by the escalation of unemployment. Counter-revolutionary economists knew that a sharp rise in the NAIRU (or minimum sustainable rate of unemployment) was liable to occur; but although classical economists were familiar with a whole list of supply-side factors which *could* have raised unemployment, the massive increase *was not in fact predicted by them.*

They neither expected the oil price shocks of 1973–4 and 1978–80, nor were they prepared for the size of the recessions which price rises would trigger off when they did occur. Indeed, the more obviously 'monetarist' economists did not cover themselves in glory over any aspect of the oil issue. They underestimated the effects of OPEC price increases on the general price level and on inflationary expectations, either by asserting that OPEC was a cartel which would soon collapse, or by overestimating the short-term downward flexibility of non-oil prices.

But whatever the *post facto* explanations, the unemployment explosion deprived the classical school of the fruits of its victory over the Keynesians. An explanation of the transitional unemployment effects of expansionary and contractionary economic policies in terms of variations around an underlying (NAIRU) level becomes much less convincing in the face of an upward leap in the NAIRU itself which no one had foreseen.

No macroeconomic school has explained satisfactorily the steep trend rise in unemployment from the 1970s onwards. The counter-revolutionaries can claim something more modest, but still important – an explanation given *long before the event* of why post-war attempts by governments to spend their way into target levels of employment would eventually fail, and why therefore such policies would be useless for dealing with subsequent problems.

A PROVISIONAL STRATEGY

A genuine counter-revolution is not the same as mere reaction. It should be able to absorb the best elements of the revolution it is replacing; or, to change the metaphor, should keep the baby while emptying out the bathwater. In this case it should be based on the contribution of both the Keynesian and Friedmanite schools.

A financial strategy which attempts to stabilize total monetary demand has a Keynesian flavour and is far removed from *laissez-faire* or faith in automatic relationships. But the qualification 'monetary' in front of 'demand' is crucial. In contrast to orthodox Keynesianism, there can be no question of injecting unlimited amounts of spending power in the hope of achieving some previously set objective for output and employment; there is thus a built-in safeguard against runaway inflation.

For the strategy involves an undertaking that governments will refuse to finance a permanently higher rate of inflation resulting from external or internal shocks. Indeed, any financial plan worth its salt must embody the slogan 'No accommodation of wage or price push'. Having established this constraint, policymakers still have a duty to try to maintain a stable growth of demand in money terms. No financial strategy can prevent a rise in unemployment stemming for instance from an increased exercise of union monopoly power. But a pre-announced policy can, if credible, minimize increases in unemployment arising from mistaken beliefs about inflation or from a sudden collapse in nominal demand.

DOES LOWER INFLATION BRING MORE JOBS?

This is a suitable point at which to examine the assertion, made by governments embarked on counter-inflationary programmes, that price stability (or low inflation) promotes jobs. Is this true? The reader who would like a straight 'yes' or 'no' will have to accept that this is one of those irritating assertions which can have several meanings that need to be examined separately.

1. At its most basic, the assertion can mean that the economy will perform better at low than at high (and therefore variable) inflation rates; and that the underlying rate of unemployment (NAIRU) will be less. This proposition is probably true; but there is no reason to suppose that the job gain from lower inflation will be anything like sufficient to put an end to unemployment worries (which will remain so long as the NAIRU is high). *Moreover, the proposition is a long-run one and says nothing about the unemployment effects of the transition from a higher to a lower inflation rate.*
2. This transition is indeed nearly always accompanied by a 'temporary' rise in unemployment (there still is a short-term Phillips curve, at least on the downward side); but given that a counter-inflationary programme is in operation, the quicker pay and price rises fall back, the smaller will be the transitional rise in unemployment. It is this distinction which understandably causes the most confusion.*

The object of a counter-inflationary strategy is to return to a state of affairs where something approaching price stability is taken for granted. Unfortunately, many people have an excessively literal understanding of what that means.

Historically, periods of price stability were not ones of zero price change. Year-to-year variations ran to several per cent; and there were decades at a time of what would nowadays be called 'creeping' inflation or deflation. The difference from today is that the direction of movement was unknowable. Prices were as likely to fall as to rise. Stability was therefore the best predictive bet; deviations from it were not so big as to destroy a person's savings, and were in any case likely to be reversed in a single lifetime.

The result was a combination of basic stability with modest short-term flexibility. If a country's terms of trade deteriorated, or if there was a harvest failure, or if real national income fell for any other reason, the burden would be spread automatically through a temporary rise in the price level without any painful renegotiations of contracts. On the other hand, pensions could be arranged on the basis that a pound was a pound and a dollar a dollar; and wage negotiators were not forced to add an uncertain inflation premium to their offers and demands.

The situation was in marked contrast to the post-Second World War period when inflation has often been high and variable and people have had to work

---

* In terms of the identity of $MV = PT$, if the counter-inflationary programme is represented by MV, the lower the level of P, the higher T – which is output – will be.

with a shrinking monetary yardstick. This makes many business calculations a gamble and causes anyone who relies on a fixed money pension to pray he or she will not live too long. Alternatively, indexation is introduced throughout the economy, thereby easing some of the inflationary distortions. But unless the indexation is carried out very carefully, the safety-valve of rising prices, which reduce real incomes in adverse economic circumstances, is removed; and there is a danger of appearing to guarantee to the population more than the entire value of the national income. An example of the wrong sort of indexation was an escalation clause like the Italian *scala mobile,* which automatically compensated wage earners for inflation. A sensible form of wage indexation would allow for the possibility of real wages going down as well as up in accordance with the market pressures of the time.

Both indexation and non-indexation are thus likely to be unsatisfactory alternatives in practice. Although in my view carefully introduced indexation is an essential second-best in inflationary times, and can even be an adjunct to anti-inflationary policies, there will be no satisfactory solution until inflation itself has been brought down to a low or zero rate.

One reason why widespread indexation cannot solve the problems of inflation is that inflation has had a social function wherever there have been any vestiges of 'money illusion'. Governments in the 1970s could acquiesce, for instance, in 'generous' public-sector pay settlements – say for the miners – in the knowledge that much of the apparent relativity gain would soon be absorbed in general inflation. Both relativity changes and the lack of them could be drowned by a rise in the general price level, and thus governments could postpone the insoluble problem of adjudicating between incompatible claims by rival interest groups. The expression of wage settlements in real indexed terms would have brought the inflation into the open straightaway.

Now, however, that money illusion is mostly gone, inflation no longer serves its social purpose of buying time by a benign form of self-deception. Little is to be lost by sensible indexation, but the systemic arguments for tolerating more than a very low rate of inflation have disappeared too.

IS THE ECONOMY SELF-STABILIZING?

One advantage of an objective for total spending – or nominal GDP – is that it entitles one to by-pass the fruitless controversy over whether a market economy is automatically self-stabilizing.

The questions about stability *sound* interesting enough. In the absence of interventionist government policies, will the economy adjust automatically to events? Are there self-stabilizing forces serving to bring it back to a normal growth and employment path after a shock? Or is the economy likely to develop an ever-growing gap between actual and potential performance – and perhaps even move into a downward spiral – in the absence of government action to sustain demand?

It is sometimes suggested that these fundamental questions lie behind the debate between the counter-revolutionary and the orthodox Keynesian. But I must confess to finding both sides extremely unconvincing and the debate between them unhelpful. The orthodox Keynesian question, echoed by many business leaders and other 'practical men' in every recession, is: 'Where is the upturn going to come from? I can't see where the demand is.' The implication is that there are no natural forces to bring about recovery in the absence of government stimulation; and that, unless it is possible to identify which specific sectors or industries will revive, the prospect is of indefinite stagnation. Indeed, the prognostications of many so-called long-term forecasters make one wonder how humanity managed any growth at all in the 99.9 per cent of its existence when the theory of demand stimulation was unknown and there was no one to predict doom in the absence of intervention.

But the self-stabilizing school is equally difficult to comprehend. There have been such things as depressions. That they are followed by recoveries does not of itself tell us that the system is functioning well. Without some empirical standard of the depth of depression to be expected and the time-scale for recovery, assertions about self-stabilization are meaningless. Nor is it enough to point to government action or social institutions (such as unions) which prevent the automatic stabilizers from working. There is no way of showing non-tautologically that the actual long-term growth path is the best that could be achieved.

Someone who is not an unreconstructed post-war Keynesian can still have worries about the self-stabilization thesis. First, he may be doubtful whether monetary demand can be relied upon to grow smoothly and adequately 'on its own'. Secondly, deviations from the underlying NAIRU rate of unemployment do occur and are not always quickly corrected. If so, large deviations in monetary demand in an inflationary or deflationary direction do matter. Technical 'monetarists' must surely share both worries. Otherwise why should they bother to advocate a stable growth of the money supply – which they think will provide the smoothest attainable non-inflationary growth of monetary demand (i.e., MV, money times velocity)? The less technical counter-revolutionary will simply wonder if the monetary rule is sufficient for the job.

The contribution of demand management to reducing deviations from the underlying rate of unemployment is not to be underrated. Such deviations, if large and persistent enough on the upward side, are indeed known as depressions. If they continue long enough they will drag up the underlying level itself. In a depression the training of labour will fall off, the attitudes, habits and skills of the unemployed will deteriorate, making them less employable when an upturn comes, and the growth of capacity will be impaired. The process by which a high actual rate of unemployment increases the rate sustainable in the longer term is known as 'hysteresis', an unhappy name for an unhappy phenomenon.

A medium-term strategy for monetary demand does not require a definitive theoretical account of the forces generating booms and slumps. It is best stated in terms of total spending, which is represented statistically by the aggregate known as money GDP, or money times velocity. A presentation in such terms avoids prejudging complex technical financial issues and is capable of explanation to a wide public. If successfully pursued, it should ensure that depression does not occur through a mass contraction of spending of the 1930s type, although it cannot prevent unemployment rising if producer groups succeed in diverting the rise in spending into higher wages and prices at the expense of jobs.

POLICY GOALS

There are four main themes to this part of the book.

First, the object of macroeconomic policy is to contribute to price stability and, to a lesser extent, to the stability of output and employment by keeping total spending (the money value of the national income measured by nominal GDP) on a steady path with the minimum of fluctuation.

Secondly, attempts to do this solely by focusing on particular measures of the stock of money are liable to come unstuck. The mere act of adopting monetary targets itself destabilizes the relationship between the money supply and national income; and the demand to hold major currencies comes from external as well as domestic holders, which adds a new element of instability.

Thirdly, there is a minimum underlying or sustainable rate of unemployment consistent not merely with price stability, but with any stable rate of inflation. Attempts to reduce unemployment below this level by increasing total nominal spending (that is spending in money terms) will generate ever-increasing inflation, with which no economic system can live, and thus prove self-defeating.

Fourthly and most importantly, if the underlying rate of unemployment is too high, the only permanent way to reduce it is by supply-side measures properly understood. By this is meant not Reagan-style tax cuts, but measures to improve the working of the labour market, to reduce 'pricing out of work' and to tackle other rigidities and disturbances which discourage adequate use of the resources of the economy.

REFERENCES

Brittan, S., *Steering the Economy*, Harmondsworth, Middx: Penguin, 1971.
Friedman, Milton, *The Optimum Quantity of Money, and Other Essays*, Chicago, Ill.: Aldine, 1969.

Friedman, Milton, *The Counter-revolution in Monetary Theory*, Occasional Paper 33, London: Institute of Economic Affairs.
Johnson, Harry, 'The Keynesian Revolution and the Monetarist Counter-revolution', reprinted in *On Economics and Society*, Chicago, Ill.: University of Chicago Press, 1975.
Lawson, Nigel, *The New Conservatism*, London: Centre for Policy Studies, 1980; reprinted in his *The View from No. 11*, London: Bantam Press, 1992.

8 Countries do not have deficits[*]

INTRODUCTION

When I was still an undergraduate, I heard that distinguished collaborator of Keynes, Richard Kahn, remark that preoccupation with the balance of payments was an example of the tail wagging the dog. He had in mind the unwisdom of basing macroeconomic policy, not on whether the whole economy was moving in an inflationary or deflationary direction, but on the modest difference between the two huge and imperfectly measured magnitudes. At a still more tender age, I had been less than completely convinced by the exhortations of Sir Stafford Cripps (Chancellor of the Exchequer under the British post-war Labour government) to export or die. Even then I had a dim sense that countries once prospered without campaigns of this kind.

I was reminded of these juvenile doubts when, as a young journalist, I went to a dinner at what was then called the Federation of British Industries in the early 1960s. The Prime Minister, Harold Macmillan, was due to give an address on the need to – guess what? – export more. An advance text was despatched. But one greatly daring conference organizer sent a message to No. 10, hinting that the speech was boring. And Macmillan duly responded: he abandoned the official text and instead looked back to an earlier world where prime ministers did not have to worry about the balance of payments and he mentioned the automatic mechanisms which regulated the flow of trade and payments in earlier years.

It was not completely clear whether he had in mind the pre-1914 gold standard or the pre-war period of floating exchange rates. He gave the impression that either was better than the post-war period when prime ministers had to award prizes for exports or launch campaigns for import-saving. Was it for this that the country's political leaders had struggled to climb the greasy pole? Needless to say, the audience was soon eating out of Macmillan's hand, especially as the economic message was surrounded by a glow of social nostalgia for these earlier years. Businessmen who had previously dismissed Macmillan's speeches as platitudinous were saying what a great orator he was, without having much notion of what he really meant.

[*] This chapter was freshly compiled in 1993 to bring together a number of heretical ideas into a coherent statement.

Further sceptical utterances were provided much later by a British Chancellor, Nigel Lawson, most notably at the Berlin IMF Meeting of 1988. His argument was that a current balance of payments deficit was not itself a matter for concern if it was the result of purely private-sector behaviour and did not reflect a public-sector imbalance. The message would have been more convincing if it had come from a finance minister of a surplus country or from Lawson himself in an earlier year when the UK current account was still in balance. But neither of these qualifications made the Berlin speech wrong.

The Chancellors who succeeded Lawson (who resigned in 1989) preferred not to stick their necks out on such matters. Some Treasury officials continued the argument for a while with the intellectually reactionary House of Commons Treasury Committee, which persisted in seeing the balance of payments in the time-honoured Crippsian way.

HISTORICAL BACKGROUND

The balance of payments preoccupation has deep historical roots. Mercantilist writers in the sixteenth, seventeenth and eighteenth centuries campaigned for a favourable balance of trade and for an inflow of gold and silver, which they mistakenly regarded as an indicator of national prosperity. But although export and import records are among the earliest of historical documents, there were no estimates of invisibles (financial earnings, royalties, travel and so forth) until well into the twentieth century. Thus for most of the world's history governments have not had the faintest idea of whether the balance of payments of their country on current account was in surplus or deficit.

The mercantilists were, however, refuted as conclusively as anything ever can be in political economy by the writers of the eighteenth-century Scottish Enlightenment, such as David Hume and Adam Smith. The mercantilist view fell into abeyance in the nineteenth century wherever classical non-interventionist economics held sway. Large current account imbalances opened up in the course of that century as the mirror image of the net capital outflows which developed from advanced countries with high saving rates to capital-hungry developing ones. Data collected by Bayoumi and Bean show that the UK had an average current surplus amounting to $4\frac{1}{2}$ cent of GNP over the period 1880–1913, which rose to around $6\frac{1}{2}$ per cent in the decade before the First World War. The Scandinavian countries had deficits averaging $2\frac{1}{2}$ per cent of GDP; Australia had a deficit of $3\frac{1}{2}$–4 per cent and Canada is believed to have had one of over $7\frac{1}{2}$ per cent in the first decade of the twentieth century.

The current balance of payments became a preoccupation during and after the Second World War, when currencies were inconvertible and capital movements restricted. It was thus difficult for a country to spend more than its current overseas earnings; and any gap had to be made up by movements of reserves or official borrowing. This is still the reality in many Third World and post-communist countries, but not in the main market economies of the west.

The full liberalization of capital markets did not occur until the early 1980s; and in some countries such as France and Italy exchange controls lingered until around 1990. Even after liberalization took place, it took time for both governments and the foreign exchange markets to become used to the limited operational value of the current balance in the new circumstances.

The best way to move from history to analysis is to start with the well-known identity that the current balance of payments surplus is equal by definition to the difference between domestic savings and domestic investment (see Figure 8.1). To say that countries should not run current deficits is to say that there should be no net international lending, which is absurd. Some academic studies make much of the finding that each country's investment has been highly correlated with its own savings. Yet such studies suffer from a lag and do not fully reflect a world in which investment crosses frontiers and, therefore, current account imbalances are normal. It is time to escape the time warp.

CURRENT BALANCE OF
PAYMENTS DEFICIT

equals

TOTAL EXPENDITURE
('Absorption')
minus
TOTAL INCOME

also equals

DOMESTIC INVESTMENT
minus
DOMESTIC SAVING

also equals

OVERSEAS SPENDING
(Imports, etc.)
minus
OVERSEAS EARNINGS
(Exports plus investment income,etc.)

Figure 8.1   Current balance of payments identities

If a country has a surplus of savings relative to domestic investment opportunities it is sensible – and in the interests of the world – that it should run a current surplus and invest the proceeds overseas. If another country has many profitable investment opportunities, but a low savings ratio, it is just as reasonable that its inhabitants should borrow overseas and the country as a whole run a current deficit. Just as conventional opinion condemned the US deficits of the 1980s, it condemned the Japanese and some other Asian surpluses, as well as the German surplus which existed before the 1990 reunification. It was wrong to do so. For these surpluses added to world savings and thus to the supply of funds available for investment.

In the world of affairs the preoccupation with the current balance has lingered long after the circumstances justifying it began to disappear. The task of the International Monetary Fund (IMF) is defined in terms of help with balance of payments adjustment. Citizens of many countries have listened to generations of exhortation to export more or accept lower wages, for the sake of the balance of payments. The debt crisis of Third World and former communist countries has been described largely in terms of their balance of payments difficulties – perhaps understandably in view of the limited access of some of these countries to the private international capital market. Much less acceptable has been the continued concern of the Group of Seven leading industrial countries, whose heads attend the western summits, with the so-called imbalances among themselves.

THE FUNDAMENTAL THESIS

Most economic data can shed some light and none should be thrown away. To say the balance of payments 'does not matter' is thus a caricature of the views of the heretics. The true argument seeks merely to dethrone this balance from its central status as a unique indicator of economic solvency and success and to relegate it to the position of an economic indicator on a par with retail sales figures, the industrial production index and the like.

The balance that people worry about is the balance on goods and services, including invisibles like banking or shipping earnings, as well as interest and dividends from overseas. The correct term is the 'current balance', which is financed by net capital inflows of one kind or another. The fundamental point about the current balance is that, unlike the Budget balance, it is not the balance of any one organization or person. It is the sum of the balances of tens of thousands of individuals and companies as estimated by statisticians.

A country such as the UK or France can have an excessive trade deficit in the same sense as a region such as Normandy or Yorkshire can have such a deficit.

How large a deficit is excessive is not known at either the regional or the national level. Nor do we need such an estimate, at least for developed countries with open capital markets. For it is companies and individuals who borrow too much or save too little; and they should be left to cope with the consequences of their own actions.

The eighteenth-century philosopher and economist David Hume disposed of the issue in a few short pages of his essay 'Of the Balance of Trade'. This had as its subject the 'strong jealousy' which still prevails 'even in nations well acquainted with commerce with regard to the balance of trade and a fear that gold and silver may be leaving them'. Equally up to date were his observations on the 'melancholy reflection' which a Yorkshireman might have about the imbalance which probably then existed in transactions with London, 'did not long experience make people easy on this head'. He struck a very modern note in observing that 'all calculations concerning the balance of trade are founded on very uncertain facts and suppositions'.

The neatest way to dispose of the problem would be to present regional balance of payments estimates for existing nations or federations. If these existed it would be possible to show without pages of tedious prose how deficits are in practice financed without the impediments of balance of payments targets and currency movements. We should also see how very different are the areas recognized as having regional problems from those which have balance of payments deficits.

But as I have not been able to find such estimates, the least unsatisfactory course is to stick to the conceptual high ground and to insist that it is individuals and companies, and not strange entities called 'countries', that undergo these deficits and earn these surpluses.

The one element of common ground is that everyone has to live within his or her own means. (Contemporary academics feel happier to say that he is subject to 'an intertemporal budget constraint'.) It is of course quite proper to borrow to build up capital assets or to finance temporary increases in consumption. There is no magic formula for saying what the prudential limit is, despite the rules of thumb that bankers and accountants have developed. The only general rule is the banality that no one's debt service to income ratio can carry on rising indefinitely.

The seemingly technical argument about overseas trade thus links up with the fundamental distinction between collectivists who think of the state as a great enterprise agency and market liberals who see the state as a civil association whose members make their own decisions and take their own risks. In this instance there is little room for argument. For since the demise of the Soviet empire, there are very few countries indeed where the government even aspires to run all foreign trade; and civil association is a closer description of reality.

The regional parallel is crucial here, as in most other parts of the argument. Yorkshire, considered as an aggregate of individuals and companies, does have a safe or warranted level of external deficit beyond which insolvencies will pile up and cash leave the county. But the inhabitants of this county have had no need to estimate it. For it is experienced at the level of persons and businesses rather than as a county aggregate. The economic liberal would take the same attitude to the UK's overseas transactions as the national economist does to Yorkshire's.

If the inhabitants of a county or region have been borrowing collectively by imprudent amounts, then it can as a figure of speech be said that the nation or region is living beyond its means. But the imprudent decisions have nevertheless been taken by households or companies. It is because their debt ratios cannot rise without limit or without losing their creditworthiness that the national balance of payments is ultimately self-adjusting, without anyone working out targets for the current balance of payments and without a national economic assessment to determine the safe level of net overseas borrowing.

There is one great difference between a balance of payments deficit for Yorkshire and one for the UK, which is of course the foreign exchange element. This reduces the prudential amount of gross – and not merely net – cross-border borrowing and lending. Thus separate currencies amount to a tax on international transactions. Indeed, this is the most important argument for a single currency – or at least irreversibly fixed exchange rates – over as wide an area as possible. Nevertheless, at the level of individual transactions the foreign currency risk is a commercial risk like any other (such as commodity price fluctuations, business cycle movements or insolvent customers) which the capital markets are no worse than governments at assessing.

On the liberal approach, the government's main fiscal task is to look after its own budget balance, which need not always be zero. It has other duties, such as safeguarding the value of the currency in which businesses transact with each other. It may also do its best to moderate the cycle of boom and bust. But on this liberal view it is not part of the government agenda to look after the solvency of individuals or companies, either separately or in the aggregate.

The clinching distinction is that private borrowers cannot of their own volition escape their debts by inflation or devaluation, whereas governments can. Left to themselves private borrowers will eventually come up against solvency constraints. This is irrespective of whether their borrowing is to finance investment or consumption. Unlike governments they cannot easily 'print money'.

The implication of everything said here is, of course, that a relaxed attitude to the balance of payments is safe so long as fiscal policy is sound and there is some anti-inflationary anchor to which policy is committed. As elaborated in Chapter 9, there can be at least four of these: a direct price-level objective, a money supply target, a nominal GDP objective, or an exchange rate target. These can be used singly or in some kind of compromise combination. If these normal safety catches are firmly in position, it is superfluous to have a further objective for the current balance of payments, which then acts as a fifth wheel causing unnecessary lurches in policy and unnecessary public anxiety.

When the government is running a structural Budget deficit benign neglect of the balance of payments is no longer so easy to justify. For the overseas deficit is no longer just the mirror image of increased overseas borrowing by individuals and companies, but also overspending by the government. In normal circumstances the appropriate response is to see it as a fiscal problem and to concentrate on reducing the Budget deficit rather than interfering with exports and imports.

What should be done, however, in a recession, when putting on the fiscal brakes might aggravate job and output losses? This will be specially true when the recession is worldwide and orders lost at home are difficult to replace abroad. The government should certainly not rush into competitive devaluation or other beggar-my-neighbour policies.

The best response lies in a modest modification of the medium-term policy I have urged in the previous chapter of sustaining the growth of demand in nominal (that is cash) terms at a rate sufficient to sustain a reasonable rate of growth, but not to finance inflation. The usual way of expressing this objective, which I have hitherto used, is in terms of nominal GDP, which is simply the GDP figures as they occur without the customary conversion into real terms.

This, however, is only an approximation to the aggregate which the government and Bank of England can and should influence. This should be expressed as total domestic demand. This includes all the components of GDP, with the exception of net exports. If this is kept to a stable and modest path, there will be room in the economy for an improvement in exports relative to imports when the world economy improves. The policy I am urging is but a modern version of the 1960s idea of 'leaving room' in the economy which would be filled by net exports when the world business cycle turned upwards, but avoids creating a domestic depression before this happens.

OPERATIONAL MEANING

The overall balance of payments always balances. The current balance, as illustrated in Table 8.1, is simply an attempt by statisticians to estimate one combination of elements in the two-way flow of trade across the exchanges.

What can actually be observed in the market place in times of trouble is downward pressure on the exchange rate. Indeed, a formal definition of a balance of payments constraint may be, as Gavyn Davies has suggested: a steeply rising supply price of external finance. But in itself this does not take us very far. A differentially high or rising interest rate premium paid by one country for international funds may reflect fundamental worries about its inter-national competitiveness. But it is just as likely to express a credibility concern about the likelihood of a government operating a tight enough monetary policy to avoid depreciation, or to maintain a specific domestic monetary objective; and the different sets of influences are almost impossible to distinguish in practice.

Of course, the foreign exchange markets will make mistakes, exhibit herd mentality and so on. But there is no evidence that government or City com-mentators are any wiser in deciding when a current deficit matters and when it does not. For temporary periods internationally co-ordinated intervention in the foreign exchange market can be used as an additional weapon, but sooner rather than later such resources are exhausted.

Table 8.1   UK balance of payments, 1992

	£bn
Goods balance	– 13.4
Services balance	+ 4.1
Trade balance	– 9.3
Investment income	+ 5.8
Transfers	– 5.1
Identified current balance	– 8.6
Unidentified ('balancing item')	+ 0.3
Identified capital movements	+ 8.3
Overall Balance	0

Source: Balance of Payments Pink Book, 1993.

THE EXCHANGE RATE

Let us suppose that the current balance of payments is regarded by the exchange markets as unsustainably weak and that they will only finance it at sharply rising interest rates. Most mainstream textbooks would in the past have treated it as a case for currency depreciation. Some readers will be surprised that I have gone so far into the present chapter before reaching the topic of the exchange rate as a balance of payments regulator.

The relevance of the exchange rate depends on the reason for the deficit. In some cases a high current deficit, especially when it has increased sharply in a short period, reflects excess demand at home, as in the UK in the late 1980s. Indeed, the main use of balance of payments deficits in such periods is as an indicator of such excess demand.

Let us suppose, however, that the government has undertaken all the obvious measures to curb excess home demand, but that nevertheless the current deficit is still higher than the markets will readily finance at interest rates which meet the needs of the domestic economy.

Prima facie this is a case for devaluation. But suppose, however, that the unsustainably high deficit persists even after devaluation. One reason may be that the trend rate of inflation is higher in the deficit country than in its trading partners. The ultimate remedy is to reduce domestic inflation; and it may actually help to lean against the wind and not to accommodate all inflationary pressures by depreciation. Severely limited accommodation might help to buy time for a gradualist reduction in inflation, as it did for France in the early years of ERM membership in the 1980s. The eventual aim should, however, be to bring down inflation and thus avoid the need for further depreciation.

The more interesting case is when equilibrium in the foreign exchange markets requires a trend improvement in competitiveness. It may be that non-price factors, such as design or delivery, are so bad that the country concerned has to reduce its prices relative to other countries. Or there may have been some sudden shock such as an increase in the price of imported oil requiring an improvement in the non-oil balance.

Say that the country is Britain. The required improvement in British competitiveness can be achieved if inflation in Britain is lower than in its trading partners. A falling pound is only another way of achieving the same effect. An entirely effective 10 per cent devaluation is equivalent to running a zero rate of inflation in traded goods prices for slightly more than three years, when other countries are inflating by an annual average of 3 per cent.

Irrespective of whether the adjustment chosen is depreciation or differentially low inflation, the adjusting country has to accept a continuing deterioration in its terms of trade and a consequent compression of real wages. The assumption made by devaluation advocates is that workers would accept a compression of real wages via the exchange rate (observable in rising prices of imported goods) which they would not accept directly via lower wage increases.

Milton Friedman has likened the advantages of flexible exchange rates to those of shifting the clock forward in spring instead of millions of people getting up earlier to enjoy the early morning light. This might be valid for a once-for-all step adjustment, as in a former communist country rejoining the world economy. But a policy of continuing or long-run depreciation is like shifting the clock every day in the hope of persuading people to rise earlier. It would not be long before they saw through the device and found it an unnecessary nuisance.

The long-term trend of sterling in the quarter-century up to 1992 was strongly downward, not only against the mark and the yen but even against the weaker US dollar. Still further depreciation – unless it was a prelude to full European monetary union – would be treated as a further confirmation that the more favourable inflation signals of the early 1990s were misleading and that Britain had embarked on a more inflationary path than its trading partners. That would do no good to employment at all – except in the eyes of those who believe that there is still a long term 'Phillips' trade-off between unemployment and inflation.

If real wages cannot be maintained at competitive levels without an intolerably high cost in unemployment, this is likely to be equally the case if the attempt to depress them is made by a low-inflation policy or long-run depreciation. Not least of the evils of the balance of payments hang-up is that what is really a labour market problem appears dressed up as currency overvaluation, a disguise which only leads to quack inflationary remedies. Unemployment is a labour market problem best treated by trying to bring pay nearer to market clearing levels. Any resulting inequities are best handled by social security reforms and ultimately by a more widespread diffusion of personal property.

'REAL SHOCKS'

Many academic economists would nevertheless say that exchange rate adjustments are still useful in dealing with 'real shocks'. By this they mean something like a harvest failure, an explosive rise in the price of a key import such as oil, or a political upheaval. The common property of these shocks is that they are not just an effect of inflation, but require some change in a country's terms of trade with the rest of the world. Here the Milton Friedman argument about summertime is said to apply. Is it not better to change one price, the exchange rate, rather than lever upwards or downwards a vast number of separate prices to bring about the required adjustment with the rest of the world?

The first thing to note is that it is only a real shock which hits different countries with different degrees of severity that provides a case for exchange rate adjustments. Most of the shocks that have hit the western world – such as Middle Eastern wars – have had a pretty uniform effect throughout the industrial west. It is hard to think of more than two such differential shocks since the early 1970s. These are the *second* oil price explosion of 1979, associated with the deposition of the Shah, which hit the UK much less severely as North Sea oil was then coming on stream. The other was German re-unification which provided an argument for a temporary revaluation of the mark.

In fact, the textbook task of transferring resources from net exports to supporting reconstruction in the east was carried out speedily without realignment. But the Bundesbank would argue that the transfer would have caused less inflationary pressure – which it had to suppress through high interest rates – had its 1990 request for a realignment been accepted.

A much more usual case is that of countries wanting to devalue in the face of an adverse shock. Indeed, the European Community orthodoxy is that the Mediterranean countries should be compensated by fiscal transfers for losing the right to devalue if they become full members of a monetary union.

There is, however, something phoney in the supposed trade-off between the gain from a monetary union and the loss of the ability to devalue. The gains from the former are real – one major business uncertainty is removed. Devaluation, on the other hand, does not provide the devaluing country with a single penny of extra resources. If Texas or Massachusetts is hit by a slump in the price of its major products, they have to accept a reduction in their terms of trade in any case, and a consequent cut in real wages, if high employment is to be maintained. All that devaluation can do is to enable this cut to be made cosmetically by an increase in prices rather than a reduction in nominal wages or their rate of increase. And the more often this cosmetic trick is tried the more quickly do businesses and unions see through it. If real wage resistance is an obstacle to adjustment after a shock it remains so, irrespective of the currency regime.

Thus the picture of Texas and Massachusetts trading off the right to change their exchange rates against the advantages of a common currency with the rest of the USA is a half-truth. Such a right may be useful if exercised once or twice in a generation, and in both directions. But I cannot help suspecting that if New England had had its own currency it would have been moved frequently downwards. Its citizens would not have seen the price rises following its devaluation as once-for-all, but projected them into the future. The Boston Central Bank would, to avoid temporary unemployment, have validated these beliefs by putting its rate of monetary expansion on a faster track. Harvard is not short of economists to rationalize these inflationary procedures. As it happens, high-technology products replaced the older textile industries and in the late 1980s New England had for a while the lowest unemployment rate in the US without the aid of a depreciating Boston dollar.

CURRENCIES AND REGIONS

Regional problems become apparent on the ground through income disparities, unemployment differentials, population movements and similar data. We can try to decide in their light how far to transfer resources to poorer regions and how far to leave them to solve their own problems; and we can do so irrespective of balance of payments estimates.

Critics say that a single currency would just be substituting regional problems for balance of payments ones. The word 'just' is a big mistake. For if we use the balance of payments as a proxy for regional problems, we often go badly wrong. Some prosperous areas will be found to have balance of payments deficits and will be wrongly diagnosed as problem cases. An example is a rapidly developing country like Spain whose payments deficit in the 1980s was the mirror image of its success in attracting capital influx. Genuine disaster areas, on the other hand, might well show current payment surpluses.

It has been estimated that one-third of all expenditure in Northern Ireland is financed by direct transfers from Great Britain, in special programmes, military outlays, UK budget expenditures and so on. If these were to be withdrawn overnight, the province could face privation, irrespective of whether it continued to use the pound sterling, switched to the Irish punt, or had a currency of its own. Yet most of the transfers are current payments and a Northern Ireland balance of payments tabulation might well show a current surplus.

East Germany was an even clearer case. In the heyday of the so-called German Democratic Republic, a precarious solvency was maintained by forcing the population to buy products made in the GDR and neighbouring communist countries. When this compulsion went and guaranteed Comecon markets disappeared, many East German products became unsaleable. Large transfers became necessary to pay East German workers wages high enough to prevent a mass exit of able-bodied people. Even with transfers from the west, unemployment reached alarming proportions.

Uncompetitive regions have in common a market-clearing pattern of real wages felt to be too low, either by some moral criteria or by comparison with neighbouring regions. In extreme cases it may be below the subsistence minimum. In any case the result is a refusal to accept such wages; and some combination of high unemployment, dependence on transfers from outside and emigration occurs.

Fortunately, I do not have to prescribe here for all the problems of poorer regions. But one suggestion I would make is that transfers and redistribution should be concentrated on individuals and families rather than areas. It is not poor regions that are badly done by, but poor people. Poor families may be concentrated more in some places than in others, but are to be found everywhere. An attempt to freeze or eliminate regional differentials or stop all net population movements would be extremely perverse. If it had been used in England at the time of the industrial revolution it would have aborted development of the North and Midlands for the sake of protecting the South.

THE UK AS BASKET CASE

Pessimists about the UK economy believe that it is like East Germany or Northern Ireland writ large. The Cambridge economists Wynne Godley and Ken Coutts, for instance, diagnose a trend since 1960 for UK manufactured imports to rise faster than exports, culminating in the arrival in the early 1980s of a secularly increasing manufacturing deficit. Hitherto the gap had been bridged by fortuitous developments such as improving terms of trade at the expense of raw material producers, the arrival of North Sea oil and a once-for-all rise in invisible earnings. As North Sea oil had passed its peak, the inference was that the current deficit would grow to a level where it could not be covered by capital inflows at tolerable interest rates and that the check would have to come from stagnant growth and even higher unemployment than the UK experienced in the 1980s.

Sometimes writers of this school seem to be arguing for a 'competitive exchange rate' and attribute UK problems to a persistent overvaluation of sterling. Yet a moment's reflection should show that everything that could be achieved by exchange rate depreciation could also be achieved by a sufficiently low rate of inflation. The devaluationists are in the end saying that UK inflation is too deeply entrenched to be tackled directly, but that it would be possible to produce the required effects via the exchange rate back door. Either way the so-called balance of payments problem is an inflation problem in disguise.

There are pessimists about the UK who go further and seem to be saying that the tendency to uncompetitiveness would still be there even if the UK rate of inflation for tradable products were eventually to fall below that of competitor countries. The core of the Cambridge case is that the world appetite for British products is so feeble and the British appetite for imported products is so insatiable that no acceptable downward shift in the terms of trade, however achieved, would maintain competitiveness and high employment. Acceptable to whom? Presumably the wage-fixing institutions in the labour market. In that case the obvious response is to try to reform these institutions rather than interfere directly with imports and exports.

The disagreement is intractable because deep-seated political differences on the role of the state become compounded with deep-seated differences of inter-pretation of British economic data (on which other chapters, I hope, throw light). But as a straw in the wind it is worth noting that in the 30 years from the early 1960s, the UK real exchange rate was fluctuating round a very stable level – the tendency to faster British inflation being offset by spasmodic devaluation. If the UK economy conformed to the pessimists' picture we would expect to see long-term downward pressure on the real exchange rate and a sharply unfavourable trend in the terms of trade.

TOO MUCH RED INK

I have deliberately left the notorious measurement problems to the end. The fact that there is a black hole in the balance of payments figures, which tends to make the UK deficit look much larger than it is, is the most easily remembered weakness. Yet even if the figures were perfectly recorded, all the fallacies of using the balance of payments as an indicator of national solvency already elaborated would remain.

Table 8.2   UK balance of payments revisions (£bn)

	1st estimate (Dec. trade figs. press notice)	1st qtly estimate (following March)	Latest available estimate (1993 Pink Book)
Current balance			
1987	− 2.7	− 1.7	− 5.0
1988	− 14.3	− 14.7	− 16.6
1989	− 20.3	− 20.9	− 22.5
1990	− 16.1	− 12.8	− 18.3
1991	− 5.8	− 4.4	− 7.7
1992	− 11.8	− 11.9	− 8.6
Balancing item			
1987	−	+ 0.9	− 2.0
1988	−	+ 15.2	+ 6.3
1989	−	+ 16.5	+ 3.1
1990	−	+ 3.4	+ 7.3
1991	−	− 4.4	+ 0.9
1992	−	+ 9.5	+ 0.3

Source: Central Statistical Office.

The most familiar weakness is the 'balancing item' of net unrecorded receipts (see Table 8.2). In one high deficit year, 1988, Britain had a favourable balancing item of over £6 billion or nearly 40 per cent of the total deficit. In 1990 the balancing item was still higher, at over £7.3 billion. These estimates moreover are the latest available after the Central Statistical Office (CSO) had spent several years trying to reduce them. From 1992 onwards the CSO seemed more successful when it came to publish its considered estimate for a whole year.

But the earlier estimates, on which financial analysts and journalists based their instant diagnoses of the British economy, still sometimes showed enormous balancing items.

A less-parochial problem is that the current deficits and surpluses of the whole world as estimated by the IMF and other international organisations, instead of cancelling each other out, cumulate to around $100 billion per annum – or nearly two-thirds of the US current deficit at its mid-1980s peak. This is the black hole in the world economy.

There is another important measurement distortion which is conceptual and not one of data. Take a country which is in balance on goods and services, but is a net overseas borrower on fixed interest terms and which uses the proceeds to accumulate equities and purchase real capital assets. The interest on the borrowing appears as a negative item on the current account. But much of the return from overseas direct investment takes the form of capital gains which do not appear in this account. The net effect is to transform a profitable two-way operation into an apparent loss. The orders of magnitude are quite large. According to a study by Clifford Pratten, a typical annual capital gain on UK fixed overseas assets is some £6 billion per annum.

A further conceptual problem arises from the proliferation of overseas investment. Trade between firms and their overseas affiliates now accounts for more than half of the OECD total. According to a report by Dr deAnne Julius, total foreign sales by US corporations were five times the value of their recorded direct exports. If the current balance of payments had been measured according to the nationality of the owners, rather than the physical location of plants, then the US would have had a current payments surplus even in 1986. By the early 1990s the US – and not Japan – might well have had the biggest trade surplus in the world.

It is meaningless to ask which is the 'correct' measure of the current balance. The only operational figure is the amount that the finance ministry or the central bank has to spend or borrow to support its currency in the foreign exchange markets. And the policy problem when these resources run dry is whether to let the currency depreciate or raise interest rates enough to prevent this happening. These questions are best discussed in terms of output, employment and inflation without getting befogged by dubious balance of payments data.

CONCLUSION

Preoccupation with the current balance of payments as a measure of national success leads to many needless worries and policy errors. Taken literally it suggests that there should be no net international borrowing or lending. The balance of payments hang-up provides a respectable gateway for protectionism, especially, but not only, in the USA. Sometimes the preoccupation imparts an inflationary bias to policy; at other times a deflationary bias: neither is desirable. Worst of all the balance of payments approach treats trade between Sussex and nearby Normandy on an entirely different basis than trade between Sussex and more distant Yorkshire. This is particularly curious when all three are supposed to be in a Single Market. Finally, as a most important footnote, the statistics are notoriously and incurably inaccurate and on the pessimistic side, thus giving a restrictive bias to policy and inciting the financial chattering classes to alarm and despondency.

APPENDIX 1: THE MYTH OF COMPETITIVENESS

Most western industrialized countries (in which we should nowadays include Japan) are suffering from similar problems: at the time of writing (1993) these are: recession or disappointing growth; high and rising unemployment; and worries about financial institutions. Yet so strong is the human instinct to blame everything on an external enemy or opponent that the only slogan under which statesmen can agree to discuss the problem is 'lack of competitiveness'. Not only are businessmen and politicians hooked on this framework, so too are some economists who ought to know better. So I must try to explain simply what is wrong with it.

The units that compete in world trade are – heaven be praised – individual businesses and not whole nations. One can still talk about competitiveness at the national economic level in a strictly limited sense. As explained in the main body of this chapter, a country may have cost levels, at prevailing exchange rates, which are so high as to undermine solvency or to threaten jobs which would otherwise be safe. In this sense the UK may have been uncompetitive – as some of us saw only with hindsight – at the ERM exchange rate at which it joined the ERM in October 1990, before being forced out less than two years later.

The UK competitiveness problem was dealt with, at least for a time, by the 1992 devaluation. In the past the benefits of devaluation were eroded by inflation. If this happens again – and it need not – then the UK will be seen to have a *real competitiveness* problem and one which cannot be tackled by monetary or exchange rate manipulation.

But if not only the UK but most other countries are in a position where labour costs are too great for high employment, then it ceases to make sense to talk of competitiveness. *For competitiveness is a relative concept; and we cannot all be uncompetitive against each other.* The last international figure whom I remember making the point was Emil van Lennep, the Dutch Secretary General of the OECD in the 1970s. Van Lennep firmly rejected any diagnosis of the common problems of his member countries in terms of competitiveness. 'Against whom should the OECD as a whole be more competitive? Against the developing world? Against the moon?' The problem was and is performance, not competitiveness.

Since then, of course, many have asserted that there is indeed a threat from the non-OECD world, in particular the Asian developing countries and the former communist countries of Europe. The real reason why these countries are unlikely to impose an unsupportable threat to jobs in the west is that they do not export to line their bank vaults with yen, dollar and D-mark notes, but in order to import. Western sales lost in home markets to these new competitors should be compensated by extra purchases by these countries of western products. Indeed, with their urgent needs for imports from the west, it is inconceivable that the developing or former communist countries should try to undervalue their currencies to maintain an export surplus. Their desire, for very good reason, is for the largest imports they can finance.*

The area against which the EC had clearly lost competitiveness in the early 1990s was the US. But the Clinton Administration was vociferous about the US not being competitive enough. The competitiveness approach thus soon deteriorates into a zero-sum game in which world output and employment seem, quite wrongly, to be fixed and in which one group can only gain at the expense of another.

These general thoughts may be of cold comfort to Western European steel, textile or coal producers who feel themselves threatened; but the threat is to staying in the same jobs at the same pay rates – not to overall job levels. If the seemingly inexorable rise in European unemployment from one business cycle to the next does not just reflect uncompetitiveness against other regions then what does it represent? John Major gave basically the correct explanation in many speeches he made in Europe in 1993 when he spoke of excessive pay rises, high social overheads, the European Commission Working Time Directive and other regulations which make labour too expensive. All these things, however, would still be a threat to jobs if they were present in all countries and blocs to the same extent.

---

* Even if they did wish to main export surpluses, in Japanese fashion, this would still not be a threat to western jobs, provided that the surpluses led to higher world investment. But as the analysis is then much more complicated, we can concentrate on the simpler case, corresponding to reality, where the new exporters import at least as much as they can earn abroad.

APPENDIX 2: THE MANUFACTURING FALLACY*

Three old codgers are sitting at their favourite café eating baked beans from a tin bearing a House of Lords crest. They decide to discuss 'economics'.

'Agriculture is the basis of everything,' says the first one, mouth full of beans. 'Everything else depends on it, you know.'

'Rubbish,' says the second ancient, banging his dish on the table. 'Without manufacturing we would have to sit on the ground and eat with our fingers. In any case we can buy all the food we want in exchange for factory products.'

'And rubbish to both of you,' says the third codger. 'Services create the demand for manufactures. These chairs, knives and forks are only needed to keep the service sector going,' pointing to Old Bill hovering by the cash desk. 'Most of the cost of our meal is service, as well.'

Old Bill has however been mugging up on his political economy and shows all three the door. 'Can't you see that the economy is interdependent?' he says. 'The consumer decides the final mix; and there are no grounds for regarding any particular sector as more fundamental than any other'.

'In any case the boundaries mean less and less. Look at Gubbins over there, a staff journalist. He is in the manufacturing sector. His drinking companion, Muggins, who works freelance for foreign papers, is in services. Funny things, statistics.'

The much-trumpeted 1985 House of Lords Report on Overseas Trade was on the same level of pleading as the three old codgers; but it contained no Old Bill to put them right. The committee was chaired by Lord Aldington, chairman of GEC, 1964–84. Its leading spirits included well known corporatists, such as Lord Kearton and Lord Ezra. The committee's motto seemed to be: 'What is good enough for GEC is good enough for Britain.' (GEC is a major beneficiary of government spending, especially on defence.)

The report is full of sentences such as 'Your committee does not believe', or 'We cannot accept ...'. But its loudest assertions are unsubstantiated; for example, that only 20 per cent of services are internationally tradable. An analysis by the British Invisible Exports Council suggests that while 25 per cent of all employees work in manufacturing, some 40 per cent work in the *internationally tradable* services sector.

Why does manufacturing have such sex appeal? Maybe because Britain led the original industrial revolution. Maybe too because large firms and trade unions are both more dominant in manufacturing than in private sectors, which makes for more effective political lobbying.

---

* This appendix is mainly based on a *Financial Times* article on the Aldington Report on Overseas Trade entitled 'Coronets and Begging Bowls', which appeared on 17 October 1985. A few paragraphs from later articles have also been inserted.

Manufacturing is also often lazily equated with 'industry', which in turn is equated with the whole of the national economy. And it is true that the output of metal boxes is easier to measure than, say, financial services or tourist provision. The Aldington Committee takes advantage of the confusion by including almost every cliché and commonplace everyone has ever uttered about the British economy, and tries to shift the meaning of these clichés by substituting 'manufacturing' when it ought to say 'output' or 'national economy'.

The Aldington report is a mirror image of a similar campaign for a US industrial strategy which Walter Mondale was unwise enough to make his own in his unsuccessful 1984 presidential campaign. The committee's own report shows manufacturing falling as a proportion of GDP in all the main industrial countries. On both sides of the Atlantic the relative decline in manufacturing has been aggravated by macro factors; the budget deficit and capital inflow in the American case, and displacement of traditional exports by oil in the British case. In both countries businessmen, impatient with these matters, sought subsidies or protection which could only set off trade wars without even improving the manufacturing balance.

The British Treasury incurred the wrath of Aldington by pointing out that North Sea oil led to a displacement of manufacturing exports; and that as the oil surplus runs off, the balance in non-fuel trade, including manufactures, will improve again. This is indeed what will happen.

A sensible policy would be to allow the real exchange rate to move to offset real forces such as the running off of North Sea oil, or differential changes in other countries' subsidies, while keeping a *firm* nominal exchange rate so as not to accommodate inflationary cost pressures (the key distinction is hardly discussed by the committee).

APPENDIX 3: A WEALTH OR SAVINGS TARGET?

Suppose one accepts that the difference between internal and external trade has been exaggerated by the balance of payments school. Even so, some will say, it is not sufficient for a government merely to keep its own budget in order and maintain an inflation or exchange rate objective. Both of these can be achieved and yet the nation can be consuming its seed-corn; that is, running down its capital stock. For this reason some economists have urged a wealth or savings objective to safeguard against inadequate savings. Unlike the manufacturing and competitiveness fallacies, a wealth objective is not a crude error and deserves to be taken seriously.

The advocates of a wealth objective have at least seen through the inadequacies of targeting the current balance of payments. They have no objection to net overseas borrowing as such. But the liabilities accruing to overseas residents are a subtraction from national wealth or capital. On the other hand, national wealth gains from the appreciation in the value of existing overseas investment, even when there is no current surplus to reinvest. It also gains from a rise in the amount or effectiveness of domestic capital, both of which can more than offset the negative effect of overseas borrowing.

The wealth objective would thus achieve more effectively what the balance of payments target attempts to do very crudely: namely, to provide a safeguard against a country enjoying a high level of consumption by living on tick and storing up trouble for the future. It would have the additional advantage that each country could pick its own wealth objective without requiring the very difficult international co-ordination that the balance of payments objectives require. There would be no beggar-my-neighbour aspects to its pursuit.

Nevertheless, there are in my view three important objections: conceptual, practical, and of principle. The national wealth can be meaningfully measured only at fairly long intervals. Currency and stock exchange fluctuations produce such erratic movements in the overseas capital component that it would be undesirable even to attempt a regular year-to-year tally. For instance the official estimates of net UK overseas assets have fluctuated in the decade from the early 1980s between below zero and £100 billion.

Even over the longer term the conceptual difficulties are immense. An example is provided by what happened to UK real national wealth between 1957 and 1985. If the market value of national assets is adjusted by a general price index, it appeared to have risen by 200 per cent. If, on the other hand, it is deflated by an index of asset prices – which reflects the sharp rise in property values relative to the general inflation rate – then the increase is only 85 per cent.

It is tempting to look for some short cut, such as a savings target (national, not personal) or an investment target adjusted for overseas indebtedness, which amounts to the same thing. A savings target became part of Liberal Democrat policy at its 1991 conference.

So-called savings incentives mainly switch personal savings from one channel to another. The crux of the suggestion is that fiscal policy should be tightened to improve the national savings ratio. Unfortunately, there is a good deal of evidence that swings in private savings tend to offset movements in government savings.

The British case is by no means unique. Between 1983 and 1991 there was, for instance, a sharp swing from deficit to surplus in the Australian budget amounting to over 5 percentage points of GDP. Yet the current payments deficit did not improve. Over the same period, Sweden enjoyed a swing towards surplus in the budget of about 6 percentage points of GDP, yet the payments deficit deteriorated. In these other countries a rise in government savings was offset by a fall in the private variety.

I do not want to go to the other extreme and say that all savings in the structural Budget balance will be offset by opposite private movements. In Germany after reunification the Budget deficit shot up and the payments surplus vanished just as the fiscalists would have expected. The weakness of the link between the Budget balance and total savings is, however, sufficient to throw doubt on hairshirt fiscal economics.

The fundamental objection to a savings target enforced through a Budget surplus is, however, one of liberal principle. There is not the slightest reason to suppose that governments, who have to bid for votes every four or five years, are better than individuals and firms at deciding how much consumption to forgo for future needs. Moreover, the whole idea of forced additional savings puts, like most such ideas, all the emphasis on the quantity as distinct from the quality of new investment resulting therefrom. The former communist countries had much higher savings and investment ratios than their counterparts in Western Europe and will spend many years coping with their economic legacy.

REFERENCES

Bayoumi, Tamin, *Saving Investment Correlations. Immobile Capital: Government Policy or Endogenous Behaviour?*, Washington, D.C.: International Monetary Fund, 1985.

Bean, Charles, 'The External Constraints in the UK', in G.A. Algosofoukis *et al.*, *External Constraints on Macroeconomic Policy*, Cambridge: Cambridge University Press, 1981.

Brittan, S., *The Price of Economic Freedom: A Guide to Flexible Rates*, London: Macmillan, 1990.

Central Statistical Office, *Balance of Payments Pink Book*, London: HMSO, annual.

Coutts, K. and W. Godley, *Cambridge Journal of Economics*, (1991).

Davies, Gavyn, *Oxford Review of Economic Policy*, special issue on the Balance of Payments, Autumn 1990.

Horam, John, *Making Britain Competitive*, London: Conservative Political Centre, 1993.

Hume, David, 'Of the Balance of Trade', in *Essays, Moral, Political and Literary*, 1741–2; Indianapolis: Liberty Classics, 1985.

McCombie, J. and A. Thirlwall, *The Balance of Payments Constraint*, London: Macmillan, 1992.

Pratten, Clifford, *Overseas Investment, Capital Gains and the Balance of Payments*, Department of Applied Economics, Cambridge University, 1991.

9   The role of the exchange rate[*]

AN ISSUE IN ITS OWN RIGHT

Should a medium-sized industrial country have an exchange rate objective? Such objectives have been a characteristic of fully fledged exchange rate regimes, such as the Bretton Woods arrangements or the European Exchange Rate Mechanism. Under the former, which prevailed from the Second World War until President Richard Nixon floated the dollar in 1971, countries outside the US obtained fixed a parity against the dollar which they changed very rarely and with the greatest reluctance. In the heyday of the ERM, to which most European Community countries adhered from 1979 to 1993, and which the UK briefly joined for the two years 1990–2, there was a similar objective against the German mark.

There can, however, be more informal arrangements, such as the attempts to stabilize major world parities within undisclosed target ranges undertaken at the Plaza and Louvre accords in 1985–7. Even without such arrangements, exchange rates have figured in monetary policy decisions all the way from an unofficial exchange rate target (such as 'shadowing the mark') to the 'taking into account' of sterling in setting monetary policy, so beloved by British Treasury officials.

How far is it sensible to have any such objective? Or should governments concentrate on what the then Chancellor, Norman Lamont, speaking after ERM membership was suspended in September 1992, called 'a British policy in British interests' without worrying too much about the exchange rate? This would of course be paralleled by 'a French policy in French interests' and so on, with all the interactions involved.

This seemingly technical question derives its sex appeal from the wider European political debate. Some of those who favoured the ERM wanted an exchange rate arrangement because they saw it as a step towards full monetary union, which in turn they believed would lead to a political union. Others detested European exchange rate arrangements for precisely the same reasons and were delighted, first when the UK was forced to leave and then when the

---

[*] Although I have drawn on material scattered in many articles and lectures, this is basically a new essay, which was obviously required after the disintegration of the original European Exchange Rate Mechanism in 1992–3.

whole ERM came apart in August 1993, because they saw these events as nails in the coffin of European federalism.

What, however, I would like to do in this chapter is to concentrate on the exchange rate as an issue in its own right, worth discussing in terms of economic policy. What is involved is simply the latest version of an age-old conflict between what might be called 'monetarism in one country' and 'exchange rate monetarism'. I shall also assume that the principal way to influence the exchange rate is by domestic monetary policy, whether this is thought of in terms of a nominal interest rate or some measure of the money supply. The highly technical and controversial question of the effect of official intervention in a foreign exchange market can be set aside: even its most enthusiastic supporters see it as no more than a short-term operation for buying time. Exchange controls (that is, controls on money moving across currency frontiers) are also not considered. Not only are they inherently undesirable distortions, but they are powerless to safeguard a seriously troubled currency – as the British Labour Chancellor, Sir Stafford Cripps, discovered when he was forced to devalue in 1949, despite the continued existence after the Second World War of the fiercest exchange controls the country had ever seen.

LESSONS OF THE COUNTER-REVOLUTION

Chapter 7 has explained the counter-revolution in economic thinking, which overthrew the belief that governments and central banks could spend their way into desired levels of employment and growth by sufficiently expansionary monetary or fiscal policies. A more plausible picture is of an underlying level of unemployment, known as the non-accelerating inflation rate of unemployment or NAIRU, consistent with any stable rate of inflation, and which can only be improved by supply-side policies to enhance the working of labour and other markets.

The great advantage once claimed for exchange rate depreciation as a policy weapon was that it enabled national authorities to stimulate their economies without a run on their currencies. In the jargon of the economics trade, countries could choose their own point on the trade-off between inflation and unemployment. If, however, such a stimulus does not lead to more growth or jobs but merely a faster or runaway rate of inflation, then the exchange rate becomes much less valuable as a policy tool. *It also becomes much less important as an exercise in national sovereignty.* For the right being exercised is that to have a faster rate of inflation in one country than in its trading partners; and what sensible person would go to the stake for that?

There is an obvious qualification to be made immediately. It is possible, as explained in Chapter 7, for unemployment to be above the NAIRU. This is what is meant by a slump or recession. During such periods inflation will fall, but at the cost of lost output and jobs. If a country enters into a currency link with its trading partners at an overvalued exchange rate, then the loss of output can be painful. The conventional historical example has been of Winston Churchill's return to the gold standard at the pre-First World War parity in 1925. (It is still not clear whether there was a similar overvaluation when sterling joined the ERM at DM2.95 in 1990, or whether it was special factors such as those associated with German reunification which drove the UK out of the ERM in 1992 and caused the ERM itself to totter a year later.)

The pains of overvaluation are a reason for taking care to enter any international exchange rate system at an appropriate level and to be prepared to make a few initial parity adjustments to seek out the appropriate rate. They do not amount to a case for flexible rates as a permanent arrangement.

EXCHANGE RATES AND INFLATION

If a country is trying to bring down and then stabilize its inflation rate it has, as a former British Chancellor, Nigel Lawson, has explained in his memoirs (Chapter 33), four main options, singly or in combination:

1.   a nominal GDP objective;
2.   a direct price-level target;
3.   a money supply target;
4.   an exchange rate objective.

Both money supply and exchange rate targets are rightly called 'intermediate objectives' because they are valuable not in their own right but as a means to stable non-inflationary growth. There is nothing illogical in favouring one of the above options in one country at one time and a different option in another country at another time.

As Lawson has written, the choice between them is mainly a matter of time and place. 'To go on heresy hunts against those whose intermediate objectives are different from one's own would be laughable if it were not for the damaging effects of such scholastic controversies on the British politico-economic debate and on the supposedly common sense Tory Party in particular.'

An exchange rate link does, however, have one clear consequence. It ties together the price levels of the countries in the arrangement. Let us imagine that there is a country called Teutonia which has managed to secure rough price stability over a long period and which puts price stability first in its monetary policy. Then let us assume that two trading partners, which we will call Gallia and Offshoria, fix their own exchange rates against Teutonia and adjust monetary policy in whatever way is necessary to maintain the link. Then inflation rates in Gallia and Offshoria will eventually approximate to that of Teutonia.(I have used these typecast names to avoid prejudging whether the new united Germany still qualifies as Teutonia.)

The case for an inflation-prone country such as Offshoria pegging the currency to that of a country such as Teutonia arises because of the enormous difficulty many countries in Offshoria's position have had in selecting purely domestic monetary targets which will provide for the non-inflationary growth of nominal demand. It may also be easier for wage bargainers to grasp an exchange rate constraint, under which they will be priced out of international markets if they engage in inflationary settlements, than to grasp money supply targets whose meaning is in dispute on the City pages of newspapers. In addition, an exchange rate objective embodied in international treaties and which is monitored in the market every day can carry greater credibility than the small print of a domestic financial strategy.

The above applies, of course, so long as the international arrangements are upheld as they were in the ERM in the 1980s. But once the arrangement is split asunder, as the ERM was after the end of July 1993 when the currency margins were widened to 15 per cent following the French franc crisis, the credibility argument is shattered and will take a time to make it convincing again.

What kind of price stability can such an exchange rate arrangement provide when in working order? It is primarily stability in the prices of tradable goods and services – tradable in the sense of moving across the frontiers of the country or region concerned. Manufactured goods are especially prominent here, but there are plenty of traded services, ranging from tourism to investment banking. Let us assume that Teutonia has complete price stability including price stability for traded products. Then market forces will ensure that Offshoria's traded products will not rise in price in the long run.

What will happen to sheltered sectors such as building, the retail trade and other services which are not so exposed to international competition? Suppose that pay and productivity in Offshoria's internationally exposed sector are both rising by 4 per cent per annum. Then, as a first approximation, there will be zero inflation for internationally tradable products. It is also likely that labour market forces will ensure that pay in the protected sector will not in the long run rise by very much more or less than 4 per cent. What will happen to the overall national inflation rate will then depend on productivity in the sheltered sector. Suppose that it rises by 1 per cent per annum. Then the inflation rate in that sector will be around 3 per cent and the national inflation rate will be a weighted average of the two sectors; that is, somewhere between zero and 3 per cent.

The most celebrated case of differential price increases in the two sectors was in Japan in the decades before 1980 when consumer price inflation was among the highest of the main industrial countries. Japan nevertheless remained internationally competitive without devaluation because of exceptionally rapid productivity growth in the manufactured sector which was exposed to international trade.

The potential difference between inflation rates among European countries with broadly similar industrial structures and linked by fixed exchange rates is very much less. According to a 1989 London Business School estimate, the potential gap emanating from differential performance in the non-traded sector is no more than 2 per cent. This has been confirmed by a Bank of England study.

Thus if Offshoria's currency is linked to a non-inflationary one such as Teutonia's, there is no way that Offshoria's inflation can soar out of control. Equally, if Offshoria's exchange rate depreciates over a long period – as sterling did when it depreciated from DM11 to the pound in 1967 to under DM3 in the late 1980s – then there is no way in which Offshoria can avoid a much faster inflation rate.

There are other arguments for exchange rate objectives beyond those of counterinflationary policy. Contrary to the predictions of floating rate enthusiasts (of whom I was one) before the adoption of generalized floating in the early 1970s, floating rates have been prone to large under- and over-shooting. The US dollar first doubled in value against the mark and then halved in the first seven years of the 1980s, in a way that did not correspond to comparative inflation performance, the balance of payments or even interest rate differentials. The cost in terms of dislocation for American firms, who first had to swing from the international to the domestic market and then to shift back again to exports as the dollar depreciated, was large. An even greater cost was the encouragement given to protectionist sentiments. It is true that from the late 1980s to the early 1990s swings between the dollar and the mark were more subdued, but there was the danger of another switchback occurring in relation to the Japanese yen.[*]

An effective international stabilization arrangement which smoothed out the worst medium-term fluctuations, without setting up an unrealistic target for

---

[*] Attempts have been made to show that the exchange rate fluctuations incurred during periods of floating rates have little impact on the real economy. One of the most interesting is that by Mills and Wood on UK experience. But there are many problems in such studies. The greatest is that floating rates are a relatively rare historical experience, and that a great deal of weight has to be placed on experience since 1972. Moreover, I doubt if the statistical concept of year-to-year volatility captures the full effects of medium-term swings in exchange rates of the kind discussed in the text.

currency operators to speculate against, would help. Admittedly the arrangement is more easily prescribed than accomplished. But there are two further objectives which require, if not a single currency, at least a monetary union or an exchange rate link so close as to amount to the same thing:

1. *Reducing money-changing or transaction costs.* These have been put by the European Commission at about $\frac{1}{2}$ per cent of GDP. This is important but hardly decisive. The nuisance value for individuals is more important than the financial costs to companies; but they can be improved by refinements in bank transfer techniques before a single currency is reached.
2. *Elimination of exchange rate risks.* The potential gains here are much greater. Uncertainty about what the pound is going to be worth in relation to other currencies is one big reason – although not of course the only one – why British businessmen are reluctant to treat the European Community as a single market in the sense that the United States is seen as a single market.

The ferocious debate, however, has not been on these issues but on whether currency links help or hinder the control of inflation and the avoidance of instability and depression.

NOT LIKE THE PRICE OF TOMATOES

Sensible domestic monetarists will avoid saying that the price of, say, sterling, is just a price like that of tomatoes and should be of no more concern to policymakers. Such sentiments do not survive a few moments' critical reflection. For unlike the price of tomatoes, the exchange rate is the link between the national price level and that of the rest of the world. If the price of tomatoes doubles, there need be no sizeable effect on inflation. But if sterling falls by 50 per cent a large number of UK prices will eventually double too.

The domestic monetarist can, however, focus on another truth. This is that if there is a pegged exchange rate between two countries, and the peg carries credibility, then interest rates expressed in the two currencies must be roughly the same. Yet an interest rate which suits one may be very unsuitable for another.

The main argument against an exchange rate anchor is that it imposes a similar interest rate policy in countries whose domestic circumstances may require very different rates. The original statement of the 'Walters critique' was that a country with a high rate of inflation would have to have the same nominal interest rate as a country with low inflation. In a sense this was too easy an answer. For it took no account of either the $2\frac{1}{4}$ per cent bands in the ERM around the central parities or the possibility of making modest changes in the central parity itself.

If, in our example, Teutonia stuck fast to a non-inflationary policy, Gallia could maintain higher nominal interest rates because of the market expectations that its exchange rate would gradually move down. Indeed, interest rates were higher in France than in Germany for most of the 1980s, but the inhibition on the extent and frequency of devaluations imposed a downward pressure on the French inflation rate. The possibility of moderate realignments just gave France a safety valve until inflation convergence was completed.

Both sides in the argument in the late 1980s failed (as so often) to envisage what the true problem would be. This was that after unification Germany required a much *higher* real interest rate than France to offset the inflationary effects of very high budgetary expenditures. By the time the ERM came apart, French inflation had for three years been less than the German rate. But the markets still had not sufficient confidence in this superior performance enduring; and currency holders came to the conclusion that an interest rate policy geared to fighting recession would be quite incompatible with maintaining the *franc fort*. Hence the run on the franc and the widening of the ERM margins to 15 per cent in August 1993.

The costs of the D-mark link could be illustrated by the behaviour of French real short-term interest rates which were nearly $7^1/_2$ per cent in 1992 compared with less than 1 per cent in the USA, which was free to set interest rates from a domestic point of view.

LIMITED INDEPENDENCE

There is, however, a tendency to exaggerate the room for real interest rate variations under flexible exchange rates. *Short-term* interest rates are then obviously much freer to vary between countries. This is not true of long-term real interest rates.

The fact is that in a world of free capital markets real long-term rates tend to converge. This is a more fundamental sense of 'not being able to buck the market' than Lady Thatcher ever had in mind in her famous remark after she stopped her Chancellor shadowing the mark in March 1988.

In a single free capital market there will be one prevailing long-term rate of interest. This long-term rate can be regarded as either the prevailing long bond rate or the expected average of short-term interest rates, appropriately discounted. These two measures must be consistent with each other; otherwise there would be easy profits to be made from moving from short- to long-term fixed interest securities, or vice versa.

In practice, bond rates in different countries are not, of course, identical. But an individual country's can differ from the going international rate – default risks apart – only by a currency premium or discount, reflecting the expected appreciation or depreciation of the currency against other main currencies.

The expected movement of a currency will, over a sufficient period of years, in its turn mainly reflect expected inflation differentials. Thus, long-term interest rates in Offshoria or Gallia can only be lower than those in Teutonia if the expected inflation rate is expected to be lower. The most optimistic likely case is that they will be expected to remain the same.

What flexible exchange rates then permit is temporary variations in either direction in *short-term interest rates*. In some circumstances, this may be a valuable degree of freedom but it is, of course, limited.

To give a specific example: US one-year nominal interest rates were 4 percentage points below German ones on 1 October 1993 and the dollar was expected to appreciate by 4 per cent against the mark over the year ahead. This may have been quite useful when the US needed low short-term rates to combat the debt overhang and the associated recession. But if you look at the gap in real interest rates over the years, the differential went first one way and then the other with a tendency to balance out over the years (see Figure 9.1).

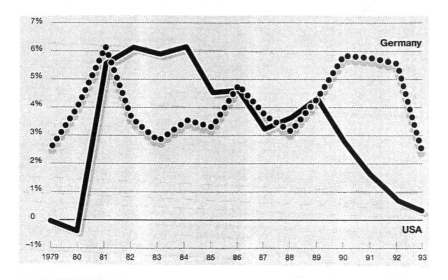

Sources: HM Treasury, and Datastream.

Figure 9.1   Real interest rates compared: three-month rates (interbank rates deflated by year's change in Consumer Price Index)

For a country trying to stabilize its currency after decades of inflation and depreciation, the choice is illustrated in Figure 9.2. If Offshoria could carry out a successful domestic monetary policy, the result might look like the line marked 'successful floating'. There would be periods – say, during domestic recession – when nominal interest rates would be lower in Offshoria than in Teutonia. There would be other periods – say, after a burst of credit liberalisation such as the UK experienced in the mid-1980s – when rates would be higher in Offshoria. There would be corresponding fluctuations in exchange rates; but over the long term there would be little trend one way or the other.

Even if those in charge of monetary policy never looked at the exchange rate and only at domestic monetary variables, their success in doing so would ensure that the exchange rate followed a horizontal trend, despite short-term variations on either side.

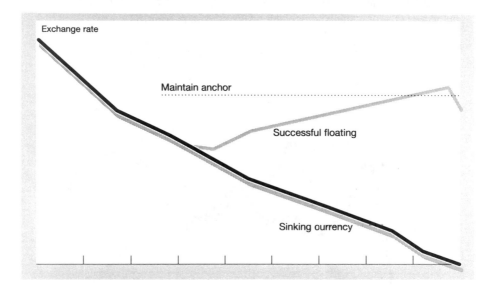

Figure 9.2   An anchor versus a floating or sinking exchange rate

A flexible rate can thus provide no more than an opportunity for a temporary deviation from the international interest norm. For instance, American short-term real interest rates could be well below those of Western Europe in 1992–3 because the dollar was regarded as depressed and likely to recover. This temporary deviation may have been useful, as was the UK move to lower short-term interest rates after September 1992. But there was no way either country could run a programme of real interest rates below prevailing international levels indefinitely.

The risks of going it alone should now be pretty clear. For in the situation shown in the figure it would be terribly tempting for Offshoria to let its exchange rate slide just that fatal bit too long. Its rulers are unlikely to know enough about monetary relationships to tighten up in time, after which inflationary expectations would become reinforced and high costs entrenched. After that the transitional output and job costs of bringing the exchange rate up to the horizontal line will seem to be (and will be) too high. Thus there will be strong pressures for Offshoria to continue on the path of inflation and depreciation shown by the diagonal line. When an anchor is available, as the mark was in the 1980s, there are thus powerful reasons for countries with adverse inflationary records and expectations to make use of it, which in the then prevailing circumstances meant adhering to the ERM.

THE BALANCE OF ARGUMENT

It is not difficult to state the factors to be balanced in deciding whether to stick to a currency anchor or to a domestically based sound-money policy and a flexible exchange rate. The advantage of a flexible exchange rate is that it provides some *temporary* scope to adopt a tighter or looser money policy than the anchor country's. The advantage of a pegged exchange rate is the reduction in transaction and uncertainty costs, combined with the greater anti-inflationary credibility that might come with the exchange rate link. If such credibility is achieved a lower nominal rate of interest might suffice to attain any given inflation goal. The reality of this consideration was shown in the 1980s when the gap between French and German nominal interest rates, both short-term and long-term, narrowed dramatically as currency realignments became rarer and smaller.

For a country with a good anti-inflation record such as Switzerland the credibility argument would not apply, and the choice about how close a link to keep with the mark would depend on whether the advantages of short-term monetary flexibility did or did not outweigh the reduction in transactions and uncertainty costs emanating from a Swiss frank–D-mark link.

The difficulty arises when there is no anchor currency available. A former anchor currency may become unsuitable because its national authorities have embarked on a more inflationary policy, as the US did during the Vietnam War. Alternatively it might become unsuitable because of a domestic shock which requires a monetary policy different from its neighbours for a stretch of several years, as was the case with Germany after re-unification.

Many economists will suspect that, if it had not been for the Vietnam War and German re-unification, some other event would have occurred to derail both the Bretton Woods Agreement and the ERM. Both depended on the good fortune that the domestic interest of the anchor currency's country coincided with that of trading partners. Even without the shocks just mentioned there would have been moves to internationalize policy so that stability did not depend on slavishly and consistently following the wisdom of the Fed and the Bundesbank respectively. Indeed, one of the avowed motives in the plan to move from the ERM to full monetary union and to replace the Bundesbank by a European central bank was precisely to reduce the financial hegemony of Germany.

Whether it would be possible, without going that far, for a committee of sound-money national authorities or central banks to provide an anchor is unknown. The European Monetary Institute, to be set up at the beginning of 1994, may provide more evidence. Although originally envisaged as a mere preliminary step before the establishment of the European Central Bank, it will be under pressure to act as a stabilizing body in its own right.

MAINTAINING NOMINAL DEMAND

The critical reader may wonder how I reconcile my belief in an objective for nominal GDP, outlined in Chapter 7, with an exchange rate anchor. (Nominal GDP can be translated in simple terms as a national – or international –cash flow objective.) When an anchor system is working successfully there is little problem. The anchor country will follow a monetary policy which is expansionary enough to permit non-inflationary growth, but tight enough to prevent an inflationary take-off. It does not matter how the policy is labelled as long as it make sense in these terms.

Troubles arise when the path for nominal demand followed by the anchor country produces excessive or deficient demand growth for a wider area. This will be a serious problem if there have been economic shocks, as in the early 1990s when the debt overhang and resulting recession argued for cheap money in many European countries, while re-unification pressures still pointed to tight policy in Germany.

At this stage the hegemonic approach no longer suffices and it becomes necessary to envisage a concerted international policy toward nominal demand, preferably among the main industrial countries whose leaders come together at the G7 summit (the US, Japan, Germany, France, the UK, Italy and Canada) or at the very least among core members of the European Community. Just as France cannot just go its own way and has had to take account of its partners' interests in trade and agriculture, so Germany will have to do on the monetary side.

This is so irrespective of the exchange rate regime. After a deep recession, such as that of the early 1980s, or a prolonged one, such as in the early 1990s, it becomes natural for commentators who are neither inflationists nor unreconstructed Keynesians to ask whether the world might not be entering a new phase, where the dangers may be at least as much those of inadequate demand and medium-term recessionary pressures as of inflation. There is no need to dismiss inflation as 'yesterday's problem' to be aware of this danger. Nor is there any need for confident predictions. It is sensible to insure against storms or fire without being sure about how likely they are to occur.

It is particularly unfortunate that some countries, including the UK, have recoiled from their experiences with both monetary and exchange rate targets by going for inflation objectives alone. At least the old simple-minded monetarism was theoretically a bulwark against depression as well as inflation. This was because of the relationship it asserted between chosen measures of money and nominal GDP. The relationship meant that, once inflation declined, output would automatically recover so long as the monetary targets held.

A collapse of confidence in such relationships does not mean that policy need be helpless. It does mean that governments and central banks cannot have an objective for inflation alone, but need one for some measure of total cash spending such as nominal GDP or aggregate domestic expenditure.

The need for such a cash objective is one that I have been trying to hammer home since the late 1970s as a way of saving the valid insights of both monetarism and Keynesianism from their misleading technocratic wrappings. The main evolution in my thinking has been on the need to move this objective to an inter-national plane. The UK departure from the ERM and the subsequent crumbling of the system itself has made such a perspective more rather than less necessary.

Irrespective of whether or not there is to be a European currency and a European Central Bank, there needs to be a concerted monetary policy for the whole Community designed to produce enough cash spending for the whole area but without resumed inflation. It was lack of such a concerted policy which undermined both the ERM and the wider attempts at a Group of Seven currency policy.

The UK's relative success in achieving a faster rate of growth than its European partners after it left the ERM in 1992 may have given an altogether misleading impression of how easy it is for a single country to go it alone in the face of world depression or stagnation. The 1992 British devaluation was a special event, taking place when downward pressures on inflation were excep-tionally severe. Indeed the Governor of the Bank of England, Eddie George, came to the conclusion that, at the original ERM parity, the UK 'might have actually had falling prices'. This would in his view have inflicted unnecessar-ily severe damage on the real economy. Nevertheless repeated devaluation in more usual circumstances will bring its normal inflationary consequences.

There is a further danger if countries try to stimulate their domestic economies by increased overseas sales on depressed world markets. In such circumstances they can only increase their share at the expense of other countries, which is a no-win game. Deficient demand may be a less frequent risk than depression-mongers suppose, and the self-stabilizing forces may be a great deal stronger. But depressed periods do occur and a concerted international macroeconomic policy would be of use here, as it would be if the more frequent danger of excess demand and inflation were to recur.

A NOTE ON CURRENCY COMPETITION

In Radical Right circles the slogan of competitive currencies became fashionable, as an alternative to both managed exchange rates and European monetary union. Exponents rarely distinguished between whether they meant competition between national currencies or the establishment of competitive private-enterprise currencies as well.

The proposals were marred by two further weaknesses. First, their proponents rarely identified the political and legal obstacles to such competition. In Britain, at least, there was nothing to stop people making contracts in marks, francs, dollars, gold cowrie shells or whatever other unit they liked. Although there are restrictions on private-enterprise note issue, deposits can be made in a great variety of outlets and denominations, subject only to prudential banking supervision.

Secondly, those who write about past periods of supposed currency competition, for example among Scottish banks in the early nineteenth century, forget to add that in those days money was automatically regarded as consisting of precious metals. The competition was not between alternative currencies but between alternative IOUs among institutions ultimately professing their readiness to convert their obligations into precious metals.

Despite experience of dealing with more than one currency in border areas, history suggests that private citizens and businesses alike find it convenient to make payments and account for transactions in a single medium and that they need extremely severe and prolonged experience of strato-inflation before they will drift to another one.

If there were to be a single European currency it would be very important for it not to be given a privileged monopoly position. There should be no question of people being forced to use it. There is indeed a very strong case, hinted at earlier in this chapter, for a common world currency as a substitute for national currencies, not merely of the European Community but of the rest of the advanced industrial world. More limited local currencies might then continue to exist side by side. Any attempt to suppress them would be a sign of lack of self-confidence by the managers of world money.

Nevertheless, as far ahead as can be seen, monetary nationalism will be a much greater threat than enforced currency centralization. Genuine economic liberals who are, for whatever reason, against a European single currency, deceive themselves if they make common cause with economic and political jingoists and slogan-mongers about national sovereignty.

REFERENCES

George, Eddie, Evidence to the Treasury and Civil Service Committee, 11 March 1993, published in *Fourth Report of TCSC, Session, 1992–93*, London: HMSO, 21 April 1993.

Lawson, Nigel, *The View from Number Eleven*, London: Bantam Press, 1992.

Mellis, C.L., *Tradable and Non-tradable Prices in the UK and EC*, Bank of England Working Paper no. 15, June 1993.

Mills, T.C. and G.E. Wood, 'Does the Exchange Rate Regime Affect the Economy?', *Federal Reserve Bank of St Louis Review*, Summer 1993.

Walters, Alan, *Britain's Economic Renaissance*, Oxford: Oxford University Press, 1986.

PART FOUR

Problems and Policies

10 The Thatcher government's economic legacy*

This essay was originally a contribution to a book examining the policy record of the Thatcher government, timed to coincide with the tenth anniversary of that government in 1989. It had therefore to be written towards the end of 1988. I have not tried to amend it in substance; the changes are limited to modest factual corrections, slight stylistic and tense improvements and adjustments to reduce overlapping with other chapters. The few comments made with hindsight are in square brackets and at the very end. The tables and charts are an exception to this self-denying ordinance. They have been updated in 1993. For there is no point in providing needlessly out-of-date statistics; and the information may have independent value.

To evaluate the Thatcher legacy, the evidence of at least one, and probably more, complete business cycles after Lady Thatcher's departure would be necessary. The Thatcher government's term of office covered almost exactly a single cycle, from the peak of 1979 to the subsequent peak of 1988–90. Attempts to update my preliminary judgements part of the way through the immediately following cycle would be more risky than helpful. For one of the intriguing features of the Thatcher years is that the economic verdict has swung about so much, depending on the time of evaluation.

INTRODUCTION AND OVERVIEW

A very conscientious economic historian, Professor Nick Crafts of Warwick, has identified the problems of the British economy as 'weak management, poor industrial relations, ineffective research and development, and low levels of vocational training'. Moreover, overmanning for a long time reduced the benefits from new technology. This is familiar and unsensational. It was the refrain of the post-war Anglo-American productivity teams, and could probably have been applied at any time over the last century.

Unfortunately, and quoting from Crafts once again, both Labour and Conservative governments were 'seduced into ill-advised dashes for growth, supporting declining industries, over-enthusiastic encouragement of mergers,

* Originally published in D. Kavanagh and A. Seldon (eds), *The Thatcher Effect*, Oxford: Oxford University Press, 1989.

and subsidies to investment'. The Thatcher government deserved two cheers for avoiding some of these traps, and for starting to reduce the difference in performance between Britain and its main trading partners.

The sources of economic growth do not lie with government. The Thatcher administration did, however, do something to create the conditions in which Britain could start to catch up with its partners and competitors. But paradoxes abound. For instance, the source of the success of the first attack on inflation in 1979–81 – and the roots of the productivity upsurge – lay in the *failure* of the intended gradualist anti-inflation programme and the administration of a short sharp shock via the exchange rate, which was unintended and due to policy errors. The growth achievement had its underside in high rates of unemployment, and all too conspicuous poverty.

THE INTERNATIONAL CONTEXT

Before going any further it is necessary to ask: how far was there an international convergence around so-called Thatcherite policies such as cutting subsidies to loss-making industries and privatization? And how far was Britain (or the US under President Reagan) out on a limb?

David Henderson, then Head of Economics at the OECD, enumerated the general movement of western governments in a market-orientated direction – a movement which international officials preferred to call 'structural adjustment' to minimize political argument. He dated the shift to roughly 1979, but believed that it was not associated with a shift of power towards conservative governments. It was also evident, for instance, in Australasia, Spain, Sweden and France, which were under left-wing rule for most of the period – although even the most revisionist of British Labour leaders continued to oppose many of the key elements of the platform.

Henderson lists four main areas. First, taxation, where there were reductions in high marginal rates of personal tax, a shift towards taxing consumption, and – less clearly – attempts to reduce exemptions and privileges. Secondly, in product markets many countries engaged not only in privatization, but in deregulation, especially in transport and telecommunications. There also was at least a *desire* to phase out industrial subsidies. Thirdly, labour markets were shaken up by the removal of controls and a shift away from centralized collective bargaining, as well as by reductions of the disincentive effect of the social security system – usually by the not very subtle means of limiting benefits. Fourthly and most conspicuously, there was the freeing of capital markets, including measures such as the abolition of credit controls and interest ceilings and allowing greater participation by foreign enterprise.

British efforts did seem in some areas greater in scope than those at least in the rest of Europe, not only in privatization and deregulation, but in the rolling back of union power. I would also highlight the phasing out of industrial subsidies. Industrial support is the one area where public spending in Britain was cut drastically, even in nominal terms. Although part of the cut-back reflected privatization or classification changes, that is by no means the whole story. Nothing like it was seen, for instance, in Germany, where regional and industrial interests triumphed over the Federal Republic's theoretical commitment to the social market economy.

Moreover, it is all too easy to forget that the post-war consensus had already been fractured before the Thatcher government came to office. Both unemployment and inflation had been getting worse in each successive economic cycle. Attempts to use incomes policy to secure stable prices without accelerating inflation had ended in spectacular failure, not only when Prime Minister Edward Heath was beaten by the miners' strike in 1974, but also when Labour's incomes policies subsequently collapsed in the Winter of Discontent in 1979. Nevertheless, partly in order to obtain union support for wage restraint, union power had become more strongly entrenched both legally and *de facto*.

Lady Thatcher clearly learned the lesson of not biting off more than she could chew. Patrick Minford reminds us that the Thatcherite ministers initially concentrated on three limited economic objectives – mastering inflation, union reform and privatization – in carefully selected and cautious order. What would strike a Martian who had only read New Right literature was how little she did to dismantle the post-war settlement, for instance in the National Health Service or the state provision of education, despite numerous and even draconian administrative changes.

Contrary to widespread belief, Margaret Thatcher did not make many speeches outlining the case for relying on market forces, Manchester liberalism, the views of Milton Friedman, or anything else as ambitious. During the Conservative period in opposition, Keith Joseph had made a number of notable speeches setting out what he then called the 'social market economy'. But in 1981 Joseph was switched from the Department of Industry to that of Education, and in 1986 retired from the government altogether.

The few ministers with an interest in economic ideas, such as Lawson, and their advisers were a good deal less intellectually interested in the micro-side than the macro-side. Their general attitude was that, whatever some textbooks might say, intervention was more often the cause of than the cure for malfunctioning markets. But innocence of the economic analysis of externalities, public goods and the like exacted its price. For the government's choice of where to pull back and where to continue to intervene was based on the strength of political resistance. For instance, privatization was hardly mentioned in the 1979 Conservative manifesto, except for shipbuilding, aerospace and National Freight. But it became a major thread when it was found easier to carry out than many other Conservative aspirations. One reason why training was neglected and under-financed for most of the period was the ignoring of the externality or spillover aspect. In other words, the incentives to individual firms to act as free riders on the training efforts of others, in the absence of corrective policies, were disregarded.

MACRO-ECONOMIC POLICY

Little of this innocence was to be found in macro-economic policy, where the major efforts of analysis were concentrated. The Medium Term Financial Strategy, introduced in 1980, was a notable innovation likely to survive changes of government. Nevertheless, many of its sentiments and even sentences were foreshadowed in the Letter to the IMF written in December 1976 by the Labour Chancellor Denis Healey. The rejection of the belief that governments could spend their way into full employment came under Prime Minister James Callaghan. The IMF was the scapegoat for, not the cause of, the turn-round. Money supply objectives, targets for reduced government borrowing, and attempts to stabilize the share of public spending in GNP, all date from 1975 or 1976. Indeed, the words 'New Realism' were first used by Peter Jay to describe the Callaghan policies when he was ambassador in the USA in the following years.

One can speculate how far the Labour government, if it had been returned, would have retained its commitment to sound finance after 1979, in the face of the unemployment explosion that would have confronted any new administration. Nevertheless, the new (or reformulated old) principles were in fact followed by socialist governments in, for instance, Australia, New Zealand and France (after the initial Mitterand experiment), as well as by centrist and coalition governments in Europe. The main odd man out, on the fiscal although not the monetary side, was the Reagan administration, which gave higher priority to low taxes than to balanced Budgets.

In Britain, Conservative Chancellors were, of course, more explicit about the meaning of sound money than the previous Labour government had been. The essential principles of the new financial approach were succinctly stated by Lawson (who took over from Sir Geoffrey Howe as Chancellor after the 1983 election) in an introduction to a book on Keynes. His recipe for economic success was:

the greatest practicable market freedom within an overall framework of firm financial discipline – precisely how that financial discipline is best applied being essentially a second-order question, though clearly one of considerable practical and operational importance.

In his earlier Mais lecture, Lawson had taken the apparently radical step of reversing the traditional assignment of instruments and objectives. He assigned to 'microeconomic' (or supply-side) policies the job of promoting conditions favourable to growth and employment, and to 'macroeconomic policy' (what others would still call demand management) the task of suppressing inflation. This reversal was old-hat, if still controversial, to those who had been following the international debate; but the British economic establishment seems to have an endless capacity for astonishment, as its reaction to the Mais lecture showed.

In fact, Lawson was not a complete follower of his own doctrines. If he had not believed that macro-economic policy had some effect on output and employment – at least in the short term – he would surely have embarked on a quick anti-inflationary kill when he became Chancellor in 1983, instead of returning to the policy of gradualism that the government had unintentionally departed from under Howe.* One disadvantage of gradualism, however, is that any policy error is likely to stall or even temporarily reverse the whole disinflation effort.

Some of the policy errors which led to a stalling of the anti-inflation effort in the mid- and late 1980s were in the realm of what Lawson rightly called second-order problems, but which nevertheless have their importance. The choice of intermediate objectives indeed troubled Thatcher's Chancellors – as it did overseas authorities – for the whole period. No less than five different sets of monetary targets were announced[†], and there were many changes of emphasis between targeting money, targeting the exchange rate, and aiming directly at total spending or income (measured by statisticians as nominal GDP): and there were increasingly well-known differences about the role of sterling between Thatcher and Lawson.

Because of these problems the Medium Term Financial Strategy was more significant for the general idea and for its fiscal aspects than for the detailed monetary numbers. The MTFS projections which did attain some credibility were on the fiscal side, where performance was 'better' than expected. Conservative Chancellors had an instinctive suspicion of making short-term adjustments in spending and taxation for demand-management purposes. Hence the same establishment economists who criticized the government for too tight

---

* This sentence does not mean that Lawson should have embarked on a quick anti-inflationary kill in 1983, but that the Mais Lecture doctrine needs modification. It was indeed better stated in his *Memoirs*.

[†] 1979–82: Sterling M3; 1982–4: Sterling M3, M1, PSL2; 1984–6: M0, Sterling M3; 1986: M0, a raised Sterling M3 target; 1987: M0.

a fiscal policy in the 1980–1 recession censured it for too loose a policy in the 1988 boom.

The thrust of fiscal policy was, first, to reduce government borrowing, and – when the fiscal outlook improved – to balance the Budget over an economic cycle. The controversial 1981 fiscal clamp-down was justified as a move towards balance in the longer term. Thatcherite Chancellors and their advisers used a bewildering variety of theories to rationalize a fiscal objective which reflected a mixture of instinct, reading of history, and opportunistically taking advantage of unexpectedly high tax revenues. The rapid shift from one rationalization to another no more than mirrored the academic debate.

HISTORICAL BACKGROUND

It is high time to move from ideas and principles to the government's actual record. Those who really want to investigate must go back much earlier, to 1973, which was a threshold year for the whole world economy. It was also the year of the Arab–Israeli Yom Kippur War, when OPEC, the oil producers' cartel, succeeded in raising the price of oil by a factor of five.

This first oil price explosion marked the end of the post-war Golden Age of growth and full employment. Growth rates subsequently fell a great deal throughout the industrial world, including Japan. Creeping inflation also gave way to that ugly combination of slow growth and high inflation known as 'stagflation' (see Figure 10.1). The rise in oil prices was probably more a trigger than a cause. The partial collapse of oil prices in the mid-1980s certainly did not restore earlier conditions of trouble-free growth. The sense that the post-war Golden Age was over was one factor behind the western economic summits inaugurated by President Valéry Giscard d'Estaing; and the Organization for Economic Co-operation and Development (OECD) marked the new mood with an inconclusive report by the specially appointed McCracken Group.

Students of British history are more inclined to remember 1974, which saw the Three-day Week, the defeat of the Heath government by the miners' strike, and the well-publicized view of senior civil servants and centrist politicians that Britain had become 'ungovernable'.

Nevertheless it was the leap in the international price of energy which strengthened the miners and weakened Heath. And subsequent events, such as the initial success of the Wilson–Callaghan pay policies and their collapse in the 1978–9 Winter of Discontent, as well as the shift of the Labour government to a form of monetarism, were a British version of a drama which was being played out on a world scale.

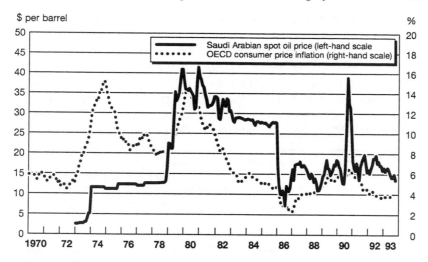

Source: Datastream

Figure 10.1   Oil prices and world inflation

Then in 1979–80 there came the second oil explosion, associated with the deposition of the Shah of Iran, which set off a further burst of world-wide stagflation. But this time the response was different. Nearly all major countries – and not just Germany and Japan – gave early priority to sound money policies; and inflation soon fell back from double-digit to low single figures. But growth did not return to pre-Golden Age rates. Unemployment continued to rise in Europe, although not in the US and Japan.

THE THATCHER GROWTH RECORD

The second post-Golden Age business cycle coincided with the arrival of the Thatcher government in 1979. Those commentators, such as Sir Donald MacDougall, who take all the post-war years as a single period, or who start from the 1960s, saw nothing very special about the Thatcher performance. What should have required comment from them (but rarely received it) was the slowdown of 1973–9 under Labour. But those who take the years after 1973 as a new phase, as is suggested by the evidence, will come to a different conclusion.

Comparisons are best made for whole economic cycles: and the best available basis is the 1973–9 cycle compared with that of 1979–88. The earlier cycle started in the Heath period and encompassed the whole of the succeeding Labour governments of Harold Wilson and James Callaghan. The subsequent period of

1979–88 includes the severe recession at the beginning of the Thatcher governments' terms of office and nearly all the subsequent recovery.

Over this last cycle output per head in manufacturing rose at an average annual rate of nearly 4 per cent (Table 10.1). Not only is this increase much faster than the negligible average recorded during the 1973–9 cycle; it is faster even than the rate recorded in the Golden Age before the first oil price explosion.

Table 10.1   UK growth rates: annual average percentage changes

	Peak to peak			Trough to trough		Other	
	1964–73	1973–79	1979–90	1975–81	1981–92	1979–88	1988–93[a]
Real GDP	3.1	1.4	2.2	1.2	2.3	2.4	0.4[b]
Output per head:							
Manufacturing	3.8	0.6	3.9	1.2	4.5	4.0	3.7
Whole economy	3.1	1.2	1.9	1.7	2.0	2.3	1.2
Non-oil	2.9	0.6	1.8	1.0	2.0	2.2	1.2

Notes
[a]   HM Treasury (November 1993 FSBR) forecasts for 1993
[b]   Average growth of real GDP 0.7% p.a. 1988–94 (using 1993 HMT forecast).

Source: Central Statistical Office.

The whole economy is much more difficult to measure, but, of course, more important. Service output has always been difficult to quantify; and all the national income estimates were undermined by some notorious discrepancies which became especially important in 1988. The estimates, for what they are worth, suggest that the average annual growth of non-oil GDP per worker increased from under 1 per cent in 1973–9, to over 2 per cent in 1979–88. This is a major improvement, but not quite enough to return to Golden Age productivity growth. Indeed, no major western country returned to these growth rates.

For many of the Thatcher years the improvement in productivity was not reflected in the growth of total output, because it was running to waste in higher unemployment. But that ceased to be true by the end. The whole 1979–88 decade saw an improvement not merely in output per head, but in the growth rate of total output (see Table 10.2). This is almost certainly too low because of the statistical weaknesses mentioned. Yet even the official estimate is nearly twice as high as that recorded in the previous economic cycle, and at long last up to or slightly above the European average, after many decades in which it was much lower.

I have stuck to estimates for the whole cycle after 1979 for the sake of caution. Nevertheless, there is evidence that the more rapid increases in productivity of the later Thatcher years were not just a temporary recovery phenomenon but a more lasting change.

Table 10.2 *International growth comparisons: annual percentage changes in real GDP*

	OECD Europe	USA	Japan	UK
1964–73	4.5	3.8	9.3	3.1
1973–79	2.5	2.5	3.6	1.4
1979–88	2.1	2.3	3.9	2.4
1975–81	2.6	3.0	4.4	1.2
1981–92	2.3	2.2	3.9	2.3
1988–94	1.6	1.7	3.2	0.7[a]

Notes
[a] HM Treasury (November 1993 FSBR) forecasts for 1994.
The peak of the UK boom of the late 1980s can be regarded as 1988, 1989 or 1990, according to the criteria used. (Peak growth was achieved in 1988. In 1989 growth was at a normal rate, but the level of output was well above trend. In 1990, the level of output itself peaked and began to turn downwards.)
   Cycles outside the UK did not always have the same peak and trough years as the UK. These differences affect particularly the trough-to-trough comparisons. The periods 1988–93 and 1988–94 have no economic significance, but are cited for purposes of record.

Source: OECD; CSO

The question is sometimes asked whether the British productivity improvement was a special case or had parallels in other countries, where governments had also gone in for deregulation and privatization and other supply-side policies. Sticking strictly to the official estimates for the post-1979 cycle, Britain did about as well as the Continental average; and the growth gap came to an end mainly as a result of slowdown on the European side.

The most clear-cut evidence of the supply-side improvement of the UK economy was the sharp recovery in profitability from the depressed level of the late 1970s and early 1980s. Excluding North Sea oil, the real net rate of return achieved by industrial and commercial companies reached 10 per cent in 1988, far higher than during the peak of the previous economic cycle, and indeed to a level not seen since the early 1960s. [At the bottom of the 1992 recession profitability remained more than twice as high as in 1981 (see Figure 10.2).]

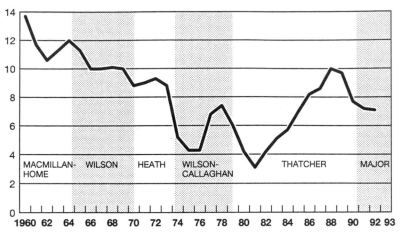

Source: *Bank of England Bulletin*, November 1993.

*Figure 10.2   Return on corporate capital: net rates of return, non-North
Sea companies*

REMAINING GAP

The level or growth of real output per head is not, of course, a measure of happiness
nor even of economic well-being. There are plenty of bads, such as pollution
or congestion or destruction of pleasant vistas, which are not measured in GDP
figures – just as there are plenty of goods such as fresh air or favourable
overspills which equally escape measurement. Attempts to correct these distortions show positive, if slower, growth rates. A high GDP is usually better
than a low one, although it is far from the only or necessarily the most important
criterion for judging the state of society or the success of its government.

To keep the growth improvement in perspective we need to remember that
the UK started and finished the 1980s with a very substantial output and productivity gap compared with its leading trading partners. Figures of absolute
levels of performance are much more difficult to estimate than growth rates;
and to be meaningful it is important to compare different countries' output at
exchange rates which equalize purchasing power rather than at market exchange
rates – a precaution not always taken.

There are many estimates in circulation which either understate or exaggerate
international productivity gaps. For instance GDP per head figures tend to
underestimate the gap because Britain has a comparatively high proportion of
its population at work. A less misleading comparison is between output per hour

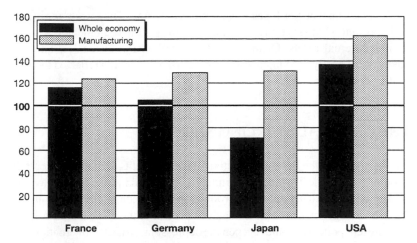

Sources: Department of Trade and Industry; van Ark, 1993.

Figure 10.3   Output per hour worked, 1989 (UK=100)

worked, which in 1989 showed France and Germany some 5 to 20 per cent ahead of Britain, and the US 40 per cent ahead (see Figure 10.3).

As for manufacturing productivity: the estimates show German and French productivity per hour about 25 per cent higher than British, and US productivity 60 per cent higher. It is, however, the very gap between British productivity and productivity overseas – the culmination of a century of comparatively slow growth – which has created the opportunity to catch up. There is no economic miracle involved in reducing the distance from richer countries employing best-practice technology; the opportunity increases with the size of the gap. The UK has at last begun to take that opportunity.

NORTH SEA OIL

The improvement in British growth and productivity in the Thatcher period could not be explained away by North Sea oil. Oil had a useful effect in the 1980s in maintaining real incomes in the face of recession and industrial shake-out. But at its peak in 1985, it amounted to under $5\frac{1}{2}$ per cent of GNP. By 1988 it had fallen to $1\frac{1}{2}$ per cent, more because of the fall in prices than because of that in production. After 1985, the North Sea rundown subtracted about half a per cent per annum from the annual growth of output; North Sea receipts accounted by then for only 2 per cent of public-sector revenues.

Nor is it true that North Sea revenues were wasted. They were, for instance, an important – but as we have seen, not the only – factor in the UK accumulation of external assets. Of the recorded deterioration in the UK balance of payments of nearly £15 billion in 1986–8, less than £2 billion reflected the change in the net balance in oil.

THE ORIGINAL STERLING SHOCK

For the origins of the British productivity improvements as of most other things, good or bad, in the Thatcher governments' economic policies, we have to go back to its first two painful years, from its inauguration in 1979 up to and after the 1981 Budget, which led to the famous protest of the 364 economists saying that 'present policies' would 'deepen the depression, erode the international base of our economy and threaten its social and political stability'.

The incoming Thatcher administration presided over a wage explosion. The annual increase in earnings rose in 1980 to the astonishingly high rate of 20 per cent before subsiding to a $7\frac{1}{2}$–9 per cent average, where it subsequently remained. The wage explosion was partly due to the knock-on-effect of the second oil price shock on the Retail Prices Index. It was also a backlash from the collapse of the Labour government's pay policies and reflected too the contagious effects of the awards of the Clegg Commission, set up by the outgoing government to terminate the public-sector strikes in 1979, but which both main political parties were pledged to honour.

The new government stoked up the explosion by the near doubling of VAT in its first (1979) Budget. Whatever the pros and cons of such a move, this was the worst possible time for it. The net result of all the various knock-on factors was a recorded rate of inflation of 18 per cent in 1980, which fed back into pay awards despite gathering depression.

But this was not all. For at the very same time when British costs were exploding anyway, there was a sharp rise in the pound, which, at its peak in 1981, was (in terms of the sterling index) 25 per cent higher than two years before. The real exchange rate, which takes into account international cost movements, rose by nearly twice as much (Figure 10.4).

The 1979–80 rise in sterling was largely an international portfolio movement due to confidence in Britain as an oil producer at a time of world-wide worries about oil supplies, reinforced by the effects of the 'Thatcher factor'. It was responsible for the rapid fall in inflation which took the government's critics and the official forecasters alike by surprise.

But it was also the proximate cause of one of the unhappiest experiences of the Thatcher period. Manufacturing employment, which had been contracting

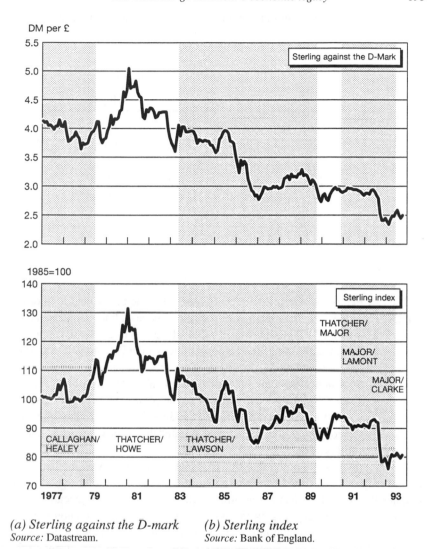

(a) Sterling against the D-mark
Source: Datastream.

(b) Sterling index
Source: Bank of England.

Figure 10.4   Movement of sterling

even in the 1970s, fell by over 2 million from its 1979 level, mostly in the early years of the Thatcher government. (Manufacturing employment fell from 8.1 million in 1971 to 7.3 million in 1979 and 5.4 million in 1983.) The number of jobs created outside manufacturing was not, initially, sufficient to prevent unemployment (of adults, seasonally adjusted) trebling from 1.1 million in 1979 to a peak of 3.2 million in 1986. Again most of the rise came in a single burst in the 1980–1 recession; but even after that it continued to creep upwards (Table 10.3).

Table 10.3   Unemployment: peaks and troughs (% of total labour force)

	UK	EC	USA	Japan
1973	3.0	2.9	4.8	1.3
1977	6.0	5.2	6.9	2.0
1979	5.0	5.7	5.8	2.1
1986	11.2	10.8	6.9	2.8
1990	6.8	8.4	5.4	2.1
1993[a]	10.4	10.7	6.7	2.5

Note: [a] August.

Source: OECD.

The pay explosion, the severe recession and the unemployment leap of the early Thatcher years were three interrelated phenomena – almost aspects of each other. The government's great mistake, especially given its gradualist approach to union reform, was to underrate the perversities of the British labour market: the attachment to 'going rates', the distaste for market-related pay, the extreme rapidity with which even temporary price explosions fed into pay, and the dominant power of 'insiders' with jobs in fixing remuneration over outsiders without. The result was that the government underestimated both the job losses in tackling inflation solely from the demand side and the underlying forces making for high unemployment.

It is now also well known that the Thatcher government was misled about the severity of the demand squeeze in its initial couple of years because it did not take the sterling exchange rate sufficiently into account, and because it did not adjust its monetary targets to take account of structural changes in the desire to hold money – including changes brought about by its own actions such as the abolition of exchange controls and the removal of the direct limit on the growth of bank deposits known as the 'corset'.

The exchange rate squeeze was doubly unintended. It arose out of monetary policy mistakes, which transformed an intended gradual disinflation into a sharp shock. Yet it had a silver lining, for the resulting pressure on profit margins led to a blitz on overmanning and a productivity spurt in industry. The unforeseen result was that what was meant to be a financial policy to reduce inflation became a highly successful, if accidental, industrial strategy. In other words, the benefits flowed from mistakes. As Professor Geoffrey Maynard wrote:

By refusing to accommodate rising costs and poor productivity with exchange rate depreciation, macro-policy imposed pressure on industry to raise productivity, lower costs, and generally move its product up market. Many firms whose managements were often vociferous in their criticism of government exchange rate policy subsequently achieved productivity improvements and product upgrading to an almost revolutionary degree.

The overvalued pound began to decline from early 1981 onwards. This was partly due to international changes. For from that time Reagan's America began to replace Thatcher's Britain as the main magnet for footloose funds. Internally the British government, fortified by the controversially tough Budget of 1981, which raised taxes despite the recession, began to worry less about the overshoot of its original target monetary aggregate (Sterling M3) and began a staged reduction of interest rates, with some temporary reversals when sterling fell 'too quickly'.

The combination of a continued world upturn, an easing of UK monetary and exchange rate policies, and structural policies to improve the British labour market eventually resulted in a turnround in unemployment. But the enhanced training and job-search programmes, and attempts to move away from national pay bargaining and going rates in the public sector, hardly began until near the end of the second Thatcher government – perhaps with the realization that ministers could hardly fight a second election (that of 1987) with unemployment still rising.

It was from the second half of 1986 that the unemployed claimant total started to fall. It did so fairly rapidly, but was in the winter of 1988–9 not far below 2 million, or nearly twice as high as when the government took office. Most seriously of all, this level of unemployment coincided with labour shortages, especially, but not only, of skilled workers, in many parts of the country, and widespread anxiety about inflationary overheating. The level of registered vacancies came back to where it was when the Thatcher government arrived in office, suggesting an increase in the 'mismatch' between vacancies and unemployment.

The claimant count was affected by a series of programmes and procedures which have discouraged marginal claimants from registering. The Labour Force survey suggested, however, that the UK unemployment data were fairly close to international survey definitions. The UK unemployment percentage remained higher than that of the US and much higher than that of Japan, although at times lower than the European Community average.

SPENDING AND TAXES

The exchange rate shock and demand squeeze gave the initial impetus to the supply-side improvement. But they cannot explain why the improvement persisted. In the words of the OECD Report on the UK:

The persistence of high rates of output and productivity growth through an exceptionally long recovery phase, judged by past performance and that of other countries, suggests that the improvements on supply-side performance is more than a transitory cyclical phenomenon.

What were the supply-side policies? The Thatcher government received both praise and blame for public-spending cuts and giving priority to tax reductions. Both were largely misplaced. In the early Thatcher years the public-spending ratio actually increased, under the influence of recession, increased demands on the social security system and electoral pledges on defence and police spending.

The public expenditure ratio reached its peak in 1982–3; but it was not until 1987–8, the government's ninth year of office, that the ratio dipped decisively below that of 1978–9, the last year of the Callaghan government. By 1988–9 the ratio had fallen to $39^{3}\!/_{4}$ per cent (excluding privatization proceeds), the lowest since 1963–4. It was projected to fall further and dip below 39 per cent in the early 1990s. But continued success in reducing this ratio could not be taken for granted once the period of boom growth and rapidly falling unemployment came to an end [an understated warning on my part!].

More fundamentally, the Thatcher government had not after nearly three terms in office reduced the range of its responsibilities for social security, health or any of the large spending areas. The result was that, because of changing needs and technology (for example, in the health service) it had to be as tight-fisted as possible simply to contain spending increases. Thus the defenders of the welfare state saw meanness and cheese-paring all round, while the Radical Right felt it had been betrayed. Indeed, by 1989 there were already signs that one key element in the government's public expenditure policy – the linking of benefits to inflation rather than income – was coming under strain.

Partly because the public-sector balance had moved from deficit to surplus, the total UK tax burden had not come down at the end of the first decade. Tax revenues, excluding those from the North Sea, still amounted in 1988–9 to a higher proportion of GDP than before the government took office. While the headlines concentrated on the reductions in the basic rate of income tax, these were more than offset by the increase in VAT and employers' contributions in the early Thatcher years, and later by the automatic effects of rising real income in bringing more and more taxpayers into higher tax zones in the later years ('real fiscal drag').

The tax rate which counts from the point of view of incentives is the marginal tax on each pound earned. Taking National Insurance and consumer taxes properly into account, this still amounted in 1988–9 to approximately 50–58 per cent, depending on family status, and only slightly less than in 1979. There was of course a much bigger cut in the top marginal rate, which on a similar basis was approximately 60 per cent for a salaried employee compared to over

85 per cent when the government took office. These very high marginal rates brought in little or even negative revenue and produced all manner of distortions not imagined by those who sneered at the incentives case. It is surely better that a country should attract high earners than push them into tax exile.

UK NO MARKET PARADISE

Greater use of competition and markets is not the same thing as reducing public spending. Many interest-group privileges – for instance, the pension funds, mortgage holders, or farmers –appear as tax reliefs. Other anti-market policies, such as quotas on textiles or Japanese cars, or so-called EC anti-dumping provisions against the Far East, do not cost the Exchequer a single penny. And the biggest burden of the Common Agricultural Policy is not the tax transfer to Brussels but the inflation of food prices above world levels.

The Thatcher government was far from a single-minded promoter of competitive markets. British Rover was sold to an aerospace company not because of industrial logic, but because of a political veto on an overseas purchaser. Quotas have proliferated on 'high-tech' and 'low-tech' imports alike, whether they come from Japan or the newly industrializing countries. Inside the European Community the British stand has been more protectionist than anyone would suppose from public denunciations of 'Fortress Europe'.

In the UK, tax subsidies to home ownership, rigid restrictions on land use, and pension fund privileges remain: and their harmful effects have been magnified by financial liberalization, in itself desirable. Rent controls have been tackled only in the late 1980s – with what effectiveness remains to be seen. On some of these issues, such as the motor car industry, Lady Thatcher was overruled by her colleagues. On others, such as mortgage privileges, she herself was the main perverse driving force.

Too many of the Prime Minister's radical urges were wasted on peripheral issues, such as the abolition of the Greater London Council and attempts to eliminate domestic rates by the Poll Tax, despite the fact that houses were already over-subsidized and undertaxed compared to other assets. No one seems to have been able to convince her that all these subsidies and privileges did not in the end benefit the young suburban couple of Tory fantasy, but spilled over into high land prices and interest rates. The combination was too often one of strident rhetoric and irrelevant action.

SUPPLY-SIDE POLICIES

Something, however, must have gone right. Because supply-side policies consist of thousands of different acts, many of them not thought of as part of economic policy and certainly not as part of one great strategy, it is extremely difficult to summarize them, let alone assess their relative weight.

The most controversial such policy was, of course, privatization. Its importance has been overrated by Conservative politicians but underrated by academic economists on the grounds that not enough was done to introduce competition into denationalized concerns. This assessment ignores the intractable problems of government relations with nationalized industries which helped to trigger off privatization and accounted for its international popularity.

It ignores, too, fundamental political economy. Such activity and interest as there has been in deregulation, franchising and contracting out, and prospects for more in future, are largely an outcrop of the privatization debate. Privatization has stirred up many corners of the British economy – less effectively than truly radical policies such as unilateral free trade would have done, but more effectively than anything else that was on the political agenda of the late 1980s.

The main effect of privatization visible by the end of the 1980s was efficiency improvements induced by the drive to sell off state industries. Impressive productivity gains emerged in a study by Bishop and Kay of firms which were publicly owned in 1979. But these findings are grudgingly reported on the grounds that 'these are changes in management culture associated with clearer commercial objectives' – as if these objectives had nothing to do with privatization.

A near-unmentionable hope is the opportunity privatization provides for the gradual erosion of union influence in a sector hitherto 100 per cent unionized – starting probably in the smaller and peripheral enterprises, out of the spotlight of publicity. Simply taking labour issues out of the political arena is a much underrated weapon on the side of common sense and market-based pay settlements.

Among other supply-side policies the OECD mentioned deregulation, ranging from the financial markets to express coaches, opticians to competitive tendering for local authority and hospital services – like all things in life, subject to abuse. The Lord Chancellor even tried to reduce restrictive practices among lawyers.

An underrated reform was the corporation tax changes in the 1984 Budget. These reduced or abolished many of the special allowances, which in the OECD's words 'encouraged purely tax motivated investment', and replaced them by a lower overall tax rate. The reform removed the pre-1984 subsidization of machinery, especially machinery financed by debt.

Strong labour productivity growth was less clearly linked than in the past to investment, which at least before the top of the 1980s boom 'remained lower relative to GDP than in earlier recovery periods'. It seemed linked instead 'to changes in organisation, with inflexibility and outdated job demarcation giving way to more rational allocations'.

FUNDAMENTALS

More important than any single policy may have been, quoting the OECD again, the 'abandoning of traditional objectives of macroeconomic policy', including the commitment to secure full employment by boosting demand or bailing out loss-making firms. The rundown in subsidies to industries such as aerospace, shipbuilding and steel may have had some parallel in other countries. But by personifying the slogan, 'The world does not owe us a living', the Prime Minister succeeded in convincing industry that the government was less likely than its predecessors or opposite numbers abroad to bail out firms or individuals from their economic difficulties.

If I were to single out two supply-side policies from the mass of detail, they would be the abolition of exchange control in 1979, at the beginning of the government's term, and union reform. The first coincided with globalization and increased efficiency of financial markets. The combination made it impossible for firms to survive with a rate of return below the going international average. In the words of one industrial economist, Douglas McWilliams:

> A consequence has been the growth in mergers, acquisitions, demergers, sell-offs, management buyouts and contracting out. Perhaps most important of all has been the increase of self-confidence. There has been both pressure to improve, and a massacre of 1970s excuses.

The same economist argues that even the short-termism of financial markets has its advantages. For the 'short term results provide the financial strength to support the longer term strategy'.

The second fundamental change was the weakening of union power, encouraged by the Acts of 1980, 1982 and 1984 covering union law. These withdrew some legal immunities (especially for secondary strikes and picketing), made union officials more accountable (for example, by secret ballots), weakened the closed shop, and put union funds at stake in case of breaches of the law.

But the greatest success came from the handling of the miners' strike of 1984-5. The spectre of Britain being ungovernable without union consent, which terrified some of the more reflective Labour ministers, as well as the Civil Service, when Labour returned to office after the Heath government's defeat, may at last have been banished. The victory over militant violence – repeated by Rupert Murdoch in Wapping – was quite as important as any economic result. The victory owed nothing to the talking classes, who insisted on endless discussions of the personality of Margaret Thatcher when the real issue was Arthur Scargill's conduct of the coal dispute.

THE GOD THAT FAILED

One disappointing aspect of economic performance under the Thatcher government was that the underlying rate of inflation stopped falling in the middle of the 1980s. British inflation rose faster than in other major countries up to its 1980 peak after the second oil price explosion, but then indeed fell more quickly (Figure 10.5). Yet the inflation decline came to a halt in about 1983, and from then the underlying rate fluctuated around 5 per cent. The UK was overtaken on the anti-inflation front by the other summit countries, including France, a traditionally high-inflation country, whose inflation rate was down, by 1988–9, to 3 per cent.

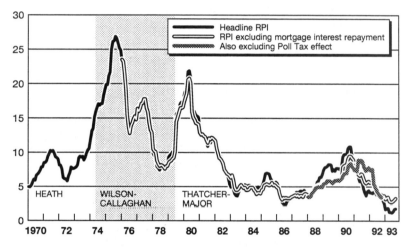

Source: Datastream.

Figure 10.5   Two decades of UK inflation: percentage changes on a year earlier (1970–93)

An underlying British inflation rate of 5 per cent means that it will fluctuate between around 3 per cent in good periods and 7–8 per cent in bad periods. The peculiar way in which mortgage interest entered the Retail Price Index magnified these fluctuations and made them more erratic.

The reason why inflation got stuck at too high a level is that total spending in money terms was still rising too quickly. When the current balance is changing, total domestic spending in nominal terms, which rose by about 13 per cent in 1988, gives a better idea of demand pressure than nominal GDP. The main significance of the 'trade gap' and the current payments deficit, which generated so much hysteria, was that they provided a safety valve for excess domestic demand – if they had not existed inflation would have been much higher.

The interesting question is *why* total spending increased so quickly in the later 1980s. The short answer is that a sharp fall in the personal (although not the national) savings ratio boosted consumption; and from 1987 onwards an investment boom added to demand pressures. The fall in the personal savings ratio and the boom in house prices and construction were, in their turn, linked to rapidly expanding credit at a time of high but stable growth. The credit boom could itself be linked to liberalization of financial markets – for example, the removal of most of the remaining constraints on the lending of banks and building societies, which began to compete fiercely to lend money.

But this explanation only puts the search back a stage. Surely one thing that monetarism was supposed to do was to give a signal when too much cash was being injected into the economy so that the Bank of England could raise interest rates in time. It was a case of the god that failed.

I have already touched on the sharp acceleration of the officially targeted broad measure of the money supply in 1980–1, when the economy was suffering an unprecedented recession. Thus, when the broad measure of money again started rising in 1985–6, Treasury economists were understandably sceptical that it meant more inflation – just as the boy who has falsely cried 'wolf' is not believed on the next occasion. The very narrow measure of money which the Treasury came to prefer ('M0'), consisting mainly of cash circulation, provided a false sense of security well into 1988.

LOST EMS OPPORTUNITY

One signal, however, could have prevented the inflationary resurgence if the government had been prepared to heed it. There was a well-established expedient for a country whose monetary indicators are erratic and unreliable. That was to link its currency with that of a country with unimpeachable credentials for price stability, such as West Germany, and keep interest rates high until the policy became credible.

The opportunity was lost in 1985, when Lady Thatcher vetoed the only serious Treasury attempt to take Britain into the Exchange Rate Mechanism of the European Monetary System. At one time this looked like a merciful deliverance. For when the oil price collapsed in 1986, sterling was allowed to depreciate further without immediate visible inflationary effect, thus giving British industry a temporary competitive advantage and stoking up the boom over the election period.

But with hindsight it became clear that the UK would have been better off without that depreciation, which was purchased at the expense of higher inflation. If sterling had joined the EMS at just above DM3.5 in late 1985, the right signals would have been given in time to tighten domestic financial policy. To be sure, the growth of output might have been less than during the hectic 1987–8 boom period, but it would also have been more durable and less plagued by doubts. The opportunity to lock Britain into a low German-type rate of inflation was thus thrown away and the fall in UK inflation came to a halt at a higher level than in the other main European countries.

By the time the Chancellor embarked on his personal policy of shadowing the mark – roughly the year up to March 1988 – it was too late. The policy started too far into the economic cycle, was maintained for too short a period, and was embarked upon at too low a rate for sterling.

UK PAYMENTS DEFICIT

How far did the emergence of a record UK current balance of payments deficit of nearly £15 billion in 1988 qualify the general picture of improvement? The deficit was almost certainly overstated; but there is no need to quibble about the emergence of a current deficit which even on a truer estimate probably still exceeded £10 billion, or 2 per cent of GDP (Table 10.4).

The horror with which it was greeted by commentators who had lived for a generation and a half with post-war payments crises was understandable but misplaced. One big difference compared with earlier periods was the emergence of a unified and liberalized world capital market. Investors in surplus countries such as Japan, Germany and the Far Eastern newly industrializing countries (NICs) needed external outlets for their savings and were short of creditworthy borrowers. There was no need for Britain or any other major western countries to go 'cap in hand' to the IMF or to other governments in search of official finance, so long as their own creditworthiness was maintained.

Another difference was that the British current account deficit reflected during the Thatcher–Lawson period private-sector borrowing rather than Budget deficits. The distinction, much stressed by the British Treasury, fell on sceptical ears. It still remains true (a) that the private sector – unlike the government – cannot default on its obligations by inflation or currency depreciation, and (b) that the growth of private-sector borrowing must eventually level off when some prudential debt-to-income ratio is reached.

The basic problem was that the investment boom of the late 1980s, super-imposed on a rising consumption trend, led to an inflationary increase in demand, part of which was deflected into imports or on to goods diverted from exports. This could not continue much longer and the true concern in 1988–9 was not the balance of payments itself, but the inflationary rise in demand of which it was a symptom. That demand could be [and was] curbed by interest rate policy, designed both to maintain a strong pound and discourage domestic lending, provided that the policy was maintained long enough and firmly enough in the face of political unpopularity.

Table 10.4   UK balance of payments 1979–92

	Current balance		Bal. item	Reserves
	£bn	% of GDP	£bn	$bn
1979	−0.6	−0.3	+1.0	22.7
1980	+2.8	+1.2	+0.9	27.5
1981	+6.7	+2.6	+0.5	23.3
1982	+4.7	+1.7	−2.1	17.0
1983	+3.8	+1.2	+1.0	17.8
1984	+1.8	+0.6	+7.2	15.7
1985	+2.8	+0.8	+1.6	15.5
1986	+0.1	+0.0	+4.0	21.9
1987	−4.5	−1.1	−2.0	44.3
1988	−16.2	−3.4	+6.3	51.7
1989	−21.7	−4.2	+3.1	38.6
1990	−17.0	−3.1	+7.3	38.5
1991	−6.4	−1.1	+0.9	44.1
1992	−11.9	−2.0	+0.3	41.7

Source: Central Statistical Office.

No policy could guarantee a 'soft landing', while the economy returned to non-inflationary rates of capital and labour utilization, and resources shifted out of the domestic sector. Meanwhile the balance of payments would take care of itself, but if, and only if, the government succeeded in reversing the inflationary tide and putting a severe limit to any depreciation of sterling.

The stability of the UK share of world net exports of manufacturing since the early 1980s was *prima facie* evidence that the UK industry was reasonably competitive under conditions of normal demand (Figure 10.6). So was the slowing down in the rise of import penetration before the 1988 boom (Figure 10.7).

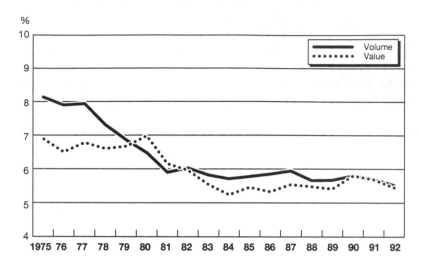

Source: HM Treasury

Figure 10.6   Share of UK exports in total world trade in manufactures

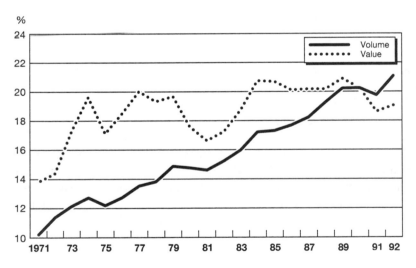

Source: HM Treasury

Figure 10.7   Share of imports of goods in total UK domestic demand
(excluding oil)

DISTRIBUTIONAL EFFECTS

It would be wrong to end this chapter on questions of monetary management. We must, before finishing, at least glance at the broader question of domestic winners and losers from the changes of the Thatcher decade. 'Glance at', for it would be impossible to cover distributional changes properly at the end of an already long chapter.

But it takes no special investigation to see that pre-tax income differentials increased greatly, a trend which started well before the Thatcher government, reflecting a world-wide change in labour markets – a change which was enhanced in the UK by the ending of the attempts at pay control and government approval of market-based differentials. More remarkable has been the extent of the widening of differentials even after tax and social security.

We are dealing with far too short a period to expect any evidence of 'trickle down' to those at the bottom. But it is worrying that the least well-off should have fared as badly as they did. This impression of near-standstill for the poor is reinforced by the social security changes. The government's stated policy was to link main benefits to inflation rather than earnings. (The statutory link with earnings for retirement pensions was severed in 1980.) The intention was to combine a near-freeze on the real value of most universal benefits – which spilled over into the middle and higher income brackets – with greater selectivity towards those with greatest need.

But even this uninspiring picture seems difficult to reconcile with the evidence of our eyes – for instance, the great increase in the number of people sleeping under the arches or in the streets and the growth in the number of down-and-outs of all ages. The official statistics cover only households. The homeless and people in institutions are excluded. There are all sorts of problems related to the under-class on the margins of society which national aggregates or conventional income distribution statistics hardly touch.

The more general question confronting the political economist is: could the poor have fared better without endangering the supply-side improvements? The tentative conclusion is 'Yes'. But it could not be done by soaking the rich or raising marginal tax rates in the middle. To improve the position of the poor in a well-functioning market economy would require an onslaught on what has been called 'the middle-class welfare state'. Redistribution and incentive alike would be satisfied by a combination of more selective, but also more generous, benefits paid through the tax system. Something like the present income tax rates and VAT rates could be combined with more redistribution, if there were an onslaught on the fiscal privileges of for example the pension funds, home owners and landowners. [The Major government made a modest start on winding down these privileges in the early 1990s – a decade too late.] The difficulties in the way of forming a political coalition in favour of such a radical social market programme are obvious. But even the masses of middle-income voters, who would bear the impact of the change, would ultimately gain from the combination of greater incentives and a quieter conscience.

Continuing in the pre-Thatcher way was not an attractive option or even possible. The task was [and remained] to remedy the black spots, while keeping the achievements.

1993 POSTSCRIPT

Unfortunately later evidence suggested that the poorest lost out in absolute as well as relative terms during the Thatcher era. Between 1979 and 1990, when the average household experienced an increase in real income of 36 per cent, the bottom tenth experienced a decrease of 1.4 per cent, according to a Written Answer provided by the Department of Social Security (18 October 1993). Even the second decile from the bottom had a zero income increase. Arguments about the relative and absolute welfare of those on low incomes can, however, be even more complicated and controversial than macro-economic disputes; and the statistical pendulum may continue to swing. The very practical problem that emerged was how best to help people of low earnings capacity to participate in labour markets at a time when market-clearing pay differentials have widened sharply against the unskilled, the less adaptable and the unlucky. (The question is discussed further in Part Four of this book.)

On more general economic performance, the Thatcher government made a start in removing some of the impediments to economic success. During the post-Thatcher years much ground seemed to have been lost again, first because of the resurgence of inflation and the high interest rates needed to combat it; and afterwards by the recession which proved more debilitating than almost anyone expected. Later, however, international comparisons moved in favour of the UK again. Recovery, if patchy and uncertain, arrived earlier in the 1990s in the UK than in continental Europe, and the economic debate moved to the labour market rigidities which the Thatcher government had taken a lead in removing. As already mentioned, the statistical dust of at least one, and probably more, business cycles will have to settle down before any firmer quantitative conclusions about the Thatcher economic legacy can be drawn.

Obviously the above chapter is not an exhaustive economic account of the Thatcher period. More, for instance, could have been said of the role of North Sea oil. I see, however, little reason to revise what I wrote about the 'lost EMS opportunity'. The EMS (or the ERM as it came to be known) did indeed provide an anchor for price stability in the 1980s, as I have explained in the previous chapter. Had the UK joined then, instead of waiting until 1990, it could have gained some of the benefits, long before the German response to unification, which came in 1990, undermined the system.

One of the main developments after Lady Thatcher left office in November 1990, was the large fiscal deficit that subsequently developed. There were many reasons for it. One was the unexpected length of the recession of the early 1990s. Mainstream UK economic opinion ascribed this recession, with a liberal dose of hindsight, to the rebound from over-lax credit policies in the boom of the late 1980s. But the continental European and Japanese recessions, which started later and were even more prolonged, suggested that deeper forces were at work than policy mistakes in a single country.

A specific British factor was the weakening of public-expenditure control in the early 1990s. It would be unreasonable to quibble with increases in recession-related expenditure especially on social security. But there were also relaxations which had nothing to do with recession but were made in the run up to the 1992 election. The poll tax gave the local authorities a heaven-sent opportunity to bump up their expenditures in the knowledge that central government would be blamed. Subsequently, some of the increased grants that an embarrassed government provided to restrain poll tax rates found their way into still further local authority spending. These poll tax effects were a Thatcher legacy; but the attempt of the Major government to show that it was less doctrinaire than its predecessor also had some unfortunate effects – for instance, the unnecessary decision to resume indexation of across-the-board child benefit payments.

Moving aside from this detail, there were broader reasons why even someone who welcomed the 1980s-style emphasis on competition and deregulation should still feel uneasy about some of the cultural aspects of the Thatcher revolution, including those that lived on under the Major government.

The economist Mark Casson has argued that the largest costs in a modern economy are transaction costs, and that these are minimized in an atmosphere of trust – in contrast to an atmosphere where everyone tries to take advantage of everyone else, and no one moves without a lawyer. An example of what could go wrong was given by a so-called right-wing member of the Major cabinet, John Redwood, in November 1993, when he spoke of the growth in the number of Health Service 'managers in grey suits', all too ready to solve their problems by closing down hospital wards.

Market economics comes in many shapes and sizes. Casson puts his finger on the mark when he writes that the supply-side package imported from the US

> comes laden with certain cultural presuppositions – amongst them the view that because people cannot be trusted, formal methods of enforcing competition between them are essential in all areas of activity. The US emphasis on the law as an enforcement mechanism is a related cultural attitude which may not 'travel' well.

He also describes how these attitudes have been borrowed from the US at a time when many successful private enterprise organizations are making their management styles more human and informal, supposedly under Japanese influence.

Many people have described the paradox that market liberalization has gone hand-in-hand with a shift of power from intermediate sources of authority to central government. They are right to detect incipient authoritarianism behind a rhetoric of free markets. But another factor has surely been an excess of caution. It is because governments have not had the courage to undertake the drastic reforms which would make, for instance, local authorities or universities responsible for the bulk of their own total financing, that Whitehall centralizers have acquired their hold. Perhaps the answer to the paradoxes generated by the Thatcher attempt to get the state off people's backs is to carry it further and really mean it.

REFERENCES

Bishop, M. and J. Kay, *Does Privatization Work?*, London: London Business School, 1988.

Brittan, S., *A Restatement of Economic Liberalism*, London: Macmillan, 1988.

Casson, Mark, *The Economics of Business Culture*, Oxford: Clarendon Press, 1991.

Crafts, Nick, *British Economic Growth Before and After 1979*, London: Centre for Economic Policy Research, 1989.

Department of Social Security, *Households Below Average Income*, London: DSS, 30 June 1993.

Henderson, D., 'Perestroika in the West', in John Nieuwenhuysen (ed.), *Towards Freer Trade Between Nations*, London: Oxford University Press, 1989.

Hoover, K. and R. Plant, *Conservative Capitalism in Britain and the United States*, London: Routledge & Kegan Paul, 1988.

Lawson, Nigel, *The British Experiment*, Fifth Mais Lecture, Centre for Banking and International Finance; City University Business School, London, 1984.

Lawson, Nigel, 'Introduction' to W. Eltis and P. Sinclair (eds), *Keynes and Economic Policy*, London: Macmillan, 1988.

Lawson, Nigel, *The State of the Market*, London: Institute of Economic Affairs, 1988.

Lawson, Nigel, *The View from No. 11*, London: Bantam Press, 1992.

Maynard, Geoffrey, *The Economy under Mrs Thatcher*, Oxford: Basil Blackwell, 1988.

MacDougall, Donald, *Fifty Years On: Some Personal Reflections*, 17th Keynes Lecture in Economics, British Academy, 1988.

McWilliams, D., *Inaugural Lecture*, Kingston Business School, 1988.

Minford, P., chapter in Robert Skidelsky (ed.), *Thatcherism*, London: Chatto & Windus, 1988.

OECD, *Towards Full Employment and Price Stability*, ('McCracken Report'), Paris: OECD, 1977.

OECD, *Economic Survey: UK*, Paris: OECD, 1988.

Robinson, W., *Britain's Borrowing Problem*, London: Social Market Foundation, 1993.

Sinfield, Adrian, (ed.), *Poverty, Inequality and Justice*, Edinburgh: University of Edinburgh, 1993.

Sprinkel, Beryl, (ed.), *Economic Report of the President*, Washington, DC: US Government Printing Office, January 1989.

Thatcher, Margaret, *The Downing Street Years*, London: HarperCollins, 1993.

van Ark, B., *International Comparison of Output Productivity*, Monograph series no. 1, Groningen: Groningen Growth and Development Centre, 1993.

11   A perspective on unemployment*

THE LUMP OF LABOUR FALLACY

One of the main reasons I took up the study of economic problems was indignation at the absurdity of unsatisfied wants side by side with idle hands, willing to work, which I believed existed before the Second World War. This feeling persists. While both price stability and high employment are, in the last resort, means to human contentment and not ends, I still attach more value to avoiding the waste of large scale unemployment than I do to price stability as a proximate objective. I also attach more value to growth than to price stability, provided that it is growth in the output of goods and services (including leisure and amenity) that people want, rather than in the products that some political leader, technologist or industrialist has decided are good for us.

These were the opening sentences of a booklet, *Second Thoughts on Full Employment Policy,* which appeared in 1975 and which I would reiterate. Unemployment has become very much worse since then. Although not so far on anything like the scale of the Great Depression, some resemblances to the 1930s are beginning to emerge. The OECD, to which the 24 principal industrial countries of the world belong, expects the jobless total of its members to reach 36 million in 1996, of which nearly 20 million are expected to be in the European Community. These estimates are equivalent to an unemployment rate of $8^{1}/_{2}$ per cent for the whole of the OECD, but getting on for 12 per cent for the European Community. On top of these, there are nearly 4 million people who have been discouraged from staying in the labour force by dismal job prospects and over 9 million part-time workers who say they would prefer to work full-time if they could.

At all times there is one seemingly ineradicable fallacy which dominates most popular discussion of unemployment. This is the belief that there is a limited amount of work to be done and that society is threatened by a chronic and increasing shortage of jobs as technology advances. This way of thinking is known as 'the lump of labour fallacy'. It is typified by remarks such as: 'I cannot see where the people who have been displaced from contracting industries like steel or coal or branch banking are going to work.' It is a maddening fallacy because, if believed and acted upon, it could halt improvements and impoverish us all quite needlessly.

---

* This chapter is freshly compiled. It draws a little upon 'Back to Full Employment: the Economic Aspect', *National Westminster Bank Review*, May 1985, and the final part of my 1985 Wincott Lecture, *Two Cheers for Self Interest.*

The fallacy rears its head when unions call for a shorter working week to combat unemployment. The same kind of attitude underlies concern about the microchip computer, the desire to reduce retirement ages or push young people into more years of full-time education, and much other nonsense.

Alarm has been expressed whenever an apparently labour-saving invention has appeared. Few people now remember the scare when the earliest type of automation appeared in the motor industry in the 1950s. But other examples go back much further – well beyond the Luddites who roamed the country after the Napoleonic Wars destroying machinery, to the sheep that in the sixteenth century were believed to be 'eating up' jobs on the land. No doubt the same charge was levelled at the inventors of the plough and the wheel.

The attitude is outrageous to reason because it means that people who could be contributing to the wants of others must be forced to retire early, to stay longer at school or have their hours of work cut against their will, because no other way is seen of using their contributions.

The lump of labour view is belied by the historical record. This suggests that neither technological progress nor growth in the working population need lead to more unemployment. In the century from 1860 UK output per head nearly trebled and the labour force doubled. The result was not mass unemployment but a six-fold increase in total output. Between 1932 and 1937, during the recovery from the Great Depression, UK employment increased by two and a quarter million, equivalent to about 3 million on today's population figures. After the Second World War, the German Federal Republic absorbed millions of refugees; and in most of Western Europe a large rundown in the farm population was not only easily absorbed, but millions of guest workers were drawn in from Southern Europe, Turkey and North Africa.

But as Matthew Parris noted from local meetings in his own period as an MP, no amount of evidence or reasoning can dislodge this fallacy, which is deeply rooted among industrialists and physical scientists as well as trade unionists and the general population. Even distinguished economists are not immune. Denis Robertson cited the saturation of human wants as a reason for inter-war unemployment. Even Keynes himself sometimes lapsed. For although his official view was that effective demand should be maintained to secure high employment, in a more unbuttoned mood he told Archbishop Temple that a much reduced working week would be necessary as well; and in the United States he doubted whether even that would be enough. (These examples are cited in Robert Skidelsky's biography of Keynes.)

THE SATIATION BOGEY

The lack-of-work view is sometimes justified in terms of the satiation or saturation of human wants. This means that as productivity rises there will be nothing more, apart from leisure, that people will be willing to buy with extra income. There is not the slightest reason to suppose that we are within miles of this state. Anyone who is in any doubt should ask how many people he or she knows are indifferent to their pay, or do not care whether they earn more or less.

If satiation did arise, we would be in a state, not of depression, but of economic bliss. Technical progress would then be enjoyed by workers in the form of voluntary reductions in the working week, effected without state or union pressure and without loss of take-home pay. Thus it would not be unemployment in the sense of enforced idleness.

If saturation were really here, few would be interested in winning the football pools; and people might well continue to work in their chosen occupations regardless of reward, as a few writers do today. We are a very long way from such a state of affairs. Saturation of human wants – even in the industrial west, let alone in poorer countries – does not pass muster as an explanation of present-day unemployment.

If a few computers could satisfy all our material wants, there would be no need to worry about increases in the money supply or budget deficits. For there would be nothing on which people would want to spend their extra purchasing power and its inflationary impact would be zero. So financial analysts who scour the statistics and the small print of government documents looking for inflationary pressures and then 'wonder where the jobs are coming from' in their more informal comments, need to rethink their mixture of ill-digested and incompatible ideas.

UNDERDEVELOPMENT

There is, of course, a sense in which there is a chronic shortage of work in many parts of the world. The Chinese government estimates that between 100 and 200 million of the rural population is surplus to requirements. But this is not the result of high technology, modernization and rapid capital accumulation, but of their *absence* in large parts of the world.

The dropping of money from helicopters to the poor of China or India would not produce a sustainable increase in employment. This is not because there are no unsatisfied needs. It is for the very different reason that there is not sufficient capital, usable land and other factors of production – including business organization and entrepreneurial presence – to allow the underemployed poor to work to meet unsatisfied needs.

It would be quite unrealistic to talk of such people pricing themselves into work when the going wage or small farm income is already close to subsistence. In Third World countries, wages in a small modern enclave may be pushed up too far above the levels prevailing in the rest of the country, resulting in excessively capital-intensive methods and too few jobs. But underdevelopment – the opposite of what the Luddites complain of – is the true cause of the great bulk of open and concealed Third World joblessness.

Underdevelopment should not, however, be a cause of unemployment in mature western countries with stationary or slowly growing populations and centuries of business development behind them. 'Should not', but sometimes is. In Britain at the time of writing, it looks as if the main barrier to full employment is not the wage pressures which develop at high rates of labour utilization, but capacity bottlenecks, which lead to pressures in the goods and service markets while there is still surplus labour.

But it is superficial to stop here. Capacity shortages in advanced western countries usually reflect policy failings or badly working markets in years gone by. The interventionist reflex, which is to bribe businessmen into investing more, will often make matters worse.

The fundamental question is why businessmen have not found it worthwhile to invest to absorb labour surpluses, which in an unrigged market should be available at modest cost. The answer usually lies in some mixture of labour market rigidities, which price people out of work, and the restrictive demand policies which are a sometimes necessary response to these rigidities.

Investment can be crudely divided into *capital widening,* which increases capacity, and *capital deepening,* which increases the machine power per worker with the object of raising output per head. In a dynamic economy with a relatively free market, such as Britain in the nineteenth century, or Germany after the Second World War, investment takes at first a capital-widening form, increasing familiar kinds of plant and equipment – no doubt embodying the latest improvements but able to suck in more workers. As surplus labour diminishes, employers have to start bidding for workers, real wages increase and capital-deepening investment quite rationally plays an increasing part.

The effect of the labour market rigidities is to stop the widening investment too early and to induce an artificial deepening too early in the process of growth. Or, as Herbert Giersch puts it: 'the unemployment that is bound to emerge under collectively agreed minimum wages (classical unemployment of the first order) is thus transformed into a capital shortage unemployment (classical unemployment of the second order)'. There can even be a third degree in which 'process innovations' – to cut costs – are encouraged at the expense of 'product innovations' – to seek new markets. These are the roots of 'Eurosclerosis'.

DEMAND DEFICIENCY

There thus are still only two acceptable diagnoses of high unemployment: inadequate demand and pricing-out-of-work. The object of my 1975 booklet was to explain, as I have tried again to do in Chapter 7, why I had 'partially changed sides' and abandoned the belief that Keynesian demand management – by which I meant monetary, fiscal and exchange rate policies – could in itself establish a satisfactory low rate of unemployment.

The words 'partially changed sides' were carefully chosen. I still believed – and believe now – that demand management had a role to play in keeping total expenditure rising in line with the growth of the nation's productive capacity, but not so fast as to finance an inflationary take-off. The main development in my thinking since then has been the growing conviction that such non-inflationary demand management would have a greater chance of success if it contained an international element.

Deficient growth of demand is as bad as excessive growth and, if sufficiently prolonged, can itself pull up the underlying level of unemployment around which fluctuations take place. Almost for the first time since the Second World War, inadequate demand became in the early 1990s an important force making for more than very temporary unemployment. In the recession of the 1980s, the annual growth of demand in nominal terms – that is total national cash flow – never fell below 6 per cent either in the Group of Seven Summit countries or the European Community or the UK. In the recession of the 1990s it fell to 3 per cent in the European Community and to 4 per cent in the Group of Seven. This is perilously close to the rate at which demand deficiency becomes a principal contribution to unemployment and inadequate growth and which Keynesian policies, at their most sensible, are designed to counteract.

There are, of course, rough and ready political and market pressures making for more stimulative monetary and fiscal policies in the face of inadequate demand. But there has been a doctrinal retrogression since the 1980s. This can be seen by looking back at the 1985 Budget speech, when the then Chancellor, Nigel Lawson, said that the Medium Term Financial Strategy was as much a safeguard against deficient as against excessive demand. In his subsequent book (p. 411) he remarks that, had the circumstances arisen, a nominal framework would 'be as vigilant as Keynes would have desired in fighting off any cumulative contraction of national or global income'.

Understandably but unfortunately, the policy which the UK adopted after its forced departure from the ERM in 1992 was stated purely in terms of an inflation target of 1 to 4 per cent per annum. Independent central banks in other countries operated in terms of price targets; and 'price stability' was defined as the sole economic aim for the proposed European Central Bank. Thus if real output were to drop in one year by 10 per cent, while inflation remained not far from 1 per cent, there would be no breach of accepted objectives and thus no obligation to take countervailing action.

Nevertheless, fears of demand deficiency in the 1990s – whether they turn out to be justified or not – cannot explain the very large increase in unemployment in the 1970s and 1980s. In the aftermath of the British boom of the late 1980s, which was generally agreed to have imposed excessive demand pressures on the economy, the claimant total did not drop below 1.7 million, or 5.8 per cent of the workforce. In the 1950s and 1960s, however, average annual adult unemployment never exceeded 800,000, or 3 per cent, in the worst years of the cycle. Something else must have been at work. Indeed, failure to reverse the upward trend in unemployment appeared in the previous chapter as one of the clearest economic disappointments of the Thatcher government. It is too soon to say whether the earlier turnround of unemployment in the UK than in other European countries in the early 1990s marked the delayed-action effects of the earlier liberalization of the labour market.

PAY AND JOBS

The word 'structural' – or, better, 'hard-core' – can legitimately be used for that part of unemployment which cannot not be permanently reduced by demand expansion. It is this element which has been rising from one business cycle to the next, and which is especially bad in Europe. The proximate explanation for this hard core is pricing-out-of-work: that is, pay and other labour costs which make workers unprofitable to employ.

With the clear failure of demand deficiency to account for the bulk of the rise in European unemployment since the early 1970s, attention naturally turned to this aspect. If the price of any particular service is raised, less will be bought – both because purchasers can afford less and because they have an incentive to substitute something else. There is no reason why labour should be different.

Thus if labour costs are too high – not in the moral sense but relative to market-clearing levels – unemployment will also be high. Of course, the concept of 'the price of labour' is a vast abstraction. Even when pricing-out-of-work regained respectability as an explanation for unemployment, mainstream economists did not lay enough stress on the need for more flexibility of relative as well as absolute wages, at a time when the relative demand for different kinds of labour was changing rapidly.

Employers often play down the pay–jobs relationship on the grounds that labour costs are only a small part of total costs, especially in manufacturing. What they overlook is that most of what they spend on supplies, materials, components and services are someone else's labour costs. For all UK employers together labour costs have typically been over 70 per cent of total domestic costs.

Even then, some employers still insist that other factors are more important than pay or even total labour costs in employment decisions: the international economic outlook, overseas competition, interest and exchange rate uncertainties and so on. But these matters are outside their control and much less under government control than is popularly supposed. As in other markets, prices are an equilibrating factor balancing changes in the supply and demand for labour, however caused. If moralistic objections prevent pay from adjusting to market conditions, there will be more unused labour on some occasions, and on other occasions more labour shortages than we would otherwise have.

How large is the effect of pay on jobs? Enough has been said to show the difficulties of estimation. But, as a very rough order of magnitude, a 1 per cent drop in UK real wages brought about by a (somewhat larger) drop in money wages might raise employment by $\frac{1}{2}$–1 per cent, say 200,000 workers, according to a published analysis by Treasury officials which appeared in 1985.

The pricing-out-of-work principle generates much heat. Exponents are accused of 'treating labour as a commodity'. Outside slave-owning societies, workers are not commodities. But they do sell their *services* in a market, a fact that no red-faced denial will change. The forces at work can be seen most clearly in direct services where householders engage plumbers, gardeners, electricians and craftsmen without the intervention of an employer or other intermediary. For given standards of reliability and service, such people's activities will be in greater demand the less they charge. If they raise their fees too much, householders will react by resorting to do-it-yourself, waiting longer between refurbishment or making do in some other way. Nor is pricing-out-of-work a capitalist phenomenon. It is equally a phenomenon of state socialism, where there are no capitalist owners to benefit from lower wages.

Accepting the pricing-out-of-work explanation does not entail the advocacy of starvation wages. (No 'ought' proposition follows from a cause-and-effect relation.) If market-clearing pay rates are regarded as intolerably low, at least three courses are open. The first, and the counsel of despair, is to accept high unemployment as an alternative. The second, and counsel of perfection, is to try to raise the market value of workers' services so that customary pay rates are no longer a threat to employment. (This is described in mainstream economic writing as 'investing in human capital', a formulation which begs many questions.) The third is supplementary payments to families with low pay packets, a course which will be supported in the remaining chapters of this book. But we should note now that such supplementation comes from the fellow citizens. The state may provide the machinery for redistribution, but the government has no resources of its own and the affordability of such payments will depend on the general level of prosperity: which is not helped by an intellectual and artistic climate scornful of business and enterprise.

THE RESERVE ARMY

Even in the most rapidly clearing markets there will be some items held as stocks, the size of which will vary with expectations of future conditions. The stocks act as a useful buffer against sudden changes in market conditions and thus help to moderate price fluctuations.

Unemployed or semi-employed workers play a similar role in the labour market. This kind of unemployment used to be called 'frictional', although there is no hard-and-fast line between this and other kinds. The resemblance between Marx's 'reserve army' of unemployed and Friedman's 'natural rate' (more respectably known as the non-accelerating inflation rate of unemployment, or NAIRU, explained in Chapter 7) is no coincidence.

It is failure to see unemployment as a reserve or margin that explains the attraction of work-sharing ideas which aim to spread out a supposedly fixed amount of work by reducing the working week or lowering the retirement age. If the total number of working hours per year is reduced the size of that surplus will not be changed; and we shall end up with the same amount of unemployment, combined with less work and a smaller national income. But even this verdict is a good deal worse than neutral if, as Giersch fears, such measures 'shorten the supply of experienced workers and of highly skilled personnel' and thus worsen the capacity constraint met by the economy in periods of expansion.

Historical comparisons are fraught with danger, but they give us the only available clues to the normal size of the reserve army. In the six decades before the First World War, UK unemployment – measured by the index of union members concentrated in the highly cyclical capital goods industries – fluctuated sharply around an average of 5 per cent. In the 1920s, which were affected by the return to gold at the high pre-war parity, it fluctuated at around 8 per cent. In the 1930s it first rose to 15 per cent at the time of the world depression and then fell to 8 or 9 per cent by the end of the decade.

It is clear in retrospect that the rates of $1\frac{1}{2}$–$2\frac{1}{2}$ per cent characteristic of the 1950s and 1960s were abnormally low. But then so have been the very high rates characteristic of most of the 1980s and early 1990s. The 5 per cent rate, equivalent to 1.3 million, which prevailed in the last few years of the Labour government's period of office in the second half of the 1970s, is much more typical of historical experience. This does not make it optimal or even satisfactory, but it at least establishes a benchmark.

Unemployed workers who find themselves in the buffer role may suffer hardship. Neither social security payments nor private insurance can be more than a partial remedy for spells out of work because of 'moral hazard'. For the higher the social insurance floor, the more selective and demanding an unemployed worker is likely to be about accepting job offers. Thus vacancies will become more difficult to fill with suitable workers and a greater pool of people between jobs will be needed.

There are two ultimate remedies. Just as modern methods of stock control have enabled economies to operate with lower levels of inventories, so they ought to be able to operate with lower labour reserves. The second remedy is to have a labour market where most of the unemployed are short-term, spending a few weeks between jobs rather than languishing for years on the dole. This is much more true of the US than of the Continental labour markets; and the UK comes somewhere in between.

MONEY OR REAL WAGES?

Mainstream forecasters have admittedly found it difficult to fit the pay–jobs relation into their models. Such models easily show how increasing pay can, at a given exchange rate, make a country's goods uncompetitive and therefore lead to a loss of jobs. Model-builders also accept that higher real pay may lead to a substitution of capital for labour, but this is a long-term influence for which they can find only modest effects within the confines of their methodology.

The most formidable logical difficulty faced by the pricing-out-of-work approach is that pay is determined in money terms. This is so whether it is fixed by collective bargaining or individual negotiation. Real wages, in the sense relevant to employers, depend on the gross profit margin superimposed on labour and other direct costs. The question arises of why employers do not, or cannot, respond to excessive labour costs by restoring margins, which would contain labour costs as a proportion of value added.

A complete theory of unemployment would have to be a theory of the simul-taneous determination of all the key prices – of goods and capital as well as labour – in an imperfectly clearing national and international economy. Needless to say, I cannot provide such a theory. Nor is there any widely accepted and illuminating theory available from economists, but only a menu of incomplete individual models.

One of the most popular of such models is that of Richard Layard, which attributes high unemployment ultimately to 'wage pressure'. By this he means attempts to secure higher levels of real pay than the economic system is capable of delivering. As he puts it: 'Unemployment is in equilibrium when it is high enough to eliminate the leapfrogging of wages over each other and to make the planned mark-up of wages over prices (the target real wage) consistent with the planned mark-up of prices over wages (the feasible real wage).' As a result, the economy has to be run with a sufficient margin of unemployment to choke off these attempts. The problem with the Layard theory is that it is embedded in the collective bargaining approach and needs a lot of massaging to fit an economy such as the US or UK where union power has been on the wane.

WAGES AND DEMAND

A much-rehearsed objection to pricing-out is that wages are a source of demand as well as of costs. If money wages are reduced will not purchasing power be curtailed as well, taking us roughly back to where we started? This objection to pay cuts was expressed by Keynes in the 1930s and re-echoed by the President of the EC Commission, Jacques Delors, in 1992 and has at all times been voiced by union spokesmen.

It would be foolish to deny that such a self-stultifying chain of events could take place. A severe deflation in which wages and prices chase each other downwards in rapid succession would be as unstable and undesirable as the more familiar upward wage–price spiral. The best way out is not to get lost in a taxonomic analysis of alternative reactions, but to make the *policy suggestion* that government and central banks should be committed to maintaining a growth of demand in nominal terms – or national cash objective – low enough to prevent an inflationary take-off, but high enough to secure adequate growth when pay and prices are sufficiently restrained. In other words, if pay moderation were to lead to a contraction in demand the authorities would be committed to compensate for these effects. In practice this would mean lower interest rates, which would stimulate both investment and consumption, and lower taxes or higher government expenditure, both of which stimulate spending.

HUNTERS AND FISHERMEN

There is surely, however, a big neglected pricing-out-of-work influence that has nothing to do with exchange rates or capital substitution and would exist in a barter economy with modest capital equipment. This arises from the output loss when people are prevented from working.

Let us try a little fable. Hunters are exchanging beaver skins with fishermen, in exchange for some of the latter's catch. The number of fish per skin is their wage. Now suppose that a dominant group of hunters succeeds in imposing a price ring in the shape of a minimum rate of exchange between skins and fish higher than the market-clearing one. Some of the skins of hunters with less elbow-power remain unsold and some fishermen find it less attractive to exchange fish; so they eat more themselves or sit in their huts.

If some Robin Hood figure destroys the price ring in skins, the quantity of marketable output and trade, and thus employment, increases both among hunters and fishermen; and this occurs in a world with no central bank, government or money but just a primitive kind of enforced trade unionism. This type of pricing-out-of-work has its effect through lowering the level of output and is almost certainly present in more complex money economies as well.

THE BENEFIT FLOOR

Even some neoclassical economists are unhappy at an account of unemployment that puts the emphasis on pricing-out-of-work or even union monopoly. Their argument is that at its height in 1979, British trade union membership accounted for only 53 per cent of the labour force. Why did not those excluded by excessive pay settlements price themselves into the non-unionized sector?

The emphasis of economists such as Patrick Minford was not on monopoly labour pricing, as such, but on the level of benefit when out of work. These economists make the benefit ratio – that is, the ratio of benefits to average pay – the fulcrum of their whole explanation. The benefit level is supposed to provide the floor or reservation wage below which it does not pay to take a registered job.

Estimates of this ratio are controversial and have varied enormously. Up to the early 1980s, it did not take much in the way of travel expenses, undeclared earnings, do-it-yourself activities and the like to eliminate the gain from taking a job for quite a large number of people in the bottom half of the UK earnings distribution. What is not controversial is that the ratio fell a great deal in the ensuing ten years. OECD comparisons suggest that by the early 1990s the UK ratio was about the lowest of all principal countries, with the exception of Japan and the US.

The pricing-out-of-work and benefit level explanations come together in the assertion that, without the dole, pay rates would drop, as people would have to price themselves into work to survive. I prefer the pricing-out formulation because it leaves space for institutional, psychological and even moral forces which – quite apart from the dole – stop pay from shifting to market-clearing levels.

According to the Department of Employment, membership of unions had fallen from a peak of 53 per cent of the employed labour force in 1979 to 37 per cent by 1992. The unionization percentage in fact exaggerates the ease with which people on benefit could price themselves into work if they so wished. More workers are covered by collective settlements than belong to unions. The public services are still heavily unionized and are also subject to 'independent' review bodies – misguidedly reconstituted by the Thatcher and Major governments –

which are engines for maintaining pay at the expense of employment. In the private sector, men, who have suffered the bulk of the increase in unemployment, are more heavily unionized than women. If men priced out of work in the union sector were to try to price themselves into work outside that sector, many would have to crowd into relatively limited and unfamiliar occupations, where wages might have to fall to subsistence or lower.

None of this is to deny that benefits affect the numbers genuinely seeking work and the terms on which they will accept it. As recent Conservative governments shrank from a full-frontal assault on the benefits system, Radical Right advisers (with some quiet support from left-of-centre labour market economists) successfully urged them to tighten the criteria for drawing benefits, through more stringent application of the availability-for-work requirement, insistence on training and drives against fraud. Benefit conditions became much stricter and benefits ceased to be an optional fallback for all.

These changes were part of a wider shock to labour markets in the 1980s and early 1990s. Union power was greatly reduced. Union legal immunities were curtailed, compulsory strike ballots instituted and the closed shop made unenforceable. Wages Councils, which fixed minimum pay in low wage industries, were much reduced in scope. Above all, there was a notable series of anti-strike victories in sectors ranging from coal mines to newspapers, where union strike power had previously been regarded as impregnable. On the positive side, the tax and national insurance system was adjusted to reduce discouragement to the hiring of low-paid workers.

Nevertheless, the influence of union pricing-out-of-work is of more than historical importance. Legislative fashions change. One of Britain's two main political parties is still very much union-based. In Germany the unions are politically influential even when the Social Democrats are out of office at the federal level. Although unions are a much smaller presence in the US than in the European labour market, they still have a strong influence on American Democrats.

At the time of writing, their influence on both sides of the Atlantic is as pressure groups for the re-regulation of labour markets and for the imposition of quite unsuitable European and American standards of minimum pay and social security for businesses in the developing countries wanting to sell in western markets. The slogan is the prevention of 'social dumping', but the practical impact is to deny opportunities and markets to workers in the poorer countries, at whose boundaries genuine fraternal feelings come to an end.

EMPLOYERS TAKE OVER THE RUNNING

Why did pricing-out-of-work continue for so long in the UK and unemployment remain obstinately high? One reason was that *employers* took over the running in pay decisions and continued to grant pay increases unwarranted by market conditions. At no time before 1992 did the nominal annual increase in earnings per head fall below $7\frac{1}{2}$ per cent. In most years earnings increases averaged 2 to 4 per cent above inflation. It was only for one year in the aftermath of the 1980–1 recession, and again at the end of 1993, that earnings increases even fell towards the underlying rate of inflation. Why then did the labour market liberalization, coming on top of two severe recessions, take so long to affect pay and jobs?

What happened could not be explained by a mechanistic model which ignored beliefs and attitudes. The labour market is the one where the Adam Smith doctrine of Natural Liberty has made least headway and the doctrine of the just reward has lingered longest. Wages above market-clearing rates give corporate executives a quiet life and a reputation among the less-thinking as good employers. Indeed, it became common for businessmen to boast of their preference for a small but well-paid labour force.

Many of my writings in the mid-1980s were directed against this mentality. The employer who prefers a small, highly paid labour force is far from being a public benefactor. He is using a queueing system based on above-market wages to sort out the workers he considers most reliable and efficient; and he is passing on to others or to the social security system responsibilities for those who are less-attuned to the work ethic or are in any other way difficult to employ but nevertheless capable of making some contributions to their fellow citizens. In terms of the Bertrand Russell quotation in Chapter 1, he is falling below self-interest rather than rising above it.

Not only does the employer who boasts of high wages and low payrolls contribute to unemployment; he is doing much less to relieve the poverty even of those at work than he thinks. The relationship between pay and poverty is much weaker than generally supposed. According to an analysis in the 1994 UK *Social Trends* some 70 per cent of individuals in the bottom fifth of the income distribution were in households without a head in full-time work. So keeping wages above market-clearing levels not only destroys jobs, but is a very inefficient method of protecting the poor, compared for instance with tax and social security measures.

THE EUROPEAN SOCIAL CHARTER

Excessive labour costs reflect not only wages, but other expenses too. Interestingly enough, one of the best lists of such items was given by the Commission of the European Community itself in its *Report* for 1984:

The wage determination system; non-wage costs; taxation; minimum wage levels;
unemployment insurance; rules governing recruitment and dismissal, the flexibility
of working hours and the organisation of work, health hazards and safety; rules
governing unions and the right to strike; pension schemes; the housing market;
training and education.

These practices are called by their proponents 'employment protection legislation'. But to the extent that they increase the cost of taking on workers, a better
name would be employment-destroying. Unfortunately, the Commission's own
Social Affairs Directorate has fought tooth-and-nail to entrench and even extend
these practices. As the British Chancellor of the Exchequer Kenneth Clarke said
in a speech in Germany in 1993, Europe's labour markets are 'over-rigid, over-
regulated and overpriced'.

Giersch has cited the specific German example of wages that result from
collective bargaining being extended by law and custom to employees and firms
that are not part of the bargaining organization. Sometimes these collective
agreements added *per capita* lump-sum increases in addition to the normal
percentage ones, which had the effect of increasing pay for apprentices much
faster than for trained skilled workers. This tended to increase youth unemployment and offset the official jawboning to persuade firms to offer
apprenticeships.

The Major government in Britain soon discerned a threat from labour market
rigidities emanating from the Continent of Europe, in the shape of the Social
Charter which was a part of the Maastricht Treaty approved in 1993, from which
the UK gained a special exemption. Many of the regulations to which the
government most objected did not come from the Social Charter as such, but
from Commission attempts to interpret earlier Community legislation. But the
spirit was more important than the letter. British ministers were remarkably
successful in gaining a second wind in their drive to free labour markets by
pointing to the contrast between the deregulated British labour market and the
ossification which they saw on the Continent and which they denounced as making
Europe 'uncompetitive'. They were able to win support from those who disliked
geographical centralization, or the loss of sovereignty to the European Community,
irrespective of their views – if any – on labour market economics.

It is however important to separate the wheat from the chaff in all these
arguments. Social charges of various kinds, whether to finance a crèche or to
finance pensions, do not price workers out of jobs if they are seen as substitutes for take-home pay, which, as a result is lower than it otherwise would be.
The basic harm of Social Charter-type provisions arises when employers are
required to make expensive changes, such as accepting shorter hours for the
same pay, which are equivalent in effect to expensive pay settlements, but are
not recognized as such. The worst effects of all are the rigidities imposed at a

micro level in preventing employers from adjusting to unexpected *changes* in market conditions, for example by increasing hours of work. All such restrictions make projects which employ much labour unattractive and risky and promote a search for labour-saving methods instead.

THE CHANGING LABOUR MARKET

The real weakness of the pricing-out-of-work thesis, as often expounded, is its timelessness - a weakness rarely spotted by the critics. Why should there be so much more pricing-out-of-work in some periods than in others? Or – to put it in macroeconomic terms – why should the rate of unemployment consistent with non-accelerating inflation (the NAIRU) have apparently been so low in the 1950s and 1960s and then risen so much first in the later 1970s and even more in the 1980s and 1990s?

There are those who think that the fault lies with the sinister hold that 'monetarist' economists acquired over political leaders. Such an explanation attributes a scarcely credible amount of influence to a few academics and commentators. It hardly explains the breakdown of post-war full-employment policies in one European country after another, irrespective of political regime.

It certainly does not explain why countries like Sweden, previously wedded both to ambitious demand management and to consensus agreements between centralized employer and union organizations – a system often called 'corporatism' – should have come adrift. Nor does it explain why, despite many other labour market and social problems, the United States did not experience a trend rise in unemployment after the mid-1970s. And it cannot explain why the famous Japanese lifetime employment system should show signs of coming apart in the 1990s.

There are at least two reasons why unemployment could have remained so low in the early post-war decades. First, there was the persistence of 'money illusion' – the belief surviving from pre-war that a pound was a pound and a dollar was a dollar. Insufficient allowance was made for inflation in pay and price behaviour; and it was therefore possible to run national economies with much tighter labour markets than before or afterwards without triggering off an accelerating inflation.

In his famous address in 1967, when he denied any long-term trade-off between unemployment and inflation, Milton Friedman nevertheless envisaged a couple of decades before pay fully adjusted to a change in price behaviour. This was more convincing, especially for the post-war decades, than the current 'rational expectations' orthodoxy which insists that beliefs about inflation, as about everything else, are adjusted quickly.

The second and perhaps more interesting reason is that post-war growth was a fairly straightforward process involving other countries catching up with best-practice American techniques. Modest traditional pay relativities between industries, and between skilled and unskilled workers, were sufficient to balance the labour market.

This post-war Golden Age came to an end with the oil price explosion when the price of that fuel rose fivefold in the wake of the Yom Kippur war of 1973–4. Tremors had already been felt in the late 1960s following the inflationary financing of the Vietnam War by the US. The inflationary outbreak of the 1970s shattered any remnants of money illusion for generations to come. A slacker labour market was from then onwards required to prevent pay and prices chasing each other upwards. In addition, the huge rise in oil and related energy prices made much energy-intensive equipment uneconomic and thus made the existing structure of capacity inappropriate.

The relative demand for different types of labour was still for a time stable enough for Central European and Scandinavian countries with strong traditions of social solidarity to hold real wages in check at modest levels of unemployment. Thus demand management – whatever label was attached to it – could be directed against inflation without large job losses. As the 1980s proceeded, however, the conditions required for these centralized agreements to work began to disappear. Traditional relativities between different industries and skills, or between areas of declining old-fashioned manufacturing industry and 'high-tech' growth areas (for example between north and south Germany) were no longer sufficient to clear labour markets. Meanwhile the rigidities imposed to obtain union consent for national economic policies became more and more a drag on performance.

LESSONS FROM THE US

Developments in the US provide a striking contrast. In 1973 the total number of jobs was very similar in the US to what it was in a group of Central and Western European countries selected by the OECD in its 1993 *Employment Outlook*. Between then and 1989 (that is, comparing two cyclical peaks) employment in these European countries rose by a bare 5 million, while in the US it jumped by 32 million. Demographic differences between the growth of population of working age on the two sides of the Atlantic could only explain about half the disparity in job growth between the two sides of the Atlantic in the 1970s and none of it in the 1980s. The differential rise in US jobs represented the country's superiority in finding work for a greater proportion of its labour force.

But there was an underside to this success. While employment rose in relation to population, real compensation per hour rose by only $\frac{1}{2}$ per cent per annum or less in the 1960s, 1970s and 1980s. Excluding fringe benefits, they actually fell in the last of these decades. Household income and spending were not hit as hard, partly because higher participation rates in the labour force helped family income, and partly because there was an increase in the share of the national income devoted to non-wage receipts, whether property income or social security payments.

Nevertheless the stagnation of pay was sufficient to convince many US citizens that the American dream was failing and that the present generation would not enjoy the same opportunities as its parents and grandparents. It was this feeling, more than anything else, that took Bill Clinton to the White House in 1992.

More striking even than the stagnation of average pay was the increase in pay disparities. Worst of all, the real hourly wages of young males with 12 or fewer years of schooling dropped *in absolute terms* by 20 per cent. The differential earnings of college graduates increased by 30 per cent relative to those with only high school education. As relative pay also rose at the top of the earnings distribution, the phenomenon became known as 'polarization'.

RISING DIFFERENTIALS

The same pressures that have expressed themselves in the US in pay stagnation have come to the surface in Europe in unemployment and non-employment (that is, workers who have left the official labour force). Nevertheless, every western country, and not just the US, has experienced widening pay differentials among those who remain in work. One method of measuring these is the 'dispersion' of earnings: the ratio of earnings in the top or bottom 10 percentile range of the earnings distribution to the earnings of those in the middle (the 'median').

In the US and the UK the widening of the dispersion started in the late 1970s. But everywhere it became more acute by the end of the 1980s. According to the OECD analysis, very little of this increased dispersion was due to structural shifts such as the move from industry to services. For the change was very similar *within* each business sector. What technological change does seem to have done is raise the market earnings of highly skilled or educated workers far more than those of unskilled ones.

Yet even within groups of similar education and experience, pay differentials grew. In a daring dive into common sense the OECD authors suggest 'an increased importance for skills not measured by educational qualifications, such as the ability to work with other people'. There was also a considerable latent demand at modest pay scales for quite basic unskilled jobs, many of them part time, which were more inclined to attract women than men. Indeed, a newspaper survey suggested that the most rapid UK job growth in 1993 was in domestic service.

The moral for unemployment suggests itself. If pay differentials have had to widen so much despite a big and ever-growing departure from full employment, how much more would they have had to widen to price all workers into jobs? Nor was it only a question of differentials. No wonder James Meade suggested that to create 2 million more jobs in Britain average real wages would not merely have to be 'restrained' but actually to fall.

FACTOR PRICE EQUALIZATION

One explanation of what has happened is based on the profound changes taking place in the world economy. A big shift has been taking place in the geographical centre of gravity away from the traditionally rich countries that make up most of the OECD membership. Associated with this has been a steep decline in the share of manufacturing in total employment in the OECD countries. In the US the manufacturing share peaked as early as 1920. Countries such as Germany – which is a real outlier with a manufacturing share of 32 per cent, very high in relation to GDP – face a shock decline in this sector as severe as anything the UK has experienced.

Two British economists (DeAnne Julius and R. Brown) caused quite a minor sensation when they speculated in a prize-winning essay that manufacturing would account for 10 per cent or less of the working population in most OECD countries by the end of the second decade of the twenty-first century. But in so doing, it would only be following a path of decline similar to that experienced by agriculture in the past 50 years. The authors see nothing horrifying in these trends. Service workers are not just 16-year-olds flipping hamburgers at McDonalds. Managers, sales personnel, brain surgeons and bankers are all in the service sector.

These events can be seen in the context of a 'theorem' promulgated by the Swedish economist and statesman Bertil Ohlin after the First World War, and restated in modern form by Paul Samuelson in most books of international trade readings. It is known as 'factor price equalization'. A 'factor' is what a businessman would call an input. Trade economists tend to group these inputs into very broad categories, such as capital, land, skilled and unskilled labour.

The so-called theorem asserts what many practical men have long supposed: that when available production techniques are similar, transport costs are low, and several other conditions are met, the earnings of 'factors' in different countries will *tend* to equality under free trade. For instance, wages of unskilled labour in the US will fall and unskilled labour in India and China rise towards a common level.

With the stagnation in US blue-collar wages of the 1980s and the rise in European unemployment, factor price equalization left the cloister and entered the world of policy argument. Indeed, some economists have been reminded of Marx's theory of the immiseration of the proletariat.

Such breast-beating has probably been premature. International studies, such as those summarized in the 1993 OECD *Industrial Policy Review*, suggest that technological change has hitherto been more important in creating these labour market pressures than either Reagan–Thatcher-type policies or international trade pressures. Research by Robert Lawrence and others suggests that the main reason for the squeeze on US real pay has been the very slow growth in productivity in the *service* sector, which now employs the bulk of the labour force. (US manufacturing productivity growth did indeed recover in the 1980s to Golden Age levels.)

Developing country exports have hitherto accounted for too small a proportion of manufacturing sales in the west to explain the downward pressure on unskilled wages. A more convincing explanation is skill-based technical change primarily of domestic origin. But whatever the position in the past, international trade movements could well impose pressures on pay levels in future. It is indeed probable that imports from developing or former communist countries will in future depress the market-clearing levels of pay among the least skilled or least adaptable groups.

FURTHER QUESTIONS

So far the debate is very incomplete. More analysis is required of likely pay trends in developing and former communist countries and how such countries are likely to spend their growing export proceeds. If this were done their emergence into the world economy might be seen as less of a threat and more of an opportunity than it is at present. Factor price equalization can be achieved by upward movement of real wages in developing countries, which could reduce or even remove the need for downward adjustments in the mature economies. This would be desirable so long as it reflected improving labour productivity and tightening labour markets in these countries rather than trade conditions imposed by the industrial west.

The implications for policy in the mature industrialized countries are not all that different whether the downward pressures on demand for many kinds of labour come from imports or from indigenous change. A familiar if clichéd response is the call for more education and training. There is also the need for more sensitive social security arrangements which will encourage people to stay in the labour market even on low or part-time pay.

Meanwhile, we can take comfort from the fundamental proposition of international trade theory and indeed of all economics. It is that voluntary exchange makes both sides better off. If free trade opens up the prospect of increasing the national income, the losses of particular groups are a distributional problem and cannot be shrugged off by references to training. The challenge is to find non-vindictive ways of redistributing income towards the losers. It is to find methods of redistribution that do not assume that all income belongs to the state. It is to find ways of compensating the casualties which do not destroy the gains from trade and technology, while providing a reasonable cushion for those against whom market forces have turned.

REFERENCES

Balls, E. and P. Gregg, *Work and Welfare*, London: Institute for Public Policy Research, 1993.

Bhagwati, J. (ed.), *International Trade, Selected Readings*, Harmondsworth, Middx: Penguin, 1969.

Bhagwati, J. and V. Dehejia, *Freer Trade and Wages of the Unskilled: Is Marx Striking Again?*, Washington, D.C.: American Enterprise Institute, 1993.

Brittan, S., *Second Thoughts on Full Employment Policy*, London: Centre for Policy Studies, 1975.

Brittan, S., *Two Cheers for Self Interest* (Wincott Memorial Lecture), London: Institute of Economic Affairs, 1985.

Brown, R. and DeAnne Julius, 'Is Manufacturing Special in the New World Order?', in *Amex Bank Prize Winning Essays*, Oxford, 1993.

Central Statistical Office, *Social Trends*, London: HMSO, 1994.

Clarke, Kenneth, 'Europe's Economic Future: Compete or Retreat?', Speech in Munich, 19 July 1993, London: H.M. Treasury.

Commission of the European Communities, *Annual Report*, Brussels, Nov. 1984.

Friedman, M., 'The Role of Monetary Policy', reprinted in *The Optimum Quantity of Money and Other Essays*, Chicago, Ill.: Aldine Publishing, 1969.

Giersch, H., *The World Economy in Perspective*, Aldershot, Hants.: Edward Elgar 1991.

Lawrence, R.Z., 'Rude Awakening: the End of the American Dream', *International Economic Insights* (Institute for International Economics, Washington, D.C.), Jan.–Feb. 1994.

Lawson, Nigel, *The View from No. 11*, London: Bantam Press, 1992.

Layard, R., S. Nickel and R. Jackman, *Unemployment: Macroeconomic Performance and the Labour Market,* Oxford: 1991.

McWilliams, Douglas, *Perhaps Marx was Right After All*, London: Centre for Economic Performance, London School of Economics, 1993.

Meade, James, *Full Employment and Inflation*, London: Social Market Foundation, 1994.

Meade, James, *Liberty, Equality and Efficiency*, London: Macmillan, 1990.

Metcalf, David, *Industrial Relations and Economic Policy*, London: Centre for Economic Policy Research, London School of Economics, 1993.

Minford, Patrick, *The Supply Side Revolution in Britain*, Aldershot, Hants.: Edward Elgar, 1991.

Minford, Patrick, *et al.*, *Unemployment: Causes and Cure*, 2nd edn, Oxford: Martin Robertson, 1985.

OECD, *Employment Outlook*, Paris: OECD, 1993.

OECD, *Employment/Unemployment Study*, Paris: OECD, 1994

OECD, *Industrial Policy Review*, Paris: OECD, 1993.

OECD, *Survey of the USA*, Paris: OECD, 1986.

Parris M., 'It is unhealthy ...', *The Times*, 21 December 1992.

Skidelsky, Robert, *John Maynard Keynes*, vol. 2, London: Macmillan, 1992.

United Kingdom. H.M. Treasury, *The Relation Between Unemployment and Wages: Empirical Evidence for the* UK, London: HMSO, 1985.

United States. Council of Economic Advisers, *Annual Reports*, Washington, D.C.: USGPO.

PART FIVE

Capitalism with a Human Face

12   Redistribution: yes. Equality: no*

BOGUS EQUALITY

On what principles should income, wealth and – most elusive of all – power be distributed? Equality is an ideal to which many pay lip service, but which they hope will not be achieved in their own lifetimes. Sensible egalitarians also accept that there must be some differences in measured income and wealth to provide incentives as well as to supply some of the personal motivations in people's lives.

Thus a very common goal has been to move towards equality, but not go to extremes. The approach has respectable antecedents. Many mainstream economists believe that there are two important goals: efficiency (which really means prosperity) and equality, which have to be traded off against each other. The more you have of one the less you have of the other; and the nearer you get to complete equality the greater becomes the price, in terms of lost efficiency, of going a little further.

The relative weight given to the two objectives are supposed to derive from some unexplained political judgement – although some economists and philosophers believe that the principle of diminishing marginal utility (which suggests that an extra pound is worth more to a poor man than to a rich man) provides an almost scientific basis for making the trade-off.

Alas, there is more than a little self-deception about these procedures. Even if there were no adverse incentive effects, many people who pay lip service to equality would hate a completely egalitarian society, if such a thing could be imagined. Unfortunately, they lack a respectable language for stating their position and do not know how to express their concern for the position of the poor and the disadvantaged other than in terms of slogans about reducing inequality.

The question of a just – or at least minimally acceptable – distribution of income and property rights has assumed a much higher profile since the collapse of communism in the former Soviet Union and its neighbours. Since then a new

* This chapter is a revised version of Appendix Two of *Beyond the Welfare State* by S. Brittan and S. Webb, Aberdeen: Aberdeen University Press, 1990. The title and first few paragraphs are from an article in the *Listener*, 23 September 1982.

class of affluent entrepreneurs has emerged, while many other people say that they have become worse off than under the communist regime. Meanwhile, in the old industrial west, market forces have been squeezing the relative, and perhaps the absolute, rewards of those in the lower part of the income distribution. How far then can we, or should we, go towards either providing a basic minimum or towards compensating for victims of change?

We urgently need some principles of redistribution which will discourage temporary majorities or pluralities from attempting unlimited expropriation. Such majorities are likely to be succeeded by radical reactionaries intent on reversing all the preceding redistribution; and the resulting alternation produces both deep personal insecurity and disturbing economic instability.

Even if we were agreed on the ideal answers, we would still have to investigate how far we could depart from market-clearing pay rates and acquired property without undermining prosperity and freedom. The answer was long ago foreshadowed by Keynes who said that there was more scope for redistribution by taxes and transfer than by direct interference in the labour market, but that there was not unlimited scope along either route.

It is tempting to say that redistribution should go on until the losses from capital outflows and emigration of highly skilled professional and management personnel suggest a halt. But opinions on when this is likely to happen are quite as wide apart as they are on the basic ethics. Moreover, the nationalistic stance forecloses any discussion of what the norm should be of the main industrial countries, taken together.

Before we come to the difficult trade-offs, we run up against the proliferation of incompatible criteria for what ought to be the case. 'Leave it to the markets' is not even a coherent slogan. For, before the market game can begin on a basis which commands support, there have to be rules determining the distribution of the stakes. Yet there is nothing even remotely approaching a consensus, even among political economists who support the market system, on how an acceptable distribution of capital and income should be determined.

Many ordinary citizens would say that income and wealth should be distributed 'fairly', as if fairness were a natural quality like redness or hardness whose presence or absence was obvious and uncontroversial. Some people would emphasize rewarding skills, some the need to give more to the lower paid, some the entrenchment of differentials, and some rewarding those doing dirty or risky jobs. There is no end to these often conflicting criteria. There is not even a *de facto* consensus on relative income levels or the ownership of property, let alone on matters of power, opportunity, prestige or influence. The lack of an accepted theory of property rights and of income distribution is a weakness both in classical liberalism and market economics.

DEFECTS OF 'MERIT'

The popular idea that pay should reflect moral merit is misconceived for the reasons explained in Chapter 6, where Hayek's objections to it were endorsed. To recapitulate briefly: an attempt to replace market determination of pay by some collective evaluation of merit would do grave economic damage, producing high unemployment in some places and at some times, and labour shortages in others.

But for all that, it would not even be just. For if inherited wealth and differences in educational opportunity could both be abolished, there would still be no inherent moral value attaching to the resulting distribution of income and wealth. As Hayek remarks:

> The inborn as well as the acquired gifts of a person clearly have a value to his fellows which do not depend on any credit due to him for possessing them. There is little a man can do to alter the fact that his special talents are very common or exceedingly rare. A good mind or a fine voice, a beautiful face or a skilful hand, a ready wit or an attractive personality, are in large measure as independent of a person's efforts as the opportunities or experiences he has had. In all these instances the value which a person's capacities or services have for us, and for which he is recompensed, has little relation to anything that we can call moral merit or deserts.

Indeed, it is one of the advantages of a market economy enjoying basic bourgeois liberties that a man's livelihood does not depend on other people's evalution of his merit. It is sufficient that he should be able to perform some work or sell a service for which there is a demand.

THE FALLACIES OF THE PIE

Near the end of Chapter 3, under the heading of 'Distribution' I looked at some concepts of fair reward and found most of them wanting. A favourite idea, as already mentioned, is that ideally we ought to have equal shares in income and wealth and that policy should aim to go as far as practicable in that direction.

But apart from all the conceptual difficulties of defining equality and the adverse economic repercussions, the idea is fundamentally flawed for the following reason. If the resources of society are regarded as one big pie to be allocated by a central authority, then the natural principle of division is equality. Departures from that principle have to be justified – just as a mother who gives children unequal shares has to show that the favoured child is bigger or better behaved, or that the child with the smaller piece has stomach trouble, is naughty or gets less for other reasons.

The equality suggested by the pie theory is notoriously difficult to define. Is it to be equal in relation to individuals or families or needs? Is somebody with greater capacity for happiness to be allowed more, as in some versions of utilitarianism, or less to offset his inborn advantage? The complications are multiplied enormously if we abandon absolutes and talk of greater equality or less inequality.

The pie theory of distribution is in itself inherently vulnerable. One Harvard philosopher, Robert Nozick, has remarked (in *Anarchy, State and Utopia*):

> We are not in the position of children who have been given some portions of pie. There is no central distribution. What each person gets, he gets from others who give it to him in exchange for something, or as a gift. In a free society diverse persons hold different resources and new holdings arise out of the voluntary exchanges and actions of persons ... The total result is the product of many individual decisions.

The weakness of the pie theory is that there is no fixed sum to go round. Individuals add to the pie by their activities and it is by no means obvious that the others should treat the results as part of a common pool.

... AND OF ENTITLEMENT

The opposite extreme to the pie theory is a historical or process theory. One leading example is the 'entitlement theory', formerly upheld by Nozick. This stated that holdings were just if they had been jointly acquired or justly transferred by gift or free exchange in the market. The doctrine applied to both property holdings and income from work.

Nozick later distanced himself from this position, saying that it was 'seriously inadequate', partly because it overlooked the 'symbolic meaning of government'. The just entitlement theory has already been criticized in Chapter 3, as giving no reason for the prohibition of state-enforced transfers logically persuasive to those who do not accept the minimal state at the outset.

To put it more concretely: the very content of property rights and the rules governing their transfer, as well as their physical protection, are the result of collectively enforced rules and decisions, which we are at liberty to change. In the words of the nineteenth-century historian, J.A. Froude: 'Without the state there would be no such thing as property. The state guarantees to each individual what he has earned; and fixes the conditions on which this protection will be granted.'

Not all policies for redistributing income and wealth inevitably involve assessing merit, measuring need or aiming to achieve equality of reward – whatever the latter would mean. There is another position. This is to accept the rankings of the actual or reformed market, but to use fiscal means to narrow differentials so that the game is played for smaller stakes. What then is needed is a view on the general shape of a tolerable distribution which does not involve a moralistic evaluation of any person or occupation. Whether this view merits the grandiose title 'social justice', which acts as a red rag to Hayek and the Radical Right, or whether it is given a less ambitious name, such as 'theory of distribution', is a matter of taste.

A CONTRACTARIAN APPROACH

The conclusion of Chapter 3 was that the least unsatisfactory family of principles was that known by the portentous name of contractarianism. The seventeenth- and eighteenth-century exponents of the social contract, such as Locke and Rousseau, half-envisaged in their very different ways some historical agreement among primitive peoples. Modern contractarians have in mind a thought experiment. The most promising approach is to ask: what are the basic rules of society governing the distribution of income and wealth (as well, of course, as other matters) that would be chosen in a hypothetical contract which it would be rational for self-interested individuals to accept as a condition of living together in society?

In his celebrated *Theory of Justice*, John Rawls made great play with the 'veil of ignorance', which is sometimes called the original position. The idea is to work out the principles on which free and rational persons concerned to further their own interests would desire their community to be run if they did not know their own social or economic place, the market value of their own talents and many other key features of their real situation. A wealthy man might like to establish principles which minimized taxes for welfare purposes; a poor man might espouse principles of an opposite kind. If people exclude knowledge of their own actual position, there is some chance of formulating principles on a disinterested basis. The veil of ignorance precludes potential oppression of the minority, or of large groups by a coalition of minorities, which can follow from uninhibited majority voting.

For all his pioneering work, Rawls's version is but one of several modern contractarians'; and the particular principles which he derives from the veil of ignorance are less persuasive than the veil itself. The principle most relevant to the present discussion is Rawls's claim that social and economic inequalities are only justified if they improve the position of the least-well-off representative person – a principle sometimes known as the 'maximin'. Rawls would therefore take redistribution via the tax and social security system to the point where any further redistribution would so impoverish the economy that the least well off would no longer gain.

This principle does not in fact follow from the contractarian starting point of the veil of ignorance. The extreme concentration on the least well off presupposes that the representative citizen under the veil of ignorance would be concerned with risk aversion to the exclusion of everything else. This is highly questionable. Somebody with a taste for gambling would be interested in seeing that there were some really big prizes in case he came out lucky: which would be quite consistent with seeking a safety net; and even a non-gambler might have an interest in the rewards available above the very bottom.

Despite Rawls's insistence in later work that a choice made under the veil of ignorance depends on 'philosophical' and not psychological considerations, I do not see how empirically established preferences can be overlooked. On the other hand, Rawls's later acceptance that his principles of justice are drawn from the values of liberal democracy rather than from timeless reasoning is a step forward.

A FLOOR CONSTRAINT

Nevertheless, Rawls still expects too determinate a result from the contractarian thought experiment. The veil of ignorance supplies a criterion of disinterestedness, and thus helps to narrow disagreements; but it cannot eliminate differences of subjective preference or lead to a unique result which all people of goodwill can accept. My own desire under the veil of ignorance would be to make sure that everyone had a basic minimum, defined at least in part in relation to the wealth of my society. This would be a safeguard in case I drew the unfortunate card and found myself at the bottom of the pack; but above that I would like to see the highest possible level of income and wealth for the representative or median citizen consistent with basic liberties (regarding leisure and amenity as an aspect of income). Above this there would be positive advantage in there being a number of rich, or very rich, people, distinct from the state.

It was therefore of some comfort to learn of psychological experiments suggesting that people do in fact prefer rules of the game which would maximize average incomes, subject to a floor constraint. I do not want to lean too heavily on small-scale tests among students; but the concept of a basic minimum above which everyone is free to rise has strong prudential and ethical resonance.

The concept of maximizing opportunities, subject to a basic floor, is of course not a single solution but a family of solutions, determined by the choice of floor; and in the experiments cited, the students did disagree on the level of the floor. The contractarian method, and the family of results derived from it, do however represent a notable improvement on the mutually exclusive viewpoints of the pie and entitlement theories. The narrowing to a discussable and quantifiable area of strongly held differences of opinion is the most that can be expected from abstract reflection.

Some readers may think that I have gone to unnecessary and tortuous lengths to justify Winston Churchill's concept of the ladder and the safety net. Others might prefer to get to this destination by different routes. But at a time when many supporters of markets do not see that they are naked without a theory of property rights and income distribution, and when many of their opponents still regard market-determined rewards as immoral, some such groundwork is necessary.

REFERENCES

Frohlich, N., J.A. Oppenheimer and C.L. Eavey, 'Laboratory Results on Rawls's Distributive Justice', *British Journal of Political Science*, 7 (1), (January 1987).
Froude, J.A., *Address to the Liberty and Property Defence League*, London, 1887.
Hayek, F.A., *The Constitution of Liberty*, London: Routledge & Kegan Paul, 1960.
Nozick, R., *Anarchy, State and Utopia*, New York: Basic Books, 1974.
Nozick, R., *The Examined Life*, New York: Simon & Schuster, 1989, pp. 17 and 286–92.
Okun, A., *Equality and Efficiency: The Big Tradeoff*, Washington, D.C.: Brookings Institution, 1984.
Rawls, J., *Political Liberalism*, New York: Columbia University Press, 1993.
Rawls, J., *A Theory of Justice*, Oxford: Oxford University Press, 1972.

13   Basic income and the welfare state[*]

UNEARNED INCOME FOR ALL

I first flirted with the idea of a Basic (or Citizen's) Income in an essay entitled 'The Economics of the Alternative Society'. It was written at the tail-end of the Golden Age of post-war capitalism, which ended around the time of the first oil price explosion in the early 1970s. During that period, growth rates were higher than at most other periods of human history and were also more stable, while unemployment was remarkably low – the idea of 3 per cent registered out-of-work would have been enough to make a British government see election defeat staring it in the face.

Nevertheless, at that time capitalism was under strong attack from the New Left and elsewhere for the life-styles it fostered. It was supposed to be based on the Puritan work ethic, which took too much of the joy and spontaneity out of life. It was also accused of fostering a consumer society, in which all other values were sacrificed in the race to accumulate the largest total of material possessions. On the face of it, the two accusations were contradictory. But doubtless, capitalism has had both these attributes at different times and among different people.

Basic Income was an attempt to cope with these and related criticisms. The idea was that an affluent society could provide a standard of living above subsistence for all. The government would stop trying to hunt down scroungers and shirkers on the welfare state. The potential shirker would be told, in effect: The community is now rich enough to give you choices. You can opt out if you wish and you will receive an allowance which will be far from princely and well below the normal wage, but will allow you to live. Alternatively, you can work and go after much larger material prizes. Or you can try to find your own compromise – for instance, using the Basic Income to allow you to take part-time or badly rewarded work, which you might, nevertheless, find more fulfilling to pursue.

Such an income should help with the problem of the underclass – although there are clearly many other factors behind the rise in the number of homeless

---

[*] This chapter is a continuation of some thinking aloud begun in a booklet entitled *Beyond the Welfare State: An Examination of Basic Incomes in a Market Economy*, by S. Brittan and S. Webb, Aberdeen: Aberdeen University Press, 1990.

and beggars, not easily amenable to an overall financial approach. Basic income would also be helpful, among other groups, to artists at the beginning of their careers, those opting for a simple lifestyle or following vocations with low or variable market returns, or students without grants. People ranging from 1960s hippies to the scholar-gypsy would be provided with a place in the sun, but would not be able to impose their values on the rest of us.

I also had much in mind the benefits which the traditional upper-middle classes derived from the possession of a modest private income which gave them a degree of independence and saved them from being complete wage-slaves. European civilization, as it developed from the Renaissance onwards, depended on unearned income and inherited wealth. Among the nineteenth- and early twentieth-century European bourgeoisie, a private income was for long a supplement to income from work – and a major element of flexibility. It enabled people to embark on careers which would not otherwise be possible and to take risks with their professions and lifestyles.

Such means must indeed play a role in the contemporary United States and Japan (for example, the Kennedys and the Rockefellers). But the lip service paid to the work ethic leads to silence on these matters. In fact, the main thing wrong with unearned income is that too few of us have it.

In the past the choice was between such an income for a few or for none. My hope was that if the productive possibilities of the new technologies were even a fraction of that claimed for them, the modest competence, which was the ideal of Victorian novelists, might eventually be possible for all citizens.

TOPPING UP LOW PAY

There was another argument for Basic Income which became especially important with the unemployment explosion of the 1980s. This stemmed from the belief of market economists that unemployment arises from rates of pay and associated costs which diverge from market-clearing levels. The real difficulty is that market economists too rarely ask: what would or should happen if market-clearing rates of pay for some workers are below the conventional minimum? (They could even be below the physical subsistence level.) In that case they are worse off with a job than on the dole. So even if the unemployed are not work-shy, they may still find it difficult to afford to take employment.

Even the fall that took place in the relative pay of the lowest earners in the 1980s and early 1990s was insufficient to price them into work in Europe. In the USA members of the underclass are often the working poor, doing low-paid menial jobs. In Europe, where benefit levels are higher, they tend to be the unemployed. The key problem for European economic and social policy is how to obtain the benefits of a flexible US-style labour market, without US poverty or ghettoes. Better than either would be a Basic Income guarantee, which would supplement the income of the low paid, so making it possible for them to price themselves into jobs.

NOT A MINIMUM WAGE

Basic Income should be sharply distinguished from a minimum wage enforced by law or collective bargaining, which has raised unemployment and reduced efficiency wherever it has been effectively introduced. Its obvious effect is to price workers out of jobs. Those most likely to suffer are exactly the people whom the proponents of such legislation say they most want to help. They include those on the fringes of the labour market or on the borderline of disablement or other incapacity, those suffering racial discrimination, inner-city youths, and all the many others who face a choice between low pay and no pay. Above all, minimum wages are a denial of the human right to sell one's labour to a willing buyer and to make one's own decisions about whether or not to take paid work at going rates.

Quite apart from the effect on the demand for labour, minimum wages are a highly inefficient way of helping the poor. Because of divergences in the number of wage earners and dependants in different households, the link between poverty and pay is much weaker than commonly supposed. According to the UK *Social Trends*, only 20 per cent of the incomes of the bottom fifth of the income distribution came from pay at all – most of the rest came from benefit. Analysed another way, more than 70 per cent of the bottom fifth of households with children consist of one-parent families or couples without full-time earnings.

A minimum wage, being work-related, is the same for the single breadwinner with a large family as for a member of a two-earner household without dependants. By contrast, Basic Income, like existing social security payments, varies with the number of dependants, both in the version where it is paid to individuals and where it is paid to households.

POVERTY NOT JUST RELATIVE

Basic Incomes have had some support from anti-poverty campaigners, who felt that the conditionality of existing income-related benefits, and the associated means tests, kept some people needlessly below the poverty line. But many in the anti-poverty movement have been understandably hesitant.

From the very beginning it has been clear that the essential condition for affording an unconditional basic minimum is that there should be a distinct and growing gap between national income per head and the target minimum. It was the lack of such a gap which destroyed the primitive experiment in guaranteed basic income at the beginning of the nineteenth century known as Speenhamland. (The Speenhamland system was named after a meeting of magistrates in the place of that name in Berkshire in 1795, which decided to make up from parish rates deficiencies in labourers' income below agreed rates. It was widely condemned for encouraging idleness and was superseded by the more severe 1834 Poor Law.)

A fully fledged Basic Income will only ever be possible if it is accepted that poverty and a tolerable minimum income are not just relative concepts. There is no need to go to the other extreme and exclude any conventional element. The organizational structure and the availability of cheap products and services, which enable very poor people to get by in the Third World, and which enabled them to do so in the west in bygone years, does not exist today. Yet it still remains true that inability to afford a video or a quadrophonic stereo is not the same as inability to buy basic food and shelter. If a relatively poor person doubles his income over time from, say, £5,000 to £10,000 per annum in inflation-adjusted terms, but still earns only one-third of the national average, it has to be accepted that he is better off than before, although not necessarily twice as well off.

The Thatcher government's decision to link benefit levels to inflation rather than earnings will enlarge the gap between benefit and pay. The process will continue, even if there are occasional real benefit upratings or if from time to time there is a government which goes back to the link with earnings. The essential condition is that the gap between the guaranteed minimum and the typical pay rates grows, however spasmodically.

It is often said that a Basic Income – or even present benefits – encourage employers to reduce wages in the knowledge that the state will fill the gap. This is not a criticism but a ground for hope. For one of the ideas is to make it easier for people to price themselves into work without driving them into abject poverty. The introduction of new, simple, low-paid jobs is the most promising quick method of reducing unemployment towards levels which we were used to in the post-war Golden Age.

Misplaced moral indignation that employers might gain should not stand in the way. In a competitive market the forces of entry and exit would ensure that employers who took on low-skilled workers at modest pay would not long obtain a better return on their capital and effort than other employers, as excess profits would be competed away. If this resulted in a lower price for the final product, the number of jobs created would be further enhanced. (Should I be wrong, the Fabian fiscal cupboard is full of ingenious ways of taxing excess profits.)

THE FADING OF THE VISION

For a time a negative income tax, which is a form of Basic Income, enjoyed a considerable vogue on the Radical Right. There was the hope that it could replace a large part of the welfare state and be much cheaper into the bargain. But it soon became apparent that it would be difficult to subsume health and education in a negative income tax; and if the effort were made, huge sums would have to be raised and transferred.

Even when the concept was confined to cash benefits, it was seen that it would be more expensive, rather than less, than the present system. By making the whole tax and benefit system more transparent, any kind of integrated tax-benefit system would reveal all the gaps where the welfare state failed to bring people up to the theoretical poverty line and would, therefore, be more expensive. (In this chapter 'more expensive' means more costly to those who are net payers to, rather than net recipients from, the tax and social security systems)

As these aspects dawned on them, members of the Radical Right backtracked quickly and, instead, espoused the Charles Murray view that benefits of all kinds encouraged a 'dependency culture'. The new line became that benefits, instead of being intended just to make up income deficiency, should be as conditional as possible.

Thus the vision of capitalism with a human face has dimmed since the early 1970s. We must try to understand why, if we are to recapture some of the elements. First, there has been the sharp fall in economic growth rates. Table 2 in Chapter 10 was originally constructed to compare UK performance during and after the Thatcher government with that of other countries. But its main lesson surely is how much growth rates have fallen in *all* the old industrial countries, including Japan.

In these decades political leaders and industrial pundits have wondered 'how will we find jobs for people in a hyperproductivity world where a few robots will produce all we need?' Yet at the very same time economic policy-makers have been preoccupied with the opposite worry about the slowdown of productivity growth so evident in the macro data.

On top of this overall slowdown has come the squeeze on average market-clearing rates of pay in general and the widening of earnings differences. The biggest squeeze of all is that on low to lower-middle market-clearing pay rates. This increases the number of workers just above the income support level who would be adversely affected by greater generosity to those on benefit.

A growing share of capital relative to labour in the national income might on the surface seem to provide a pot of gold from which a Basic Income might be financed. But, on reflection, the idea seems less attractive. A big squeeze on post-tax profits would – if not passed on – reduce both the return on investment and the means of financing it at a time when accelerated investment in capital-widening projects is required to promote employment (as explained in Chapter 11). Moreover, much of the increased return to capital accrues, not to a few plutocrats, but to pension funds and small savers (including holders of government savings bonds), whom it would be neither attractive nor politically easy to tax in draconian fashion

'CRISIS OF THE WELFARE STATE'

The climate for Basic Income has been worsened by what is often called the 'crisis of the welfare state'. The debate has been triggered off by the very sharp rise in total general government outlays among the European members of the OECD – from 35 per cent of GDP in 1970 to over 50 per cent in the early 1990s. Social security spending was not the only reason for these increases, but welfare state expenditure of all kinds was indeed responsible. The Scandinavian countries, and especially Sweden, which were already top of the league, experienced the sharpest increases, taking Sweden to a peak public spending ratio of some 67 per cent. This was followed by a draconian curbing of Swedish welfare benefits.

In all countries, the slowdown in economic growth was, of course, a big influence in holding down the denominator of the public sector to GDP ratio. But changes in the numerator were even more important. On the social security side, the forces at work included: improved benefits; demographic shifts; and changed social attitudes which led to a greater takeup. (The line between being less inhibited about exercising citizen rights and scrounging on the state is, of course, notoriously difficult to draw.) In any case, the resulting rise in taxation led to an increased wedge between the wage costs of the employer and what the worker received. Even in the UK after 15 years of Conservative government the wedge was about 50–58 per cent at the margin, if employers' contributions and indirect taxes are included – as they should be (Chapter 10).

In fact, the British public spending ratio rose much less than that of most other European countries; and the UK which was in the middle of the league in the early 1970s was near the bottom in the early 1990s. Despite this relatively restrained performance, social security expenditure was the most rapidly rising component of public expenditure. It was running in Great Britain in 1994 at £84 billion per annum and represented 12–13 per cent of GDP. It had grown at an average annual rate of 3.7 per cent in real terms in the previous decade and a half. But contrary to popular supposition, the main reason was not benefits for the unemployed but higher expenditure on pensions, the sick, the disabled and families. Excluding the effects of unemployment, the underlying increase was still 3 per cent per annum, appreciably above the prevailing growth rate.

Looking ahead to the year 2000, the Department of Social Security's central assumption is of a rise in social security expenditure averaging just over $2\frac{1}{2}$ per cent per annum, a fraction of a decimal point above the projected national economic growth rate. The assumption is that unemployment will fall by a quarter and that as a result real growth will be slightly above trend while the slack is being absorbed.

Thus a superficial British response to the crisis of the welfare state would be to say: 'What crisis?' There is indeed likely to be a temporary stability in the cost of providing for the old because the dependency ratio – the ratio of people over 65 to those aged 15–64 – is expected to stabilise or decline slightly, while it is rising in other countries. But in the twenty-first century even the UK can expect a large rise in this ratio – from just over 22 per cent in the year 2000 to over 33 per cent in 2040. Germany, France and Japan face much higher ratios still. Even the projected containment of British costs up to the end of the twentieth century depends on governments continuing to tie benefits and the basic pension to inflation and not to pay levels, and also on the more stringent tests which have been introduced, especially for unemployment and invalidity benefits.

A far more immediate threat than the slow ageing of the population in the twenty-first century is the dramatic drop already taking place in the proportion of men still at work in the 55–64 age range. This fell in Britain from 86 per cent in 1977 to 65 per cent in 1992. The pattern here is for workers in that age group to be persuaded to take early retirement during periods of recession, and not return to work during the upturn. David Willetts expects the proportion at work in this age group to fall below 60 per cent. In many Continental countries the ratio is already much lower.

The phenomenon can be regarded as one of joblessness – an addition to the total of unemployed and non-employed. It is also a burden on the welfare state, because of both the reduction in the tax base and the increased calls on benefits such as invalidity payments. Worst of all is the great waste in human terms. As Willetts says: 'Such men cannot easily be categorised either as retired or conventionally unemployed.' The majority in that age group have left work because of redundancy or dismissal. But most of them do not regard themselves as either unemployed or retired. It is quite extraordinary that at times of improved health and life expectancy people should be discouraged from taking up paid work at so early an age.

There has been a similar trend at the bottom of the age scale. Pressures and incentives introduced under the sacred name of education and training now make it unusual for teenagers to take paid work at the official school-leaving age of 16. Within the space of two decades – 1975 to 1995 – the normal span of a man's working life will have dropped by nearly a third. The premature retirement of so many men is one reason why many more women have entered the labour market. With self-imposed burdens of this kind, no wonder that the welfare state is under pressure and public perceptions of living standards lags well behind the statistics of national growth rates.

This shortening of the working life-span is the culmination of many influences. There is the instinctive tendency of so many employers to respond to overmanning pressures by edging out older workers. There is also prejudice against their recruitment, despite a mass of evidence that they are more reliable and effective in many jobs.

The moralistic prejudice against undercutting must take a lot of the blame for making it difficult for people – whether young or senior – to price themselves into jobs; and prime-age workers are doubtless glad to be without their competition. There are also specific practices which encourage premature retirement. There is the convention that workers should retire at top pay rates. The convention is reinforced by the provision in most pension schemes for pensions to be based on the last few years of working life, which makes workers themselves reluctant to stay in their posts when they may be earning somewhat less than at their peak. Public policy could have an effect here through tax and pension legislation. But the first need is to be aware that we have suffered an infliction rather than found a neat way of dealing with unemployment.

THE TAX BURDEN

Many academic economists take an excessively narrow view of the distortions caused by high taxes. Typical studies look at how hours of work respond to tax rates in specific establishments, or in questionnaires. Not surprisingly, these conclude that marginal tax changes have but a modest effect, except perhaps on women in part-time work who can vary hours. As Assar Lindbeck notes, such calculations cover only very few types of tax distortion: 'the consequences for the choice of job, work intensity, the desire for promotion and the incentives to invest in human capital are seldom included'. He remarks that high marginal taxes are like tariffs, which favour production in the domestic household – and also in illegal economic activities – at the expense of exchanges in the regular market.

There is a deep-seated aggregation problem in ascertaining voters' wishes on public spending versus take-home pay. Opinion poll after opinion poll suggests big majorities for increased welfare expenditure of all kinds, even if it means higher tax rates. Yet actual elections show voters turning away from the political parties that have increased the tax burden or seem most likely to do so.

The discrepancy does not necessarily reflect hypocrisy or cynicism. Many people genuinely favour increased spending in chosen areas and are prepared to pay higher taxes to do so. But when the different spending choices of all citizens are added together the result is a much greater tax burden than they are prepared to meet. This is an old public-finance problem known as 'full line supply'. Voters have to buy combined policy packages and cannot pick and choose according to individual taste as buyers can in a supermarket.

While this chapter was being written in early 1994, there was a public outcry against the tax package introduced in the last Lamont and first Clarke Budgets, which was expected to subtract 3 per cent from household disposable income over the two years 1994–96 to reduce the Budget deficit. This hardly suggested a public willingness to accept the much higher package which would have been necessary to boost the welfare state as well.

THE TORN NET AND SHAKY LADDER

It would be wrong just to throw in the towel in the face of current pressures on the welfare state without making a few suggestions about remedying the obvious weaknesses at tolerable cost. It is still worth undertaking a summary of the key features of Basic Income, both because they highlight present weaknesses and because it might be possible to achieve some features of BI incrementally without committing oneself to going the whole hog. It should not be seen as a messianic movement whose aims have to be achieved in total or not at all.

What, however, needs to be reformed? No system of state-provided financial rights can cover all the varying personal problems which drive people into degradation and despair. But, despite the high sums expended, the welfare state has not succeeded even in providing the standard safety net for which its founders, such as Beveridge, hoped.

Very nearly a half of all British benefits are accounted for by National Insurance payments, such as retirement pensions, invalidity and sickness benefit (and, for a minority of eligible cases, unemployment benefit). These are paid irrespective of means and are financed by employer and employee National Insurance contributions. They are essentially tax payments. The system is called pay-as-you-go to distinguish it from the funded schemes normal in the private sector where contributions are paid into a fund, the investment of which finances all the benefits. Thus, contrary to popular belief, recipients of National Insurance contributory benefits, such as state pensions, have not paid for them in any actuarial sense.

Next in importance are non-contributory income-related benefits designed to support those not eligible for contributory benefit, or whose benefit is inadequate to standard needs. By far the most important example of these is now called Income Support, on which many pensioners and most unemployed rely. The name is one of a succession of labels that have been invented to take the sting out of what was once known as National Assistance, and which ultimately goes back to the medieval Poor Law. A much more recent benefit is known as Family Credit, designed to supplement the incomes of low-paid working families with children. Housing Benefit, which accounts for much larger sums, is designed to provide help in paying rents and some local authority taxes. All these top-up benefits are subject to a test of means and are withdrawn as income from other sources rises.

Finally, there is a group of miscellaneous benefits where entitlement neither relates to contributions nor varies with income. Of these, overwhelmingly the most important is Child Benefit, which is paid to all parents, rich or poor, and is not taxed. Additional benefit is provided where children are cared for by a single parent.

Yet, despite this great array, there are still loopholes which prevent people from claiming the conventional minimum. First, there is incomplete coverage. Family Credit, for instance, is not available to childless working families. Then again, unemployed claimants can be disqualified if their condition is regarded as voluntary or if they are involved in an industrial dispute. A benefit may also be withheld or reduced if claimants have capital in excess of certain moderate limits (£8,000, apart from the value of a residence, for Family Credit and Income Support in 1994); and Income Support is lower for adults under 25.

A particular problem with means-tested benefits is that of inadequate take-up. Some of the estimates of non-take-up give an exaggerated impression, as it is quite rational for households to avoid detailed scrutiny of their affairs if their net entitlement is likely to be very small. But even in terms of the *value* of unclaimed benefit, the take-up percentages are disappointing, particularly in the case of Family Credit.

It is not only the safety net, but the ladder of opportunity that is in a shaky condition. This is because the high rates of benefit withdrawal, when the unemployed obtain work, or people with low incomes move up the earnings ladder, produce serious disincentives to work, effort and savings, known as the unemployment and poverty traps respectively. By these traps I do not mean that income is literally lower or the same if an unemployed person takes a job or an employed person obtains a better one. The trap exists if the withdrawal rate for benefit is so high that the gains from the better job are negligible. The very high implicit marginal tax rates of 90 to 100 per cent which used to affect some lower-income households have been nearly eliminated, but at the price of increasing the number of households paying marginal rates of 70 per cent and over – amounting to more than 500,000 in 1993.

THE SYSTEMS COMPARED

How does Basic Income differ from existing social security benefits? Nearly all existing social security payments are contingent. Even the contributory benefits depend on certain conditions prevailing – such as unemployment, sickness or age. One idea behind Basic Income is to move away from this kind of conditionality and to make a payment to everyone. Basic Incomes have many other names, such as Citizens' Income, Social Dividend or Minimum Income Guarantees. They are all inherently the same; and so is a negative or reverse income tax.

Basic Incomes could be paid across the counter like state pensions – this is called the Post Office Principle. Alternatively, they could take the form of a tax credit, which would be set off against income tax for those with sufficient tax liabilities, but received as a positive payment from the state by those with insufficient liabilities.

For all the sound and fury, the distinctions between the two methods of payment are essentially administrative. The important differences relate to the size of basic payment and the rate or rates at which it is withdrawn or taxed away as income comes in from other sources.

The straight dotted line on Figure 13.1 illustrates a pure Basic Income or negative income tax scheme. The horizontal axis shows original income. The vertical axis shows net benefit received or tax paid. The bent line can be seen either as an improved and streamlined version of the present system or a modified Basic Income scheme. It can in fact be regarded as a reasonable approximation to the tapering-off system now applied to Family Credit, Housing Benefit and local tax benefits. It does not fit the contributory benefits or Income Support even approximately. (The biggest idealization in the figure is the elimination of the overlap where people are receiving benefits, but simultaneously paying tax, thus causing a temporary steepening of the withdrawal line to the right of T.)[*]

The pure Basic Income would abolish the distinction between selectivity and universality. The credits would be universal; but as income rises they would be withdrawn from everyone at a single rate. Everyone would be subject to the same means test as is now imposed automatically with income tax. Income would indeed be redistributed towards the less well-off, as those in the lightly shaded area gain. But the reform need not be confiscatory for those at the top if a single cut-off rate is observed. Then there is indeed no gain to be had from the confiscatory marginal tax rates of 83 and 98 per cent rates which made the UK a tax accountant's paradise under the Healey regime of 1974–9.

---

[*] The reader is also warned that in much of the writing on these subjects, final income rather than net taxable benefit is plotted on the vertical axis. The two presentations are equivalent, but I believe mine to be more direct and it avoids implying that all income derives from the state.

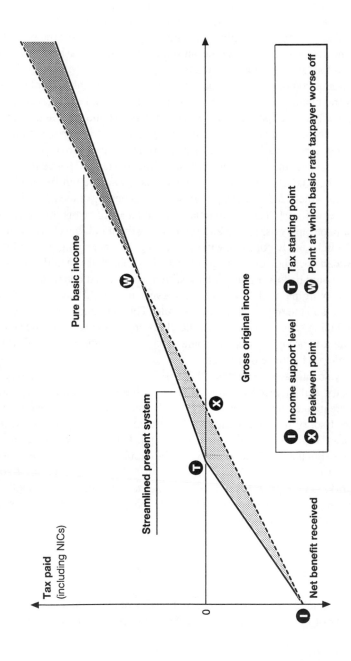

Figure 13.1 Basic income and streamlined present system

The slope of the line labelled 'Streamlined present system' represents the withdrawal rate at which benefit falls as original income rises. Beyond the point T, where benefit is exhausted and tax begins, it shows the marginal tax rate (including employees' National Insurance contributions), which amounted for most employees to 35 per cent in 1994. The withdrawal rate, which can be regarded as an implicit marginal tax rate, is much steeper for the poor than for people nearer the middle. This is because the former suffer the benefit withdrawal rates and the latter the tax rate, which is a good deal less.

Numerous complexities have been omitted to simplify the presentation. There are several changes of slope in marginal UK tax rates. For instance, there has been since 1991 a 20 per cent lower rate band for income tax. On the other hand the slope becomes shallower and less progressive at the upper earnings limit, where employee's National Insurance contribution ceases to be paid. The slope grows steeper again when the higher rate of income tax (40 per cent since 1988) begins. There is also some overlap where tax is payable but benefit is not yet exhausted, which leads to a temporary severe steepening of the implicit marginal rate to the right of T. These refinements would need to be taken into account in any complete analysis. But an attempt to bring them into the chart would make it incomprehensibly complex without altering the underlying principles.

The chart does, however, bring out that the withdrawal rate under a pure Basic Income would be lower than with existing means-tested benefits. On the other hand, the marginal withdrawal rate that everyone would have to suffer would be higher than the present marginal tax rate. This is bound to be the case in any self-financing scheme. In terms of the chart, the shaded area to the right of W would have to bring in enough revenue to pay for the improved benefits or lower taxes enjoyed by those on the left.

In any social security system, there is a three-way trade-off between cost, generosity and disincentive marginal rate effects. The high marginal rates which create the poverty trap stem from the rate at which benefits taper off as incomes rise. If the system aims for the greatest generosity at lowest cost the withdrawal rate is likely to be extremely high. This will have the advantage of selectivity but the disadvantage of very high implicit tax rates at the bottom end of the distribution, thus taking away most of the gain from moving to higher-paid work. On the other hand, if benefits are tapered off very gradually, these poverty trap effects are reduced; but either the cost is prohibitively expensive or the benefits are far too low.

DECONSTRUCTING BASIC INCOME

In our original paper Steven Webb outlined a modest scheme for integrating two types of income-related benefit: Family Credit and Income Support with income-tax. The idea was to provide a guaranteed income for all households at the conventional subsistence minimum governing these schemes. It would have amounted in 1994 terms to about £44 for a single adult over 25 and around £115 for a typical family with two children. Webb also stuck to the existing practice in income-related benefits in tying the new benefits to households rather than individuals, which is rank heresy to many Basic Income campaigners.

Nevertheless, even the limited proposal that we did consider would have cost in 1994 some £34 billion per annum on a no-losers basis. More realistically, if financed from personal direct taxation, the basic rate of income tax plus employee National Insurance contribution would have to rise by 15 percentage points: to 50 pence in the pound starting from 1994 levels. The personal allowance would go except for a small disregard, and be replaced by a tax credit.

If we are to rescue anything from the idea it is essential to consider how the cost of it could be reduced. By far the most logically extensive economic study of alternatives (which is yet free of social security technicalities) has been made by James Meade. Here I can only offer a few pointers for those who want to start with a less exhaustive approach.

The best chance of advance is to unpack the Basic Income idea into its components to see how it can be introduced by stages, starting from the present. In so doing people of all views should be able to discover why the latter fails to provide even a conventional subsistence minimum for all.

I list first the most controversial aspects which are either prohibitively costly or towards which some people would object on principle, and then go on to the more modest components where action could be taken much sooner:

- *Unconditionality* The Basic Income would be made available to all with no conditions about incapacity, availability for work and so on. Nor would there be questions about capital ownership.
- *Uniform withdrawal rate* There would be a uniform withdrawal rate at no more than the normal tax rate, including employee National Insurance contributions.
- *Payment to individuals* Many proponents of Basic Income regard a shift from a household to an individual basis payment as essential (despite its absence from the Webb scheme which was drafted in terms of households).
- *Post Office Principle* Under BI, people would have the option of receiving BI across the counter, as Child Benefit is now received. This would help with the problem of incomplete take-up which arises from the reluctance of potential recipients to come forward at social security offices.
- *Integration* Alternatively, recipients could offset their Basic Income receipts against income tax, thus making or receiving a single payment without 'churning'.

- *Generality* Working adult families on low incomes without children would for the first time have their incomes topped up. (UK Family Credit at the time of writing only supplements the incomes of families with children.) The 100 per cent withdrawal rate for Income Support for working-age adults would thus be trimmed back.
- *Non-discrimination* There would be no discrimination in size of payment to working-age adults – in the UK the under-25s now receive less as a deliberate act of policy.
- *Adequacy* This is inevitably subjective and controversial. But some existing benefits – for example, for adults under 25 and for households with low earnings but without children – do not even aim to provide a conventional minimum.

The lower items in the list demonstrate some of the improvements that could be achieved by building on the present system without waiting for the full merging of the tax and social security systems. The latter is an administrative move often wrongly seen as the heart of all BI and negative income tax ideas.

Any government could quite inexpensively take a first step and extend family credit to single people and childless families, individuals and households. This move would have cost only about £350 million per annum in 1994 – trivial by the standards of modern public finance.

In principle, the extension of Family Credit to all adult workers would eliminate the extreme forms of the unemployment trap. For anyone deemed to have a full-time job will have his or her income topped-up to minimum levels and will always gain from taking employment. But whatever reforms are made, it is difficult to imagine a swift and easy transition from Income Support to Family Credit for some of the people on the fringes of the labour market.

It would thus also help if the withdrawal rate for Income Support for adults of working age could be reduced below 100 per cent and preferably brought in line with the 70 per cent taper used for other income-related benefits. Specifically, it would encourage people to take spasmodic, casual or part-time jobs that do not qualify them for Family Credit and to take them on a legal basis.

The removal of discrimination against younger adults will arouse strong passions. The discrimination was put in by the Thatcher government to encourage the work habit and to discourage young people from moving away from their families to other parts of the country where they did not have assured jobs or accommodation. As young people did nevertheless move – and often with good reason – this discrimination has increased the number of homeless and the size of the underclass in general. A middle-of-the-road approach might be to eliminate the discrimination but make young people's benefits conditional on genuine attempts to find work or to train – as they are supposed to be for the over-25's.

Of the more radical ideas higher up the list, it is the uniform withdrawal rate that I would most readily put on the back burner. The very high cost of Webb's simulation, as of other schemes, arises from reducing the withdrawal rate for benefit so that it is no higher than the income tax rate. High marginal rates for all taxpayers are then necessary to eliminate completely the high 'poverty' marginal rates at the bottom.

This would be a doubtful bargain at present. High implicit rates of tax arise at the bottom end of the income scale because of the attempts to combine adequate support with some control over costs. Attempting to eliminate the high implicit tax rate at the bottom altogether would mean that any extra sum available for poverty relief would spill over to help people well above subsistence in the shaded area to the left of *W* in Figure 13.1. To compare high 'poverty taxes' at the bottom of the income scale with lower income tax rates higher up is to compare like with unlike. The withdrawal of a benefit is not the same as the levying of a tax, unless one believes that all income belongs to the state.

To distinguish a Basic Income which tolerates a high withdrawal rate from the pure concept, it might be best to call the former a modified Basic Income. A modified but unconditional Basic Income would be represented by the bent line, *ITW*, on the figure. To argue for retaining a steeper withdrawal rate for benefits than the general tax rate is to argue in favour of retaining selectivity. This is common sense when resources are scarce. If £1 billion per annum more resources became available, what would be a better use of it: to increase the basic benefits, which is all that the poorest receive, or to reduce the withdrawal rate (that is, to flatten the line *ITW*) so that much of the gain spills over to those who need it least?

If there are any doubts about priorities for people of working age, there can be none about pensions, where the subtleties of work incentives do not apply. The majority of pensioners are not on or below the poverty line. But a minority do need Income Support to keep them above it. Modest funds spent in increasing Income Support for the elderly and providing it in a more user-friendly way would do far more good than much larger sums spent in increasing the basic pension.

Yet the centrepiece of the British Labour Party's policy in several elections has been a substantial rise in the basic pension, to be followed by annual re-rating at the faster of prices or earnings growth. The Labour governments of the 1960s and 1970s both started off with an across-the-board pensions increase which they spent the remainder of the Parliament paying for. This exhausted their redistributionary zeal, or at least means; and they were extremely strapped for cash for other kinds of redistribution, both towards low-income families and towards the poorest minorities among the old. Across-the-board increases in state pensions – and for that matter Child Benefit which John Major unfroze and then relinked to prices – are a wasteful and inefficient means of helping the poor; and while politicians may need to buy votes, the rest of us should resist emotional blackmail.

I am more reluctant to abandon unconditionality: the 'modest competence' available to all. It is difficult to say in advance how many people would want to take advantage of an unconditional income guarantee at Income Support levels to drop out of the official labour force or cut their hours of work, and how their numbers would compare with those taking jobs for the first time, because it paid them to do so. In any case, voters do not feel either rich enough or sufficiently laid back to tolerate intentional subsidies to those opting out of paid work.

But I would still like to avoid postponing the whole project indefinitely. One suggestion is a partial Basic Income. This has been suggested by the person who has done more than anyone else to promote the cause in the UK, namely Hermione Parker. It was also the approach chosen by the Liberal Democrats in the run-up to the 1992 election. Such a partial Basic Income would have the advantage of introducing the principle of non-work incomes for all. To start with, it would have to be little more than a token payment, but it would be something on which to build.

When we come to the argument between the administrative integration of tax and benefit and the Post Office Principle, it is an argument about means among reformers. The advantage of the Post Office Principle is that the 'caring parent' (usually modern jargon for the mother) of a family could be made the recipient of benefits intended for herself and her children without being dependent on her partner to hand over the cash. The advantage of integration is that the mass of two-way payments between the citizen and the state could be netted out so that the principal breadwinner would either receive or make a single payment.

It is said that assessment for tax benefit must always be separate because benefit needs fluctuate week to week according to family circumstances and need. Tax, on the other hand, is adjusted for under- or overpayment once a year. I have myself suggested a good liberal compromise whereby the 'caring parent' could opt whether to receive benefit across the counter or allow it to be netted off against her own or her partner's tax bill.

In any case, changes could be made to make benefit assessment more like the tax variety and less like a medieval inquisition. While capital holdings can never be completely irrelevant – or we would have eccentric millionaires with houses full of Picassos drawing benefit – the typical benefit drawer is not full of clever financial tricks for transforming income into capital and is more concerned with meeting the household readies. Much higher levels of capital disregard would probably make little difference to the cost of social security. At least this is a conjecture worth investigating.

Too much of the discussion about making benefits more like the tax system and less like the Poor Law has been of a Great Leap Forward kind. We are extremely unlikely to wake up one morning to find either a completely integrated tax–benefit scheme or benefits available to all at the Post Office with minimal scrutiny. But a great deal can be done incrementally.

TOWARDS CONCLUSIONS

Social security is often treated as an instrument of redistribution. Yet between two-thirds and three-quarters of gross welfare benefits (including education and health as well as social security) are effectively paid for by the same person at another time in his or her own lifetime. (See, for instance, the Economic and Social Research Council Report by Hills.) It is therefore tempting for non-paternalists to say that only the one-third of genuine redistribution should be retained, leaving people free to make their own decisions about smoothing expenditure over time. But before coming to any such conclusion we should hold on to our safety belts – here a very apt metaphor.

For the estimate of two-thirds lifetime recycling is an average over millions of people. It is impossible for the individual to know beforehand how the vagaries of life in terms of illness, unemployment and so on are going to affect him. Some people will receive back from the state far more than two-thirds, others much less. Moreover, if a person has been improvident in providing for adversity his fellow citizens will not be happy to see him starve or live in the gutter. Knowledge of this fact creates a moral hazard which will make it rational to underinsure and undersave.

On the other hand, it is also common knowledge that state benefits are never likely to provide more than some conventional minimum. People wanting to maintain as much as possible of their living standards in adversity will be well advised to take out their own insurance.

Drawing the threads together, one is led to envisage a three-deck structure. First, there will be a partial Basic Income for all, unconditional and not means-tested. Secondly, there will be income-related benefits intended to bring people up to a conventional minimum which will rise with inflation, but only partially with income. Thirdly, over and above these supports, people will make their own arrangements.

This is a neat, but not entirely satisfactory, picture. Many of the risks of life are not in practice or even in theory insurable. Cover might be obtained for a few months of unemployment or illness, but not for many years of impaired earnings capacity. This represents a problem for people above the poverty line who have nevertheless been victims of change in the demand for their skills or whose activities have been displaced through changes in the pattern of international specialization. There is a limit to what the social security system or even private insurance can achieve here. Indeed, if everyone were compensated against all change, there would be no pressure ever to shift employment, occupation or activity.

The task of cushioning people against specific economic industrial shocks is better carried out by the kind of special payment that has been developed in the United States under the name of Adjustment Assistance for those hit by imports. Another model is the social payments that will gradually replace farm price support in the European Common Agricultural Policy – but without the wasteful component of compulsory withdrawal of land from cultivation. Something too may be gained from studying past British schemes to compensate workers in specific industries, such as the mines and textiles.

A careful trawl through these and many other projects should provide some lessons for the future. The problem with them is that taxpayers' aid is channelled to those who are geographically and industrially concentrated and therefore highly visible on the political scene. Yet no extra help is provided for even greater numbers of affected people who are less politically visible because they are thinly spread over many industries, occupations and areas.

WIDER OWNERSHIP

The most valuable guarantee against adversity is some non-wage and non-benefit income for a much larger number of people than has been customary in the past. In public discussions of earnings and income there is almost a conspiracy to overlook property income. In 1992, for instance, income from work, including self-employment, accounted for 66 per cent of personal income. Some 15 percentage points of the remainder was accounted for by social security and other government grants. This left 19 per cent – much the most rapidly growing component – coming from private pensions, rents, dividends, interest and so on. Moreover, there is important income in kind from property, whether the value of owner-occupied housing or the amenity value of land, which is not included in the official personal income statistics.

Nigel Lawson, when UK Chancellor, characteristically let the cat out of the bag by speaking of the emergence of a 'nation of inheritors'. Indeed, inheritance is likely to play a much greater role than superficial talk of the enterprise culture suggests. But it will still be only a relatively small number who will inherit substantial sums.

Privatization has introduced a large minority to share ownership at the cost of selling state assets at less than the maximum the government could obtain. It has thus extended the number of private shareholders, but as a percentage of total equity their holdings have not done better than stabilize at around 21 per cent since 1989. The great bulk of shares is in the hands of pension funds, insurance companies and, increasingly, overseas holders.

Nevertheless, more could be done to spread ownership in a redistributive way. In 1978 Barry Riley and I suggested that the income from the state's stake in North Sea oil should be handed over to individual citizens, the right to which could be realized in the capital market. Later on I suggested that privatized shares should be handed over 'free' to citizens instead of being sold to private investors.

Although these opportunities were missed, experiments have been made in places further afield. Citizens of Alaska have been receiving per capita dividends from the state's revenue from its North Sea oil. But the biggest attempts are now being made in the former communist countries of Central and Eastern Europe. Here enterprises are being denationalized where there is no investing public with means to purchase the privatized stock. Citizens of some of these countries have been provided with vouchers, either free or at negligible cost, with which they can acquire holdings in groups of former state enterprises.

The uncertainty and lack of sophistication of mass investors in countries where the tradition of private investment has atrophied makes them a prey to financial sharks, who purchase the vouchers from the original citizens at a fraction of their likely long-run worth. Yet despite these shortcomings, the experiments may still provide lessons for the older capitalist countries of the west.

The passing on by inheritance of the residential property of the first generation of UK citizens to have been mass owners of homes will itself do something to disperse ownership. It should not take too much ingenuity to push the trend somewhat further into non-residential types of property so that more people have some cushion of modest wealth to fall back upon in the face of life's shocks and are not wholly dependent on their wage packet or the state.

No scheme for distributing shares can eliminate the tendency, remarked upon by David Hume two and a half centuries ago, for property to become concentrated again through the vagaries of chance and ingenuity, even if the initial distribution is even. Nevertheless property ownership could still be much more widely spread than it is at present.

REFERENCES

Barr, N., *The Economics of the Welfare State*, 3rd edn, London: Weidenfeld & Nicolson, 1993.

Brittan, S., 'The Economics of the Alternative Society': reprinted as Chapter 3 of *A Restatement of Economic Liberalism*, London: Macmillan, 1988.

Brittan, S., 'Privatisation: a Comment', *Economic Journal*, (March 1986).

Brittan, S., 'The Politics and Economics of Privatisation', *Political Quarterly*, 55 (2), (1985).

Brittan, S. and B. Riley, 'A People's stake in North Sea Oil', *Lloyds Bank Review* (1978). Reprinted in C. Johnson (ed.), *Privatisation and Ownership*, London: Pinter Publishers, 1988.

Brittan, S. and S. Webb, *Beyond the Welfare State: An Examination of Basic Incomes in a Market Economy,* Aberdeen: Aberdeen University Press, for the David Hume Institute, 1990.

Department of Social Security, *The Growth of Social Security*, London: HMSO, 1993.

Dilnot, A., J. Kay and C.N. Morris, *The Reform of Social Security*, Oxford: Oxford University Press, 1984.

Hills, J., *The Future of Welfare*, York: Rowntree Trust, 1993.

Hills, J. *et al.*, *Investigating Welfare: Final Report of the ESRC Welfare Research Programme*, London: Suntory–Toyota International Centre, London School of Economics, 1993.

Johnson, P., G. Stark and S. Webb, *Alternative Tax and Benefit Policies for Families with Children*, Commentary C18, London: Institute for Fiscal Studies, 1989.

Lindbeck, A., *Overshooting, Reform and the Retreat of the Welfare State,* Seminar Paper no. 552, Stockholm: Institute for International Economic Studies, 1993.

Lindbeck, A., *The Welfare State, Selected Essays*, Aldershot, Hants.: Edward Elgar, 1991.

Meade, J.E., *Liberty, Equality and Efficiency*, London: Macmillan, 1993.

Minford, P., 'The Poverty Trap after the Fowler Reforms'; reprinted in *The Supply Side Revolution in Britain*, Aldershot, Hants.: Edward Elgar, 1991.

Murray, C., *Losing Ground*, New York: Basic Books, 1984.

Parker, H., *Instead of the Dole*, London: Routledge, 1989.

Willetts, D., *The Age of Entitlement,* London: Social Market Foundation, 1993.

Finale

14 Some presumptions of economic liberalism*

INTRODUCTION

Economic liberalism is a convenient name for one family of ideas. It is based on a wider ideal of personal freedom of which the economic aspect is only part. The ideal certainly derives from the classical liberalism of the past. 'Classical liberalism' may conjure up a picture of high-minded people in frock coats. But its modern extension covers the revolt of the young in the 1960s in favour of 'doing their own thing', the enjoyment of alternative lifestyles, including that of hippies, MPs with exotic sexual tastes, and flower children, as well as that of bond dealers in the cities of London and New York.

A liberal in my sense does not have to pretend to derive all public policy from one stated goal. If he calls himself an *economic* liberal, he must obviously attach some importance to prosperity and living standards as well as freedom. Moreover, economic liberalism is not and cannot be a rigorous set of deductions from some ethical theory combined with already established causal relations. (Nor can any other set of beliefs meant to guide action.) Economic liberalism is best seen as part of a tradition encompassing figures such as Richard Cobden and John Stuart Mill, or Ludwig Erhard in our era. It can only be fully understood in the context of specific events and developments. No liberal could have had anything to do with the ill-fated 1993–4 Back to Basics campaign of the UK Major government, which, whatever its original intentions, soon became an exercise in Grundyism.

One cannot pretend that the economic liberal tradition is in good shape. If we tried to find the present-day successors of Cobden, Mill or Erhard (themselves of course rather different individuals), it would have to be mainly among academics – and not all that many even among them – on the American side of the Atlantic.

* This chapter is a slightly shortened and amended version of the 1989 Mais Lecture given at the City University under the title *A Restatement of Economic Liberalism*, and published by the City University Business School. It was republished by the Social Market Foundation in 1990 with a Preface in which I summarized the similarities and differences between the social market and economic liberal traditions, putting most emphasis on the similarities. Readers interested in this aspect are referred to the SMF version.

Indeed, I must admit to not having been much impressed by the claims to a wider belief in personal freedom of the pro-market economists whom I first encountered. They were alive to the denial of choice arising from restrictions on imports of cars and textiles, but took as a fact of life much greater invasions of liberty such as peacetime conscription. (I refrain from anecdotes about purely university matters, except that one well-known 'liberal economist' played a key role in sending down an undergraduate before he could take his degree, for publishing an allegedly blasphemous poem.) It was not until I came across Milton Friedman, and learned that he had spent more time in lobbying against the 'draft' than any other policy issue, that I began to take seriously the wider philosophic protestations of the pro-market economists.

In the political world, there has developed a tragic chasm between the two sides of the liberal tradition. Those who care most about civil liberties, open government, limitation of police powers and similar matters have drifted to the left, while those who have been most concerned with economic liberalism have drifted to the right. Both sets of ideas have become impoverished as a result.

To an economic liberal, what has gone wrong with the movement to market economics in our day is not that it is too extreme or not extreme enough, but that it has been divorced from a wider commitment to personal freedom. Unfortunately, it is often just those political leaders who claim to be most against state control of economic life, who have most reservations about freedom of personal and artistic expression. But because the main political outlet for the explicit expression of market ideas has been among conservative politicians, free-market supporters have too often turned a blind eye to the total package offered by the latter.

THE MORALS OF MARKETS

The greatest obstacle faced by the market economy throughout recorded history is the belief that it is based on, or encourages, selfishness, materialism or acquisitiveness.

We know that the self-interest doctrine is an over-simplification. Institutions concerned with health and education are usually non-profit-making even when their services are sold for cash; and there are good reasons why this should be so. (Even so, those who run those institutions know if they ignore the self-interest of the staff and pay less than the going market rate, they will lose valued members – not only caretakers and cooks, but scientists and physicians.)

Nor do we need to play down professional motivations. A great musician or surgeon will often have a strong sense of vocation and not just play or operate for the money. A doctor or teacher should have some responsibility to his patient or pupil over and above the search for fees, and so on. Market rates of pay have their effects at the margin. They bring in the less-dedicated who might otherwise have chosen a different field of endeavour, and they affect even the dedicated in their choice at the margin between work and leisure. (X might be a surgeon even if he were not paid for it. But he would perform fewer operations.)

Thus the 'Invisible Hand' is pretty pervasive, even though it does not explain everything. It upsets more people by its apparent sanctioning of greed than by its economic reasoning. Their worries will need to be tackled if a modern form of economic liberalism is ever to establish its moral legitimacy. There are numerous ways in which market economics can be presented without overemphasizing the greed motive. Self-chosen aims can be emphasized at the expense of merely selfish ones. We can say, as Denis Robertson once did, that the economist economizes on love: that is, he has to make it go the furthest possible way without wasting it in spheres where lesser or baser motives would serve. We can point out that the altruistic businessman should strive harder than his rivals to make profits and differentiate himself by what he does with his gains. Finally, we can point to specific examples. For instance, it would have been the height of social folly to have sold coal or oil at artificially low prices during the energy shortages of the 1970s.

Here we reach the heart of the matter. We do not always have the *knowledge* to assess the effects of our actions on other human beings, especially those more remotely affected by them. For this, if for no other reason, we need *prima facie* rules of conduct. Examples are: 'Don't tell lies', 'Do not steal', 'Keep promises' or, in the public sphere: 'Observe international treaties'.

The Adam Smith self-interest doctrine takes its place as one of the more surprising *prima facie* subordinate maxims of conduct in a broadly utilitarian system of public morality. Its essence is that, *in some areas and under certain conditions*, the use of markets avowedly based on self-interest will prove more beneficial than an overt attempt to achieve the public good directly. The suggestion is that in matters such as buying and selling, or deciding what and how to produce, we will do others more good if we behave *as if* we are following our self-interest rather than by pursuing more altruistic purposes.

There will be occasions when the normal citizen will suspect that the 'Invisible Hand' is giving the wrong signals, even in spheres where he might expect it to apply. No maxims of political economy can then absolve him from exercising his own moral judgement. The absence of effective legislation should not excuse a chemical company that pollutes the air – although the competitive advantage gained by an unscrupulous firm over others suggests that the law should be put right soon, so that the public-spirited firms are not forced out of business.

But I risk being too pious. I would rather record my conviction, that people in the grip of greed often do much less harm than people in the grip of self-righteousness, especially when that righteousness is harnessed to the supposed needs of a collectivity or given some theological or metaphysical justification. In terms of the Bertrand Russell quotation on page 31, people, especially in public life, more often fall below self-interest than rise above it.

RELATION TO MAINSTREAM ECONOMICS

There are distinguished economists who reject the 'Invisible Hand', not because it is immoral but because they believe it impossible to say very much in general terms about either the working, or the desirability of a market economy.

Consider for instance this summary by a modern general equilibrium theorist, Frank Hahn, of what he believes can be rigorously demonstrated. There must be an economy of many rational agents. All production must be under constant returns to scale. There must be no externalities or public goods or other complexities or complications. In addition there must be available binding contracts stretching indefinitely ahead even for goods which will only be available in the future, including conditional contracts. (For instance, I will deliver 15 bales of hay on 1 October in ten years' time, but only if rainfall that summer has not exceeded the average.)

Then, and only then, there exists an allocation of present and future goods on which no agent can improve without making others worse off; and there also exists a set of prices at which this allocation would be achieved and clear markets. (This statement is sometimes called the Fundamental Theorem of Welfare Economics.) In any case the required conditions are clearly not fulfilled in reality. There are, for instance, too few markets stretching far enough ahead.

This kind of analysis may throw doubt on markets, but does not tell us how governments could improve on markets or even the direction which intervention should take. The rigorous study of the optimal allocation of scarce resources among a known present or future population with given tastes employing known techniques may have its value as a mathematical research programme. But, unfortunately, it bypasses the most important role of markets as evolving institutions reacting to unforeseen change.

By contrast economic liberals put more emphasis on markets as a discovery procedure in a world where tastes and techniques are changing and information scarce and expensive. (That this view is still often described as 'Austrian', as if it were something foreign and exotic, is itself revealing.) Markets are means of disseminating information diffused among millions of human beings (who will not be conscious of all the information they possess). This information is transmitted in the form of signals – price changes in flexible markets, but also shortages and surpluses where price changes are delayed by habit or law. These signals provide an incentive to meet unsatisfied needs and to move resources from where they are no longer required. Wants, techniques and resources are not given, but are constantly changing in part due to the activity of entrepreneurs who suggest new possibilities (whether digital records or cheap stand-by transatlantic flights) which people did not previously know existed.

The view of markets as a discovery procedure and co-ordinating mechanism is now common property to many economists, irrespective of their politics, especially in the United States (away from the eastern seaboard). But it is still 'double Dutch' to large numbers of Oxbridge graduates who have been brought up to suppose that they have only to diagnose a departure from perfect competition for the case for the markets to collapse; and that they are then free to propose any ingenious intervention that occurs to them or just follow their general political predilections.

To be fair to Hahn, he is well aware of the signalling and discovery aspects of markets and gives full credit to Schumpeter and Hayek for insisting upon them. But because there is no rigorously formulated body of knowledge concerning 'the behaviour of a market economy when it is not in a coherent state which we call equilibrium or, nowadays rational expectations equilibrium', he prefers to call these contributions 'political economy', to distinguish them from 'scientific economics'.

MARKET FAILURE

A shift to the discovery procedure view of markets by no means establishes a case for *laissez-faire*. Just like language and law – those other products of social evolution with which Hayek compares it – the transmission and incentive mechanism of the market can be improved. So shifting attention from the static allocation of resources to the market as a discovery procedure does not remove the issue of intervention.

And of course we have always known of many cases where the 'Invisible Hand' did not work or required supplementation. Many were cited by Adam Smith himself. Externalities have long been known. There are costs and benefits which do not appear in the profit and loss accounts of those responsible. A familiar negative example is the damage caused by a smoking chimney. A positive externality or spillover is the benefit from training a person who then leaves to join another firm. Another related example is that of public goods, such as defence or pleasant urban vistas, which confer indiscriminate benefits. In other words, one person's consumption does not diminish that available to another. A less-familiar example is television transmission.

The old term for most of these examples is 'market failure'. A modern label which captures most of the relevant cases is the Prisoner's Dilemma (see

Chapter 1). This is based on a classic American example where two prisoners, who follow their own narrow private interest and confess, receive a harsher sentence than if they had stood by their thieves' code of honour and followed the rule 'Never confess'. How does one decide whether Prisoner's Dilemma aspects – suggesting either public intervention or moral restraint – or 'Invisible Hand' ones – suggesting leaving matters to market forces – are more important in particular instances?

DEFECTS OF THE POLITICAL MARKET PLACE

Mainstream economists differ from market liberals in remaining content with a case-by-case approach. But even on that basis it is necessary to compare like with like.

Too often the case of intervention is made without asking whether the human beings who will have to carry out that intervention have the knowledge or the motivation actually to improve matters. The defects of real markets are implicitly compared with the hypothetical actions of a benevolent and omniscient dictator (as frequently – in the more technical writings – for reasons of mathematical convenience as from deeply-held convictions).

Research into the political economy of government (sometimes called public choice) has highlighted various likely governmental shortcomings. One particular distortion has recently come to the fore. If there are no constraints on state action, individuals have a much stronger incentive to invest resources in political activity and to try to use the state machine to supply them with goods (or contracts on favoured terms). The activity is now called 'rent seeking'. People vote to obtain a government that will favour either council tenants or private home owners; managers of enterprises divert their efforts into keeping on good terms with ministers and officials, or sitting on time-wasting committees and keeping *au fait* with the latest governmental fads and fashions; and, at local level, find it wise to keep in with the authorities who dispose of the more desirable school places or subsidized homes.

The idea that politicians and officials are themselves in a market place, like oil salesmen and car salesmen, has taken an astonishingly long time to penetrate the British economic establishment. (One British official to whom I pointed out the existence of the economic analysis of political behaviour replied that he was very sorry but he was not up on psychoanalysis.)

Many of the defects of the political approach appear not only in specific acts of intervention, but in the cumulative effects of many such acts in enlarging the political sphere. *To a liberal the market is not just a piece of machinery to manipulate but a device that has evolved – imperfect and capable of much*

*improvement – which reduces the number and range of decisions which have
to be taken by coercive organs after a struggle for votes, power and influence.*

The biggest disease of the modern extended state is that it becomes neither
a provider of public goods, which cannot easily be provided by the market, nor
a vehicle for redistribution to the less fortunate, but an engine for the provision
of private benefits to interest groups. Political pluralism, which seems political
as a struggle and compromise between interest groups, was a harmless doctrine
– even a benign protection against more ambitious ideas of the state – when
government controlled a small proportion of resources, but becomes extremely
harmful when government has a major say in the disposal of around half of the
national income.

The reason for this degeneration is well known – namely, the concentration
of benefits from intervention among specified and loud-voiced groups and the
dispersal of losses among the mass of consumers and voters. What is less well
known is that many major interest-group benefits do not appear in public
spending or taxation figures. The main cost of the Common Agricultural Policy
is not the budgetary transfer to Brussels, but the imposition on the consumer
of food prices far above world levels. The cost of mortgage interest relief, or
relief from capital gains tax on owner-occupied residences, appear only as
allowances against tax, and are buried away in a subsidiary table in the British
Public Expenditure documentation.

The American economist Mancur Olson has pioneered the analysis of the
pernicious effect on economic growth of interest-group privileges in mature
democratic countries. But even more important has been the corrupting effect
(sometimes corrupting in the straightforward sense of temptation to bribery) of
the state as feeding-trough, rather than umpire or keeper of the rules. The
ultimate danger is of a Hobbesian state of nature at the collective level in which
we all have to join aggressive interest groups for our own defence, and in
which the absence of rules or norms provides an incentive to predatory raids.

A FEW GUIDELINES

There is no philosopher's stone: no simple criterion for distinguishing between
government interventions which improve the functions of a market economy
and those that take us a few steps further along the road to serfdom. But it is
possible to state a few presumptions or guidelines or maxims which, taken
together, give a few clues:

1. (a) *Non-paternalism.* Individuals should be treated as if they are the best
        judge of their own interests.

    (b)   Desires that individuals have to coerce or down-grade other people (*negative interdependence effects*) should have no weight in public policy.

2.   *General rules* should govern policy, with a minimum of discretionary power for publicly appointed officials – or private bodies engaged in backstage pressure – over their fellow men and women.

3.   Where possible, *market remedies* should be used to treat market distortions. This implies not only a preference for price mechanism remedies, but also where possible for the assignment or modification of property rights.

4.   We should try to *limit the domain of political activity*, even though we cannot make out the exact circumstances in advance.

I have given the essential background to these presumptions in an earlier book, *A Restatement of Economic Liberalism*. I will just note here that these presumptions interact with and qualify each other.

The first set of presumptions can be skipped because most mainstream economists claim to hold at least 1(a) (non-paternalism) and because I have already discussed 1(b) (so-called interdependence effects) exhaustively in Chapter 3 on utilitarianism.

The second presumption, in favour of general rules, needs a little more elaboration. F.A. Hayek, who called it the rule of law, argued that it would be sufficient to eliminate intervention harmful to personal liberty or a market order, and I can claim to have examined the convention more thoroughly than many professed Hayekians. Unfortunately, it does not succeed in doing this. There can be coercive general rules – for instance, a ban on any criticism of the principles of Marxism-Leninism. Nor would general rules prevent a great deal of oppressive economic intervention, such as exchange controls or foreign travel bans.

But although it is not a cure-all, the concept of a government of laws rather than of men is one of humanity's greatest discoveries and perhaps the most important single protection of freedom. The case for general rules is partly one of efficiency and good government. At best, the official using his discretion will play safe and back the respectable and the well-known. At worst, there will be widespread corruption. But much worse is the subjection of one human being to the arbitrary power of another. *The greatest argument for the European Community is that, for all its maddening aspects, it is firmly based on the rule of law – an aspect to which many so-called market economists remain blind.*

I have already touched on the case for my third maxim, the use where possible of market and price mechanism-type remedies. But an economic liberal will put a different slant on such remedies to a mainstream economist. The latter will generally put the case for paying the market rate to recruit members of the armed forces, or for financial measures to protect the currency instead of foreign travel controls, in terms of efficiency. The liberal will be most concerned to recapture freedom, with any gain in efficiency seen as a bonus.

Similar considerations apply in the environmental field. The great advantage of road pricing over licensing of cars in urban areas, or of selling fishing permits at a price high enough to prevent overfishing, is that the choice of how far to pay the charge, and how far to cut down the activity in question, is left to the individual or firm – within a framework that ensures the desired overall result is achieved.

We can often go one stage further. Many adverse externalities or Prisoner's Dilemma cases arise because property rights are insufficiently defined. The principle 'polluter pays' is an attempt to redefine a property right so that the owner of a chemical plant that emits pollution into a stream has to pay for the damage he inflicts downstream.

New and redefined property rights are also relevant to 'macro' problems, such as whether it is possible to have a 'soft landing' after a period of inflation and excess demand without too great a check to output and employment. Earnings increases are notoriously resistant to downward pressure; and the conventional response to a demand squeeze, especially when profits are starting from a high level, is to slow down recruitment and as a last resort dismiss non-hard-core workers. Matters could be different if wage contracts were to contain a large profit-related element so that adjustment to squeezes can be more through pay and prices and less through output and employment than in the past. Insiders who have *de facto* property rights to jobs may be more willing to accept profit-related elements in pay if recently hired outsiders are excluded from the bonus element.

The fourth and most important guideline – the need to limit the domain of the political – is the most difficult to state precisely. For there is no sphere of human activity that can *a priori* or forever be removed from political responsibility. The nearest I can approach a general maxim is that whenever one new sphere of activity is brought into the political sphere we should seek to remove another from it. The inherent bias of a democracy is to expect too much from government action. But such action is likely to be more effective if limits are placed on what it can be expected to achieve. If ministers and officials are made to feel responsible for everything, their feelings of responsibility for tasks that are indisputably theirs – whether safeguarding the currency or removing unnecessarily harsh prison regulations – are diminished to vanishing point.

One reason for trying to limit the economic role of government may surprise some fellow economic liberals. This is that there is for the foreseeable future going to be such a large role for government in what is now called the welfare state area that there is no room for any avoidable load elsewhere.

I can best explain my contention by saying that there is no established liberal position on the distribution of income and wealth. We cannot just dispose of the matter by showing, as we easily can, that complete equality even of opportunity, let alone of outcome, is on close examination deeply unattractive, if not intellectually incoherent. Nor is it enough to point out that the wealth of the rich is not necessarily the cause of the poverty of the poor. Neither proposition establishes the desirability or even legitimacy of any particular distribution of entitlements to wealth and income.

REVIVAL OF THE SOCIAL CONTRACT

The revival of social contract theory, explained in more detail in Chapters 3 and 12, is the most promising foundation for a new liberal theory of entitlements. Although John Rawls's version is the best known, it is part of a larger family of contractarian doctrines. In place of the historical social contract of seventeenth- and eighteenth-century writers, the modern idea is to work out the principles on which free and rational persons, concerned to further their own interests, would desire their community to be run if they did not know their own social or economic place, the market value of their own talents and many other key features of their real situation – what Rawls calls the 'veil of ignorance'.

A major advantage of the new social contract approach is that it precludes the potential oppression of the minority which follows from uninhibited majority voting. Contractarians place less reliance on majority voting than the conventional democratic theorists. Representative institutions and majority voting are simply possible decision procedures which may be laid down at the constitutional stage as the way to take second-order post-constitutional decisions.

The contractarian assertion is that everyone would gain from some restraint on the power of the majority of the moment to do what it likes, including those who for the moment belong to that majority. The gains would come from greater security and predictability. The implicit bargain is a trade-off in which the affluent agree to a reduction in their property rights (in both their non-human capital and the earnings from their own talents) in return for a limit on state redistribution. The better-off make a sacrifice in previously held wealth in return for more certain enjoyment of the remainder. As for the worse-off: in return for a limit on the amount of redistribution that they could obtain via the ballot box, they become more secure of the redistribution they already have.

Nor can one claim that contractarian thinking has reached the stage where it could form a basis for either the reform or the entrenchment of different parts of the welfare state. In *A Restatement of Economic Liberalism* I simply accepted that economic liberals could and did have different attitudes to redistribution and asked how much redistribution and of what kind was compatible with basic freedoms. The analysis, written when egalitarianism enjoyed more support than it does today, could become relevant once more.

I highlighted two very pernicious forms of redistribution. One was attempts to control specific prices and wages, which could, if pressed too far, lead to the direction of labour. The other was what I called specific redistribution, which derived its appeal from plausible slogans such as 'Nobody should be able to buy privileged education for his child or better medical treatment simply because he has more money'. (The right of the citizen to buy private health or education was under fundamental challenge in the 1970s and could be so again.)

Some of the support for such statements is based on a simple mistake of economic analysis: the belief that educational, medical and similar services are in inelastic supply – which they may be in the short run, but not in the long – and hence that 'queue-jumping' by those prepared to pay fees deprive others of vital services. Beneath the mask of social concern is a use of state coercion to limit freedom of choice.

By contrast there is no way of ruling out on liberal grounds generalized fiscal action to affect the distribution of income and wealth, although, if pushed beyond a point very difficult to define in advance, efficiency and prosperity could suffer so badly that governments are tempted into illiberal expedients.

NO DISMANTLING WELFARE STATE

These statements are essentially defensive. On the positive side, the usual market liberal view is that redistribution in cash is preferable to services in kind, because it respects individual freedom of choice. But I have never seen the welfare state as a promising area for large reductions in public spending. Let us look at them briefly in turn.

Housing is clearly a private, not a public, good in the economist's sense; and there is nothing to be said for expensive state intervention. But by the early 1990s housing policy had little direct public expenditure cost in the UK (if we treat Housing Benefit as basically social security).

Health is a much more difficult area. There are technical reasons, due to the economic characteristics of insurance, why privatization is unlikely to provide effective or adequate health care.

Similar 'moral hazard' reasons apply to basic *pensions*. I am not persuaded that the same technical reasons apply to *education*.

Social security is in most advanced industrial countries much the largest sector of public spending. But it is already paid by definition in cash rather than kind. And although I favour dropping the fiction of national insurance and moving as far as possible towards integrating tax and benefit, it is a snare and delusion to suppose that such a reform offers an easy way of reducing the social security bill.

By placing too many hopes on reforming the welfare state, free-market radicals are letting the interventionists get away with too much perverse interference in what used to be the heartlands of the market economy: trade, industry, agriculture. Even after the experience of the 1980s, in which many governments have professed devotion to competition, we have a full enough agenda in these areas without entering the much more complex emotive area of privatizing the welfare state.

BUSINESSMEN'S ECONOMICS

This is a good place to introduce what I call 'businessmen's economics', which is often a much greater threat to economic liberalism than anything of a more left-wing flavour – if only because market economics and pro-business policies are so often confused in public discussion.

But an equally important reason for highlighting them is that if many kinds of state activity and intervention are either unavoidable or extremely difficult to run down, it is all the more important – for much wider reasons than the narrowly economic – to avoid overloading the political agenda with policies based on these fallacies.

Here are a few examples of the kind of fallacy I have in mind:-

1. The idea that a country or group such as the EC must be a key producer or exporter of products in areas such as aerospace or nuclear arms. It does not have to be so at all.
2. The view that some sectors of economic activity are inherently superior or inferior; for example, 'I really don't believe myself that the USA is going to become a nation of hamburger stands, Chinese restaurants, laundries, banks and computer operators. I think we have to have some sort of manufacturing sector.' The relative role of these different sectors is better determined by the most distorted and imperfect of markets than by the instincts of the self-important.
3. The view that an increase in exports or reduction in imports must always be to a country's advantage. This is just plain wrong.
4. The assertion that 'we', meaning governments, have to decide, for instance, what to do 'when UK oil runs out', whether to be self-sufficient in coal or allow imports. Again, there are available self-adjusting mechanisms, highly imperfect, but upon which it is most unlikely that government will improve.

All the above are primitive fallacies which one does not have to be a *laissez-faire* fanatic to reject. Why, for instance, should the British or French Cabinet determine the size of the nuclear power programme, the choice of reactor or the structure of the nuclear industry? In the much smaller Swiss electrical power system, the choice of reactor is made by the utilities concerned and two different systems are in successful operation. Other examples of misplaced energy include the arm-twisting of motor companies to buy national components. Then there is the strong preference for home-made products in the public sector or, worst of all the 'Voluntary Export Restrictions', forced on Japanese and developing country exporters of cars, consumer electronics or textiles to the USA and the European Community.

The most ridiculous aspect of the whole debate is that businessmen argue that market economists are cynical and myopic and that they are the long-sighted statesmen. My examples are mostly drawn from an excellent exposition of common fallacies by David Henderson. But whereas he calls them 'do it yourself economics', I prefer to call them businessmen's economics – for two reasons. First, it highlights the difference between market liberalism (or the social market economy) and mere pro-business policies. Secondly, there is no fallacy, however pernicious, that has not been supported by some highly sophisticated economists. In the academic world demand for a certain type of product creates its own supply, and many highly trained economists in Cambridge (Mass.) are at the moment of writing engaged in rationalizing the business demand for protection under slogans such as 'the need for an American industrial strategy'. Here is an area where the USA could learn from European experience, but is determined not to do so.

DEVELOPMENTS IN FINANCIAL MARKETS

I cannot end without a few remarks on financial markets, which have always provided some of the most controversial aspects of capitalism in practice. If we are to have dispersed ownership, there has to be a secondary market in paper titles to business property and less-tangible assets such as government debt. The speed and ease with which such titles can change hands are important for efficiency and the freedom of action of citizens with even the most meagre financial holdings.

There is nothing to regret in the disappearance of cartel arrangements, such as fixed commissions in the London Stock Exchange or other restrictive practices, including the enforced separation of trading from brokerage – akin to the distinction between barristers and lawyers and many other arcane procedures and restrictions inside the legal profession. Nor is it such a bad idea that banks or building societies should have to pay competitive rates of interest on depositors' money, including the accounts on which cheques can be drawn.

There is much to be said even for the unpopular activity of take-over battles. A widely recognized problem of modern organizational theory is that of the 'principal agent'. How does one find incentives for a senior civil servant, health service manager, head of a monopolistic public utility or managing director of a private-sector corporation to act in the interests of those to whom he is responsible – in the latter case the shareholder – rather than to follow his own goals? To secure the maximum return on shareholder's assets is normally in the interest, not merely of the shareholders, but also of the nation. It is not in the interest of the poor or the unfortunate that assets should be inefficiently or under-utilized. The reformer may legitimately wish to change the distribution of equity ownership, but not – if he is sensible – to hold down the return on capital.

On the other hand corporate managers left to themselves may well follow objectives such as a quiet life, or profitless growth, or – at the other extreme – safety-first cash mountains. Without the threat that in the last resort underperforming management will be replaced by a more successful one, a vital incentive to performance is missing. In continental Europe the role of keeping management up to scratch is often played by large banks. But is this closed-door method of decision really preferable? And does not the close connection between banks and corporations provide large concentrations of power at least as objectionable as American or British corporate conglomerates?

We need not so much 'take-overs' as 'take-over battles'. (Monopoly and merger law must of course always be there as a long-stop to prevent business concentrations which threaten competition.) Those of us who favour decentralization and are suspicious of big battalions will be happiest when the outcome of a takeover fight is an internal revolution in the threatened company, which is then able to repulse the bidder. But unsuccessful take-over bids cannot exercise their galvanizing role if there is not at the time a threat of success. The first take-over fight I remember was when ICI made a bid for Courtaulds in the early 1960s. The bid was unsuccessful; but it did succeed in shaking up the Courtaulds management and led to the emergence of the late Lord Kearton, who had a thoroughly beneficial effect there before he decided to venture elsewhere as an industrial statesman.

To the extent that financial institutions do take too short-term a view, a likely reason is that they are too managerial. Much financial business is now carried on by salaried employees, often young, ambitious and energetic, but who are judged by their performance over three-month periods – or, in very liberal establishments, perhaps over a year. Most of the traders and principals today are employed by institutions such as pension funds, protected by tax privilege, which are under no pressure to act as profit maximizers, but merely not to do conspicuously worse than their peers in any period.

Stabilizing speculation is more likely if many participants are using their own money and can decide for themselves whether to back a longer view. It was the old-fashioned capitalist, with ample personal resources of his own, who could afford to take the long view. The suntraps of the world are full of prematurely retired, cantankerous characters who backed their own long-term judgements against the fashions of the moment.

This is a problem with which we may just have to live. The spectacular increase in the number of private shareholders associated with privatization has been in individuals holding a handful of shares, who can hardly be expected to play the role of stabilizing speculators. In any case, large fluctuations in financial asset values have been characteristic of the history of capitalism and indeed of all systems with a market-related sector.

Obviously speculative bubbles and overextended or imprudent credit expansion can occur. The job of central banks, which now have to act together across frontiers, is not to 'know better', but use their lender-of-last-resort power to ensure that failures of particular institutions or markets do not spiral into a general contraction of money, credit or purchasing power, as Bagehot taught several generations ago. But Bagehot did not explain how the problem of moral hazard could be resolved without keeping people guessing which institutions will be rescued and on what terms. The occupational temptation of central bankers is to rescue too many rather than too few, both of institutions and countries.

As a cautious risk-averse person, I welcomed the emergency packages that the IMF and the central bankers put together in 1982 and immediately afterwards to avert country default in the Third World debt crises of that period. Market prices, however shadowy, eventually came to exist for most Third World debt; and the time came for the banks to make their own deals with the debtors, with some degree of write-off and without calling on the taxpayer for a contribution.

MONEY AND CURRENCIES

Unfortunately, those on the free-market side have not presented a very happy spectacle either. They put too many of their eggs into two baskets: the belief that there was a stable predictable relationship between something called money and price level or the national income; and the view that floating exchange rates were the best way for different national currencies to co-exist.

Neither doctrine is an essential part of market economics of any variety. It would, of course, be convenient if all we needed to cope with the world's macroeconomic problems was a monetary constitution in each country instructing the central bank (a) to increase a defined measure of the money supply by a pre-determined percentage amount; and (b) not to intervene in the foreign exchange markets. But it would be astonishing if the world were so kind to us; and it is sad that the free-market economists allowed themselves to be identified so exclusively with these two doctrines.

The defects of monetarism, in the narrow sense, are that it concedes too much power to government policy, underrates the influence of competition in providing monetary substitutes, and takes official statistics far too much at their face value. None of this should have been surprising. The invention of new monetary instruments to replace old ones – and competition between currencies – was bound to become more important as communications improved further, capital markets became even more closely linked, and controls on both financial institutions and on currency movements across frontiers were abolished.

Floating exchange rates were probably the least bad method of weathering the decade or so after the collapse of Bretton Woods in 1971, a period which also saw two oil price explosions, and two waves of double-digit inflation. Nevertheless, the combination of national economic policies hardly led to a harmonious development of exchange rates. The dollar doubled against the German mark in the five years up to March 1985. Then in the subsequent two years it halved. One did not need to have a view of the *right* exchange rate pattern to conclude that if the 1980 and 1987 dollar rate was right, then the rate of 1984–5 was absurdly high. The unsustainably high dollar of the middle 1980s had longer-term ill effects, as it put immense commercial pressure on the sectors of the US economy involved in exports or subject to import competition. But as the very high dollar did not last, any adaptations which were made proved to be a mistake. American producers of traded goods had to rebuild market shares after their overseas competitors had entrenched themselves and were prepared to see their margins squeezed.

Unfortunately, it is a big leap from recognition of exchange rate misalignments to devising an improvement. Many of these problems were tackled automatically under the gold standard, and we may have yet to return to some kind of commodity-related standard. We cannot pretend that such a standard is around the corner. In the meanwhile market liberals should not sneer at the groping and often fumbling attempts to evolve a world or European monetary order. Stable money in the broadest sense has always been regarded by the wisest economic liberals, from Hume and Smith onwards, as a vital background condition for the operation of markets and it is a legitimate sphere for official action, even of an imperfect kind.

Exchange rate objectives are unfashionable at the time of writing. Rather than try and guess if and when they will become fashionable again it is more important to reiterate the lesson that *on their own* they will never be enough. When such targets are under strain, should the onus be on strong currency countries to loosen their internal policies or on the weaker countries to tighten theirs? The world rate of inflation and demand growth become indeterminate if exchange rates are the only guide.

One suggestion, worth repeating, is that the level of nominal world interest rates might be adjusted upwards or downwards if aggregate national income in money terms (combined nominal GDP) in the participating countries threatens to exceed or fall short of objectives. The distribution of national interest rates around this average would then be adjusted to help the key currencies to stay within their target zones.

CONCLUSION

Important as these arguments on financial strategy are within the liberal camp, they are often overrated. They would certainly be the wrong note on which to conclude. I am more concerned by a wider issue.

In 1973 I wrote a book to persuade the open-minded reader that the right kind of market economy could be an instrument of human freedom as well as a way of satisfying human wants. Since then, a strange paradox has arisen. The case for the market is now more widely accepted politically; and it is less of a lonely, although it is still a minority, voice in intellectual circles. The virtues of decentralization, deregulation and dispersed ownership – not only of personal property but also of the means of production – have become almost an orthodoxy.

Yet something vital is missing. The market case is now almost always put forward in terms of prosperity, efficiency or 'accepting hard realities'. The discussion about the bearing of different forms of economic organization on freedom has all but disappeared. Moreover, a great deal of present-day capitalism is not based on liberal-individualist values. Many commentators have noted that the successful capitalism of East Asia is based on a very different Confucian tradition. Thus, while in the early 1970s one of the main tasks of economic liberals was to put the competitive capitalism to supporters of 'permissiveness' (a derogatory name for freedom), their task now is at least as much to explain to upholders of the market the role of personal freedom.

The movement of institutions and technology has been favourable to market liberalism. The movement of ideas has been much less so. There is understanding of markets as a form of co-ordination superior to collectivist compulsion. But belief in personal freedom, on which the whole approach rests, has taken some knocks, which I trust will prove temporary.

The most realistic hope is not that one political party will be captured for classical liberalism or the social market economy, but that different aspects will be advanced by different groupings. Although we need to think of how to put together the political coalitions which will advance liberal ideas in practice, this cannot be a substitute for much-needed further thought on the content and development of the ideas themselves.

People may make many mistakes in the use of freedom, and nature or society may hold many unforeseen snags. But in the end the dangers from freedom are far, far less than the dangers from those on the left and right alike who deign to tell fellow citizens how to live. The absurdities produced by the moral authoritarians and the economic collectivists alike will always provide the supporters of freedom with a chance, so long as their supporters are prepared to meet the challenge.

REFERENCES

Bagehot, W., *Lombard Street*, original edn, London, 1873.

Brittan, S., 'Capitalism and the Permissive Society', 1973; the main parts are reprinted as the first three chapters of *Restatement* (below).

Brittan, S., *A Restatement of Economic Liberalism*, London: Macmillan, 1988, pp. 80–111 and 138–43.

Hahn, F., 'Market Economics', in R. Skidelsky (ed.), *Thatcherism*, London: Chatto & Windus, 1988, Ch.6.

Henderson, D., *Innocence and Design*, Oxford: Basil Blackwell, 1986.

Olson, M., *The Rise and Decline of Nations*, New Haven, Conn.: Yale University Press, 1982.

Peacock, A., H. Willgerodt and D. Johnson, *Germany's Social Market Economy: Origins and Evolution*, London: Macmillan, 1989.

Peacock. A. *et al.*, *German Neo-Liberals and the Social Market Economy*, London: Macmillan, 1989.

Rawls, John, *A Theory of Justice*, London: Oxford University Press, 1972.

Index

accelerationist hypothesis *see* non-accelerating inflation rate of unemployment (NAIRU)
Alchian, A. 71
Aldington Committee 162–3
altruism 40–41, 61–2, 267
anchor currency, availability of 175–6
   see also deutschmark, exchange rate link with; dollar, parity against
Armstrong, William 11
Armstrong Committee 15
Australia, balance of payments of 146, 164–5
Axelrod, R. 40

balanced-budget principle 109
balance of payments
   with budget deficit 151, 152
   exchange rate as regulator of 152–4, 157
   historical background 146–7
   measurement problems 158–9
   operational meaning of 151–2
   as proxy for regional problems 156
   real shocks and 153, 154–5
   regional 149–50
   as sum of individual and company balances 148–50
   Thatcher government and 204–5
   undue emphasis on 129, 135, 145–6, 148, 150–51, 159–60
   see also under names of individual countries, e.g. United Kingdom
balance of trade 146, 148–9, 152
balancing items 158–9, 205
Banker 10, 14
Bank of England 110, 170, 177, 195
Bank Rate 8, 11
Barry, B. 88, 98–9
Basic Income Ch.13
   administration 252, 255, 258–9

and average pay rates 244–5
compared with existing social security benefits 252–4
components 255–6
concept of 242–3
crisis of the welfare state and 247–9
distinct from minimum wage 244
partial 258, 259
proposals for introduction 254–9
to supplement low pay 243–4
tax burden of 246–7, 249–50, 255
unconditionality of 255, 288
withdrawal rate 252–4, 255, 256, 257
basic theorem of welfare economics 58, 268
BBC licence fee 15–16
Bean, C. 146
beliefs, moral 29–32
Bentham, Jeremy 66–7, 70, 72, 73, 87, 96
Bretton Woods Agreement 130, 135, 136, 166, 175, 280
Brittan, Samuel
   and *Bogus dilemma* 13
   at Cambridge 5–7
   at Chicago University 18
   committees served on 15–16
   and democracy 19–20
   at Department of Economic Affairs (DEA) 12
   early political beliefs 3–4, 12
   and exchange rates 12, 14–15, 19, 21, 22–3
   family background 3, 5
   at *Financial Times* 7–10, 12
   influence of Friedman on 5, 13–14, 266
   interest in psychology 4–5
   'Jay-Brittan' period 20–22
   knighted 23
   at Nuffield College, Oxford 18